# MARIAN BURROS

## 20-Minute
## M·E·N·U·S

*Simon and Schuster*

NEW YORK ◆ LONDON ◆ TORONTO ◆ SYDNEY ◆ TOKYO

**Simon and Schuster**
Simon & Schuster Building
Rockefeller Center
1230 Avenue of the Americas
New York, New York 10020

Copyright © 1989 by Foxcraft, Ltd.

Designed by Karolina Harris
Manufactured in the United States of America

1   3   5   7   9   10   8   6   4   2

Library of Congress Cataloging in Publication Data
Burros, Marian Fox.
20-minute menus/Marian Burros.
p. cm.
Includes index.
1. Quick and easy cookery.   2. Menus.   I. Title.   II. Title:
Twenty-minute menus.
TX652.B857   1989

641.5′55—dc19                                      88-38823
                                                            CIP

ISBN 978-1-9821-2336-9

# ◆ ◆ ACKNOWLEDGMENTS ◆ ◆

The man behind the stove is my husband, Donald Burros. All who buy this book are indebted to him, as I am, for his honesty in evaluating the 20-minute meals that were put in front of him.

My husband has a keen palate and a concise style for describing what he doesn't like: "Can it."

From time to time my children, Ann and Michael, made their own contributions, for which I am also grateful.

I would especially like to thank my editor, Carole Lalli, who did what few editors do anymore. Edit.

And thanks to my agent, Susan Lescher, who kept both of my feet on the ground; to Lisa Kitei, who handled the publicity on my previous book with such relish and enthusiasm and with such an open mind that it will once again be a pleasure to work with her.

*Marian Burros*
*Bethesda, Maryland*
*November, 1988*

# ACKNOWLEDGMENTS

# ◆ ◆ NOTE FROM THE AUTHOR ◆ ◆

*After my last book of quick-cooking menus—Keep It Simple—30-Minute Meals from Scratch—appeared on* The New York Times *Best-Seller List I received a lot of mail thanking me for making life easier, but the letter I cherished most came from a man who was a single parent.*

*He wrote: "You have made it possible for me to give up TV dinners, hot dogs and baked beans, and even, I confess, peanut butter sandwiches on occasion, in order to feed myself and my kids.*

*"I am indebted to you forever. And so are my kids."*

To my husband, Donald Burros,
who on February 15, 1988, washed the
dinner dishes for the first time in 28 years
of marriage and has been doing them ever since.

# ◆ ◆ ◆ ◆ CONTENTS ◆ ◆ ◆ ◆

# ◆ ◆ ◆ ◆ INTRODUCTION ◆ ◆ ◆ ◆

*20-Minute Menus* makes you an offer you can't refuse: an answer to the time-taste-health dilemma that confronts everyone who has to cook dinner for a family.

I have spent the last three years creating 100 first-rate dinner menus for two or three people that can be put on the table in 20 minutes, from the moment the cook puts on the apron (assuming the cook wears an apron). And I did it in the evening, after I came home from work. Believe me, I was too tired to spend more than 20 minutes concocting enticing combinations.

Yet there is not a frozen dinner in the lot and no convenience foods, unless canned tomato puree qualifies. Instead, these 20-minute meals are made with fresh, raw ingredients.

Because there are millions of people out there just like me, the need for these quick meals seems logical. Otherwise, what would account for the staggering increase in sales of so-called gourmet frozen dinners and the steadily rising number of shops and supermarkets selling prepared food? The total market for take-out and home-delivered prepared food had reached an estimated $60 billion in 1987. Even upscale restaurants have gone into the carry-out business.

As a *New York Times* poll in the fall of 1987 revealed, despite the feminist revolution, women, whether they work outside the home or not, still do most of the cooking and shopping.

Ninety-one percent of all married women shop for food and 90 percent of all married women cook. Eighty-six percent of married women who work outside the home do the cooking, while 90 percent of the married women who work outside the home do the shopping.

So it's easy to see why they are anxious to get their shopping and cooking done quickly. The annual nationwide survey of food-shopping habits conducted for the Food Marketing Institute has, in recent years, consistently shown that a majority of shoppers choose where they shop based on the speed of the checkout counters. In addition, many shoppers indicate they will buy packaged meat rather than take the time to request a different cut, or will patronize a convenience or "gourmet" store rather than a less expensive supermarket because it is quicker. In almost every age and income bracket shoppers are more worried about their time than their money. The length of the average supermarket visit has dropped from one hour to 20 minutes.

By using this book, your visit should drop to 10 minutes.

People are equally anxious to get dinner on the table quickly. So another *Times* poll result makes perfect sense; 20 percent of those surveyed said they spent 15 minutes making dinner at night; 29 percent spent 15 to 30 minutes; another 28 percent 30 to 60 minutes.

And most people who spend 30 minutes fixing dinner think that's 10 minutes too long.

Doreen Mott, associate director for consumer services at Good Housekeeping Institute said: "We used to feature a 30-minute dish. Now it's a 30-minute menu and readers keep writing to ask, "Could you get it down to 20 minutes?"

I don't know if the Good Housekeeping Institute has been successful, but I have been.

So, if you find quick meals prepared by others too costly or tasteless or too loaded with fat and other undesirable ingredients, if you want to have more control over what goes into your body, have I got a book for you!

For those with an iota of curiosity, along with a healthy dose of skepticism, such a concept may stretch the bounds of reality.

And skepticism is probably increased with the further news that these meals are healthful, generally in tune with the latest Dietary Guidelines for the United States and the Surgeon General's Report on Nutrition and Health: reduce fat, sodium and cholesterol; see that your caloric intake is moderate; increase carbohydrates and fiber.

The food tastes wonderful, too.

So where's the catch?

The catch, if you can call it a catch, involves the configuration of the dinner plate and the preparation technique. The plate no longer has one mound of meat surrounded by a mound of vegetables and another of starch. At least two of the elements are combined: the protein and the starch, the vegetable and the starch or the vegetable and the protein. In a few instances all three components are cooked in one pot and you have the proverbial dinner-in-a-dish.

---

### ◆ *Hints for a 20-Minute Cook* ◆

Cooking a complete dinner in 20 minutes calls for a different game plan. You prepare as you go along, not in advance. This is important information to grasp because it runs counter to the way many of us were taught how to cook.

Don't think about completing one dish before going on to start another; use the same equipment and pots and pans for more than one chore. And whenever possible rely on others to do some of the preparation. That doesn't mean hiring a kitchen helper. It means using what you find in the supermarket—not prepared foods but ingredients that are already cut or trimmed or chopped, such as those found at a salad bar. Such cut-up items are referred to throughout the recipes as "ready-cut." Using partially prepared ingredients has even been given a name: step cooking.

The preparation of the meals depends on organization and simplification. It is not difficult to learn the rules, but speed is the operative word—so you can forget about radish roses and peeled tomatoes.

Certain procedures become luxuries to be put aside for fancier weekend cooking. Among them are careful measuring; long marinating of food to tenderize it; slow roasting or braising; peeling and seeding tomatoes. For 20-minute meals, broiling, boiling, sautéing, steaming and poaching are the best techniques.

One of the most important aspects of this method is reading the recipe through before cooking the food. Cooks are always advised to do that but it is absolutely essential when time is a factor.

A game plan for quick cooking is also a must, and each menu includes one. The object is to begin with the dish that takes the longest to prepare and then to move back and forth between the recipes so that everything is ready at the same time. Not all the menus require the full 20 minutes to prepare and cook. And a few take a bit longer, but none more than 25 minutes. The game plan, however, is just a guide. You may find that you will do some of the steps in a different order.

Cooking times are not always specified in the recipes. If you follow the directions and the Game Plan, the dishes will be ready when you are—in 20 minutes.

No time has been allowed for chatting on the phone, reading the mail, watching the TV, saving your toddler from disaster or arguing with someone about setting the table. It is a given in this plan that someone other than the cook will set the table. Anyone between the ages of three and ninety is capable. And, by the way, if I could get my husband to wash the dinner dishes after 28 years of marriage, there is hope for everyone. Even as I type this, he is working at the sink!

Cooking dinner in 20 minutes is not for people who have never used a stove. It isn't that the techniques used are complicated—it's just that in order to be efficient in the kitchen you have to know your way around. The novice certainly can cook these meals. It will just take longer.

And generally certain assumptions have been made: even though most recipes do not specifically say to wash fruits and vegetables, meat, fish and poultry, it is a given that they should be washed.

While you need a food processor for quick preparation, you do not have to have the most up-to-date equipment. I cook these meals on a 25-year-old stove in a 25-year-old kitchen. And without the aid of a microwave oven.

Desserts are not included, so if you want to add one, it will have to include a stop at the fruit stand, bakery shop or ice-cream freezer.

If you cannot purchase already cut-up vegetables, you can still make the meal, but in some cases you will have to process them yourself; add one to five minutes' preparation time.

Every salad bar has a different assortment of ingredients, so be prepared to adjust, but never buy cut-up tomatoes: they taste terrible.

PLEASE DO NOT TAKE THE AMOUNTS IN THE RECIPES TOO LITERALLY; IF YOU DO, YOU WILL WASTE PRECIOUS TIME IN THE GROCERY STORE TRYING TO FIND EXACTLY THE RIGHT AMOUNT.

◆ If a recipe calls for an 8-ounce onion and there are only 9- and 10-ounce onions, buy the larger onion and either use more onion or discard a few tablespoons when you cook.

◆ If the package of chicken breasts is one pound instead of 12 ounces, freeze the extra or make a larger meal and have the leftovers for lunch.

◆ If you cannot find tiny new potatoes, use larger ones and cut them up. Besides time, however, the reason whole, small potatoes are preferred over cutting them before cooking is that when they are cut, much of the Vitamin C ends up in the cooking water instead of staying in the potato.

Amounts have been given in ounces as well as a rough equivalent in cups, and I emphasize *rough,* so don't take the cups too literally, either. They are included for the convenience of those who have leftovers at home and don't have a scale for weighing them or don't want to bother with one.

If you've been around a kitchen long enough, you can eyeball amounts and don't have to worry about measuring out 1 teaspoon of this or that.

In many instances alternatives are offered: if fresh pasta is not available, dried is recommended. The same is true in most recipes with herbs. But there are many more substitutions that can be made and an experienced cook knows how to make them. The recipe may not turn out the same, but that's not the point: if it tastes good and the meal can be made in 20 minutes, that is the bottom line. This is not classical French cooking we are talking about!

The items on the shopping list that accompany each menu include the actual amount needed in parentheses. Obviously you cannot buy 1 tablespoon of parsley but it helps to know what you actually need. And that way you are reminded that if you already have some left over you may not need to buy the ingredient.

Here are some other points to keep in mind:

If you use a toaster oven for broiling instead of the broiler in the stove, it will take longer to cook the food. Toaster ovens do not get as hot as oven broilers.

About 25 percent of the recipes are for three people, but there may be only two of you. Instead of taking the time to figure out what two-thirds of the recipe should be, make the whole thing and take the leftovers to work.

If you have to double the recipes for a meal, add three to five minutes to preparation time.

---

## ◆ Hints for More Healthful Meals ◆

While these are definitely not recipes for dieters, they are recipes for people who want to eat healthful food, maintain their weight and enjoy the pleasures of eating. There have been some important changes in the way we eat over the last 15 years: some of them fit right in with the Surgeon General's Report and Dietary Guidelines. The healthier meals have smaller portions of meat and larger portions of vegetables and grains. The calories derived from fat are fewer.

Throughout this book you will see these changes if you look for them: the portions of meat are never more than 6 ounces instead of the 8-or-more-ounce portions that were once so prevalent. In some meals the meat is an accent, not the main component. There is a sizable group of menus in which there is no meat at all.

But all the techniques used to improve the nutritional status of the meals without affecting the flavor are painless. And all of them can be adapted to other dishes.

They include such simple techniques as draining off excess fat, removing excess fat from meats and using leaner meats.

In addition these are some of the suggestions that will help:

Substitute low-fat or non-fat yogurt for sour cream.

Substitute non-fat or low-fat cottage cheese or low-fat ricotta with low-fat or non-fat yogurt for cream.

If you use equal parts of yogurt and cottage cheese or yogurt and ricotta you will have a fairly thick sauce; to make it thinner increase the amount of yogurt to get the right consistency. Process the mixture in a food processor to make it smooth, but do not heat it or it will separate. Yogurt alone can be heated if it is first mixed with cornstarch to prevent separation; use 1 tablespoon of cornstarch per 1 cup of yogurt.

Sauté in wine, vermouth, broths instead of oil, if desired, and add a small amount of butter or olive oil after cooking, for flavor.

Use nonstick pans. The best chefs do this today to keep fat down. You will notice that most of the recipes call for some range in the amount of sautéing fat, whether it's oil or butter. If you use a nonstick pan you can usually use the smaller amount.

Make salad dressings of equal parts oil and vinegar, using a mild but intensely flavored vinegar such as balsamic or raspberry. At most use the ratio of 2 parts oil to 1 part vinegar rather than the traditional 3 to 1.

To keep fat at 30 percent of calories, figure that you can add ½ teaspoon of pure fat for every 50 calories of relatively nonfat food; a slice of bread can take 1 teaspoon of butter; 1 cup of cooked rice can take 1 tablespoon of butter or oil.

Salt is not used in any of the recipes: herbs and spices and other seasonings make up for it. Try lemon juice, vinegar and hot pepper in place of salt; use lots of garlic and onion.

For those who want to use salt, just remember to adjust for ingredients such as soy sauce and anchovies.

When choosing oils, remember, olive oil is the healthiest because it is mono-unsaturated. A new mono-unsaturated fat on the market is canola, which is less expensive than olive oil and has no taste.

When you are not using a mono-unsaturate, use a polyunsaturated fat such as corn oil or safflower oil, but do not use them exclusively. Several scientific studies suggest that ingesting large quantities of polyunsaturated oils causes cancer in test animals.

As long as you do not have a serious cholesterol problem and keep your total consumption of saturated fat down to less than one third of your total fat intake, there is no reason to use margarine instead of butter.

If you want to cook brown rice in 20 minutes, combine the rice with twice the amount of water and allow it to soak overnight or for the day and then cook as you would white rice.

The ordinary supermarket can be your ally in your battle to have healthful meals in 20 minutes: it can also be your enemy. You have to be a smart shopper.

Believe me, your supermarket manager is ready, willing and anxious to help you: he wants you to shop there instead of going to a carry-out or a restaurant so the cutting and chopping is being done for you and things are being offered in small portions. Where once every package of pork chops contained at least four, now just as many contain two. Even supermarkets that don't have salad bars have packaged cut up vegetables like carrots and broccoli. There are lots of low-fat and low-sodium products, too.

Let's take a look at the supermarket to see what ingredients are offered that can help you to get in and out quickly and to get the meal on the table in 20 minutes or less.

## ◆ At the Supermarket ◆

### MEAT DEPARTMENT

Chicken comes either as boneless, skinless breasts or tenders, or even smaller as nuggets, which are bite-size pieces of white meat. All of the chicken recipes in this book call for chicken breasts because they cook so quickly. Occasionally I have seen boneless chicken thigh meat, and if you find it, it can be substituted in some recipes calling for chicken breasts.

Turkey breasts are sold boneless or in slices, and turkey meat is also sold ground.

Lamb is cut as chops or is ground.

Beef is cut in cubes as well as steaks, and, of course, ground.

Veal is scalloped or cut into chops or ground.

Pork is cut into chops, trimmed into tenderloins or ground.

## FISH DEPARTMENT

Most fish is sold as fillets or steaks.

Some seafood, like crab and shrimp, comes already cooked; shrimp is frequently available shelled and raw.

Oysters are often sold shucked.

Scallops, of course, are the original fast food.

## STARCHES

There are many forms of grain and beans that cook in under 20 minutes, including long-grain white rice. There is no need to buy instant white rice: the cooking method for long-grain white rice described with each rice recipe is foolproof.

In addition, all of the more exotic rices, such as the wonderfully nutty Indian basmati, the creamy Italian arborio and such American rices as Texmati and pecan rice cook in less than 20 minutes.

Should you want to use brown rice in a 20-minute meal, see page 18 for the simple trick that makes that possible.

Of course, there are all the fresh pastas and the thin or small dried pastas, plus bulgur, precooked couscous, kasha or buckwheat groats and instant polenta or cornmeal. And even though red lentils are seldom seen in supermarkets, they are readily available in natural-food stores and in Indian markets. They cook in less than 10 minutes and taste just like green lentils. Even quinoa, the nutty grain that has recently made its way north from South America, is turning up on supermarket shelves.

## VEGETABLES

Cut-up raw and blanched vegetables are available by the pound at salad bars in fruit and vegetable markets, supermarkets, delicatessans, even some fast-food restaurants.

Fresh garlic packed in oil is sold in the refrigerator case at many supermarkets;

some of these preparations contain salt or preservatives so check the label carefully for the variety that contains only garlic and oil.

Fresh herbs are frequently available.

## PACKAGED GOODS

There are a few good-quality canned products that are indispensable: tomatoes, tomato puree and tomato paste—and there is almost always at least one version that has no added salt, if that is a concern.

Corn niblets are also quite good.

Canned beans are useful but the label must be checked: some contain preservatives.

There are three frozen vegetables that make good substitutes for fresh: peas, corn kernels and lima beans.

Also handy are frozen chicken and beef stocks, if they are free of monosodium glutamate.

And now there are at least two national brands of canned chicken soups that are free of salt and monosodium glutamate: Campbell's and Health Valley.

Now let's take a look at some of the things in the supermarket that make shopping there more difficult than it used to be. The descriptions on labels are often very difficult to decipher. The only place on the label where you can be relatively certain the information is accurate is on the ingredient statement listing ingredients in order of predominance.

But elsewhere, products touted as "natural" or "lite," or "preservative-free" beckon the unwary.

Here's a quick lesson in wariness.

## NATURAL

Natural has come to mean absolutely nothing at all except for the foods over which the U.S. Department of Agriculture has jurisdiction—poultry and meat products.

At U.S.D.A. natural means "minimally processed and no additives."

Otherwise, you can never be sure when you see the word on the label how the manufacturer chooses to interpret it.

Is a spaghetti sauce made with the usual recognizable ingredients plus "natural flavorings," really natural? If it is, why won't the manufacturer list what those natural flavorings are?

If a cheese calls itself natural but it has smoke flavoring in it, is it natural?

## NO ADDITIVES

Sometimes, instead of calling itself natural a product will say "no preservatives." But does that mean it is free of all artificial ingredients? Not at all. No preservatives means just that. There may still be artificial color and/or artificial flavor in the product.

## SUGAR-FREE

If a product is labeled sugar-free it means it has no sucrose. It may however have fructose, molasses, honey, corn syrup, aspartame (brand name Equal) or saccharin. All you can be sure of is that it has no sucrose.

## REDUCED CALORIES AND LOW CALORIE

Reduced calories has a specific meaning according to the U.S. Food and Drug Administration. The product must contain one-third fewer calories than the food with which it is comparing itself. A product labeled low-calorie cannot have more than 40 calories per serving.

## REDUCED AND LOW SODIUM

If a product has at least 75 percent less sodium than the product it replaces, then it can use the term "reduced sodium."

For a product to be labeled "low sodium," it can contain only 140 milligrams of sodium or less; very low sodium, 35 milligrams or less; sodium-free, less than 5 milligrams per serving.

## FIBER

There are two kinds of fiber: soluble and insoluble. Wheat bran is insoluble fiber, which may help prevent colon cancer; it is good for constipation and diverticulosis.

Soluble fiber, which lowers cholesterol, is found in oat bran.

## FORTIFIED

Foods that are fortified contain some nutrients that were not originally found in the product at all or more of a certain nutrient than was there in the original. Adding Vitamin C to a can of root beer would be an example of fortification.

## ENRICHED

When processing removes a nutrient from a product and the nutrient is returned to the product after processing, the product is considered enriched.

When whole wheat flour is processed into white flour, and the white flour is made into bread, the bread is enriched, returning some, though not all, of the nutrients lost in the processing.

## SELECT BEEF

Once called good grade, select beef has less fat than either prime or choice grades. That makes it somewhat less tender and chewier, but if it is cooked properly, for less time than it takes to cook prime or choice, it is quite good, and much healthier than those grades.

## LIGHT

Or "lite." At this writing it means nothing except at the Agriculture Department. It can refer to the color, the texture, the taste, the weight. It may even have to do with fewer calories or fat, but there is no way to know without careful reading. Some "light" products have more calories or fat than the original versions. Different government agencies with jurisdiction over food and beverages have different rules.

At U.S.D.A., in order for a meat or poultry product to be called light it must have 25 percent fewer calories, 25 percent less fat, 25 percent less sodium or 25 percent less breading than the traditional product it imitates.

## NUTRITIONAL CLAIMS

As of this writing the Food and Drug Administration has proposed to allow food products to carry nutritional claims. For example, a milk carton might say: high in calcium. Even though the milk is also high in fat, it would not have to include such a disclaimer on the label.

Judging by the nutritional claims already being made in advertising, people will be even more confused than ever about the true nutritional worth of any given product.

A can of a national brand pea soup now says, "good source of fiber," but says nothing about the high level of sodium in the product.

Is such information useful to consumers?

## NO CHOLESTEROL

Because a product has no cholesterol, it is not automatically good for you. It may still be extremely high in fat.

Vegetable oils, for example, contain no cholesterol, but they are not a product that a health-conscious person consumes in large quantities.

Just as dietary cholesterol may increase your blood cholesterol level, too much fat can do the same thing, especially saturated fat.

The good news is that shellfish are not off-limits to people on low-cholesterol diets.

For most Americans, the reason their cholesterol is too high is because they eat too much saturated fat, rather than because they eat too much cholesterol.

There is a proposed federal regulation to govern cholesterol claims, but so far it is just that—a proposal.

## LOW FAT

The Agriculture Department has a definition for low fat; their regulation governs meat and poultry products only.

Lean means no more than 10 percent fat by weight; extra lean means no more than 5 percent fat by weight.

This proposal, however, does not apply to ground beef: lean ground beef, by U.S.D.A. definition, is 25 percent less fat than regular ground beef.

---

## ◆ Pantry for a 20-Minute Kitchen ◆

To keep shopping time to a minimum you will have to keep a pantry of staples on hand. In addition to the usual items, the staples you choose reflect what you like to cook and your family likes to eat.

This list calls for ingredients used repeatedly in the book. Pantry staples have three definitions: ingredients used so often, such as lemons and yogurt, that they are handy to have on hand all the time even if they do not last indefinitely; ingredients that have a long shelf life, such as dried herbs and condiments, and are used often; ingredients that have a long shelf life but are not used very often. This makes it so much easier to prepare a variety of the more unusual dishes. Sesame paste, Sichuan peppercorns, rice wine vinegar, hoisin sauce and Japanese horseradish powder (*wasabi*) for many of the Oriental dishes; Parmigiano Reggianno, top-quality olive oil (kept in the refrigerator if you don't use it too often) and balsamic vinegar for those who like an Italian accent are typical examples.

Foods in this last category are handy to have because a trip to a special store is often required to buy them. Obviously each cook will pick and choose among these items for the tastes that appeal.

On the other hand, a few items you might think of as belonging in your pantry, such as onions, are not included because it is quicker to buy them already cut from a salad bar, if they are available. But obviously you are going to work out what you want to have on hand for yourself. These are simply suggestions.

There are, however, some ingredients that are not always available, and it helps to keep a supply on hand. If you cannot find fresh herbs regularly, freeze them when available and simply add them to the dish directly from the freezer.

You can do the same thing with ginger. Freeze whole pieces, and then when you need some, remove the piece from the freezer and, without defrosting, grate coarsely.

If you want to prepare your own minced garlic in oil, simply mince the garlic in a food processor, place in an airtight glass container and cover with the oil of your choice.

To help those who do not have access to good-quality foods, I have included a list of mail order companies (see page 235). For the last seven years I have written a Christmas mail-order gift column for *The New York Times*. From those lists and from other articles, I have culled the very best of the mail-order items.

Organic foods are noted as such. For more and more people the purity of the food supply is becoming a serious consideration. The number of small farmers raising organic crops is increasing, and some of them sell by mail. The products listed here are excellent. The fruits and vegetables are especially good when winter sets in, though I do not recommend ordering lettuces by mail: they do not seem to be able to survive the trip. In the summer, of course, most of us have access to some local organic crops. Whether or not your first concern is the purity of the food, you will love the flavor: it is better than any standard supermarket produce.

## HERBS AND SPICES

*Allspice*
*Basil—fresh, frozen, dried*
*Bay leaves*
*Caraway seeds*
*Cardamom, ground*
*Chervil—dried*
*Chile powder—hot and mild*
*Cilantro, fresh*
*Cinnamon, ground*
*Coriander seed, ground*
*Cumin, ground*
*Curry powder*

*Mustard—powdered*
*Nutmeg, ground*
*Oregano—fresh, frozen, dried*
*Paprika—preferably sweet Hungarian*
*Pepper—freshly ground black, ground white, ground red (cayenne), Sichuan*
*Poppy seeds*
*Rosemary—fresh, frozen, dried*
*Sage—fresh, frozen, dried*
*Savory—fresh, frozen, dried*
*Sesame seeds*
*Tarragon—fresh, frozen, dried*

Fennel seeds
Ginger—fresh, frozen, powdered, pickled
Marjoram—fresh, frozen, dried

Thyme—fresh, frozen, dried
Turmeric

## CONDIMENTS

Anchovy paste or whole anchovies
Beans, salted or fermented black
    (Chinese)
Capers
Catsup
Cheese—Parmigiano Reggiano
Chili paste, hot, with garlic (Chinese)
Chili sauce
Cornmeal
Cracker crumbs
Fish sauce (called nam pla in Thai
    cooking or nuoc mam in Vietnamese
    cooking)
Hoisin sauce
Honey
Hot pepper sauce
Maple syrup
Molasses, unsulphured, dark
Mushrooms, dried, wild
Mustard—Dijon and grainy
Nuts—almonds (slivered); peanuts
    (unsalted, roasted); pecans; pine

Oil—olive, peanut, corn or safflower,
    Oriental sesame, hot chile, walnut,
    canola
Olives—black or green, packed in brine
    or oil—French, Greek, Italian
Oyster sauce
Raisins
Sesame paste—Oriental style (or
    creamy peanut butter)
Shallots
Sherry, dry
Soy sauce, reduced sodium or light
Tomatoes—sun-dried, paste, puree and
    whole, no salt added
Vermouth, dry
Vinegar—balsamic, cider, red and white
    wine, rice
Wasabi—Japanese horseradish
Wine—red, white and rice (called mirin
    in Japanese cooking and shaoxing in
    Chinese)
Worcestershire sauce

## PASTAS AND GRAINS

Thin pastas such as linguine, spaghet-
    tini or angel hair
Small shells
Thin egg noodles

Couscous
Bulgur
Lentils, red
Rice—white, basmati, arborio

## BASICS

Beef stock, bouillon or broth, preferably
    unsalted
Bread crumbs
Butter, unsalted
Chicken stock, bouillon or broth, prefer-
    ably unsalted
Cornstarch
Eggs

Flour, unbleached
Garlic minced in oil (the variety that
    must be refrigerated, free of additives)
Lemons
Milk—low-fat or skim
Orange juice
Sugar—white granulated, brown
Yogurt—plain low-fat or non-fat

# ◆ *Equipment for 20-Minute Meals* ◆

Your kitchen needs to be stocked with certain equipment and utensils. This is the minimum, and adequate when cooking for up to four.

Keep in mind that if your knives aren't sharp, if the lids don't fit on your pots, if you try to cram four hamburgers into a five-inch skillet—you will not be able to cook quickly.

But having the proper tools does not mean great expense; it means eschewing the gadgets and spending the money on a few good things, all of which are listed below. A food processor is essential in the execution of 20-minute meals, and a good investment in any case.

## TOOLS FOR QUICK COOKS

*KNIVES, FORKS, SPOONS*
*Chef's knife*
*Paring knife*
*Bread knife*

*2 stirring spoons, one slotted*
*1 large fork*

*POTS AND PANS*
*14-inch skillet with lid, preferably nonstick*
*Sauté pan with lid, preferably nonstick*
*6-quart pot with lid*

*2- to 3-quart pot with lid*
*Steamer or holder for steaming that fits into pot*
*Aluminum baking sheet*

*OTHER UTENSILS*
*Graduated set of stainless steel bowls*
*Spatula*
*4-sided grater*
*Set of measuring spoons*
*1-quart measuring cup*
*Set of ¼-, ½-, ⅓- and 1-cup measuring cups*
*Large colander or strainer*

*Can opener*
*Bottle opener*
*Whisk*
*Vegetable peeler*
*Hand juice squeezer*
*Pot holders*
*Food processor*
*Toaster oven*

# 20-Minute
## M·E·N·U·S

# $\mathcal{F}$ISH NIÇOISE ◆ COUSCOUS ◆ BRUSSELS SPROUTS ◆ ◆ ◆ ◆

*For this recipe, you can use flounder, sole, cod, scrod or perch.*

## FISH NIÇOISE

- 1 teaspoon olive oil
- ½ teaspoon minced garlic in oil
- 1 teaspoon paprika
- ½ teaspoon dried marjoram or thyme
- 4 tablespoons tomato puree
- ⅓ cup dry white wine
  Freshly ground black pepper to taste
- ¼ cup French, Italian or Greek pitted black olives, packed in oil or brine (about 12 large)
- 12 ounces white fish fillets (flounder, sole, cod, scrod or perch)

1. Heat oil in a skillet large enough to hold the fish. Sauté garlic and paprika in the oil for 30 seconds.

2. Add marjoram or thyme, tomato puree, wine and pepper. Simmer about 2 minutes.

3. Pit olives.

4. Wash fish and cut into 2-inch pieces. Add to sauce with olives and simmer, covered, for about 5 minutes, using the 8 to 10 minutes to the inch of thickness rule.

**Yield:** 2 servings

## COUSCOUS

- 1 teaspoon unsalted butter
- ½ cup couscous (precooked)

1. Following the directions on the couscous package, bring water to boil; stir in butter.

2. Add couscous, cover and remove from heat, allowing couscous to absorb water, about 3–5 minutes.

**Yield:** 2 servings

## BRUSSELS SPROUTS

8 ounces Brussels sprouts

$\overline{1}$ Bring water to boil in steamer.

$\overline{2}$ Wash and trim Brussels sprouts. Steam for 7–10 minutes. Drain and serve.

**Yield:** 2 servings

---

### ◆ *Game Plan* ◆

*Prepare sauce for fish.*
*Boil water for Brussels sprouts.*
*Clean Brussels sprouts.*
*Boil water and butter for couscous.*
*Pit olives and add with fish to sauce.*
*Cook Brussels sprouts.*
*Cook couscous.*

---

### PANTRY

*Olive oil*
*Minced garlic in oil*
*Paprika*
*Dried marjoram or thyme*
*Tomato puree*
*Dry white wine*

*Whole black pepper*
*French, Italian or Greek black*
   *olives*
*Unsalted butter*
*Couscous*

---

### SHOPPING LIST

*12 ounces white fish fillets*
   *(flounder, sole, cod, scrod or*
   *perch)*

*8 ounces Brussels sprouts*

# BROILED FISH WITH RED PEPPER PUREE ◆ POTATO AND CUCUMBER SALAD ◆ ◆ ◆ ◆ ◆ ◆ ◆ ◆ ◆ ◆

*This recipe contains a simple method for making red pepper puree. The peppers are not roasted, but are sautéed with onions, to produce a lovely, sweet taste. The puree nicely complements any emphatically flavored fish.*

## BROILED FISH WITH RED PEPPER PUREE

8 ounces whole red bell pepper or 7 ounces sliced (ready-cut) (1½ cups)
8 ounces whole onion or 7 ounces sliced (ready-cut) (1½ cups)
1 tablespoon corn oil
12 ounces strongly flavored fish fillets, such as mackerel or bluefish
1 teaspoon reduced-sodium soy sauce

1 Heat broiler; line broiler pan with double thickness of aluminum foil.

2 Wash, trim and seed whole pepper and put through julienne or shredder disc in food processor; drain excess liquid.

3 Peel and trim onion; quarter and slice with same disc; drain.

4 Heat oil in 10- or 12-inch skillet and sauté pepper and onion until they begin to brown, about 10 minutes.

5 Wash and dry fish. Broil fish, skin side down, in broiler pan 2 inches from heat source, about 7 minutes.

6 When vegetables are cooked, stir in soy sauce and puree in food processor.

7 Spoon puree on dinner plates and top with fish.

**Yield:** 2 servings

## POTATO AND CUCUMBER SALAD

9–12 ounces tiny new potatoes
1 small Kirby cucumber or ½ small regular cucumber

1 Scrub potatoes but do not peel; place in pot with water to cover. Cover pot and boil potatoes until tender, about 18 minutes.

½ cup plain low- or non-fat yogurt
½ teaspoon white wine vinegar
⅛ teaspoon dry mustard
½ teaspoon ground cumin
¼ teaspoon ground coriander seed
Freshly ground black pepper to taste
1 tablespoon finely minced red onion
1 tablespoon chopped fresh cilantro leaves

2 Scrub Kirby cucumber or peel regular cucumber. Cut into small cubes.

3 Combine yogurt, vinegar, mustard, cumin, coriander seed and pepper in bowl large enough to hold cucumbers and potatoes.

4 Finely mince onion and add to bowl with cucumber.

5 When potatoes are cooked, drain and cut into halves or quarters, depending on size, directly into serving bowl. Stir to coat with dressing.

6 Wash, dry and chop fresh cilantro; add to salad.

**Yield:** 2 servings

---

## ◆ Game Plan ◆

*Heat broiler. Scrub and cook potatoes. Shred and sauté pepper and onion. Broil fish. Prepare salad. Puree pepper and onion; add soy sauce. Drain potatoes, cut up and add to salad. Chop fresh cilantro and add to salad. Spoon puree on plates and top with fish.*

---

### PANTRY

Corn oil
Reduced-sodium soy sauce
Plain low- or non-fat yogurt
White wine vinegar

Dry mustard
Ground cumin
Ground coriander seed
Whole black pepper

---

### SHOPPING LIST

8 ounces whole red bell pepper or 7 ounces sliced (ready-cut)
8 ounces whole onion or 7 ounces sliced (ready-cut)
12 ounces fish fillets, such as mackerel or bluefish

9–12 ounces tiny new potatoes
1 small Kirby cucumber or small regular cucumber
Small red onion (1 tablespoon)
Fresh cilantro (1 tablespoon)

# BROILED FISH ON COLD TOMATO VINAIGRETTE ◆ CREAMY POTATO SALAD ◆ ◆ ◆ ◆ ◆ ◆ ◆ ◆ ◆ ◆ ◆

*The hot fish and cool sauce provide a nice contrast.*

## BROILED FISH ON COLD TOMATO VINAIGRETTE

3 tablespoons olive oil
2 tablespoons balsamic vinegar
2 teaspoons ground coriander
½ teaspoon minced garlic in oil
1 teaspoon minced fresh parsley
1 teaspoon minced fresh tarragon
1 teaspoon minced fresh oregano
2 ripe medium tomatoes
Freshly ground black pepper to taste
18 ounces fish fillets (tuna, swordfish, sea trout, mackerel or sea bass)
Olive oil for brushing on fillets

1 Heat broiler and cover broiler pan with aluminum foil.

2 Beat together the oil, vinegar, coriander and garlic.

3 Mince parsley, tarragon and oregano in food processor, if desired, and add to dressing.

4 Thinly slice tomatoes in food processor or chop coarsely by hand; add to dressing with pepper.

5 Place fish fillets on broiler pan and brush lightly with oil. Broil about 2 inches from source of heat, allowing 8 to 10 minutes for each inch of thickness.

6 Spoon a bit of dressing on serving plate. Top with fish and pour remaining dressing over fish.

**Yield:** 3 servings

## CREAMY POTATO SALAD

20 ounces tiny new potatoes
1 cup plain low- or non-fat yogurt
1 cup low- or non-fat cottage cheese
1 teaspoon ground cumin

1 Scrub potatoes but do not peel; place in pot with water to cover. Cover pot and boil potatoes until tender, about 18 minutes.

2 Combine yogurt, cottage cheese and cumin in food processor and process until mixture is smooth. Spoon into serving dish.

4 heaping teaspoons fresh
cilantro leaves, coarsely
chopped, plus some for
garnish
Freshly ground black
pepper to taste

$\overline{3}$ Remove cilantro leaves from stems.

$\overline{4}$ When potatoes are cooked, drain and cut in halves
or quarters directly into serving bowl. Mix with
dressing and sprinkle with cilantro and black pepper to taste.

**Yield:** 3 servings

---

### ◆ Game Plan ◆

*Prepare and cook potatoes.*
*Heat broiler.*
*Prepare dressing for fish.*
*Broil fish.*
*Prepare dressing for potato salad.*
*Drain potatoes and add, cut up, to bowl; mix with dressing.*
*Spoon dressing on plates and top with fish; top fish with remaining*
*dressing.*

---

#### PANTRY

*Olive oil*
*Balsamic vinegar*
*Ground coriander*
*Minced garlic in oil*

*Whole black pepper*
*Plain low- or non-fat yogurt*
*Ground cumin*

---

#### SHOPPING LIST

*Fresh parsley (1 teaspoon)*
*Fresh tarragon (1 teaspoon)*
*Fresh oregano (1 teaspoon)*
*2 ripe medium tomatoes*
*18 ounces fish fillets (tuna,*
  *swordfish, sea trout, mackerel*
  *or sea bass)*

*20 ounces tiny new potatoes*
*Low- or non-fat cottage cheese (1*
  *cup)*
*Fresh cilantro (4 teaspoons)*

# *F*ISH ON BED OF SALSA ◆
# BOILED NEW POTATOES ◆ ◆ ◆

*Southwestern ingredients have become increasingly popular throughout the country and add a wonderful zest to dishes.*

## FISH ON BED OF SALSA

½ jalapeño chile
¼ cup plus 3 tablespoons chopped fresh cilantro
20–24 ounces ripe tomatoes
5 ounces whole red onion or 4 ounces sliced (ready-cut) (1¼ cups)
1 lime
Freshly ground black pepper to taste
12 ounces fish fillets (sole, snapper or flounder)
½ cup plain low- or non-fat yogurt

1 Remove seeds from jalapeño and quarter. Coarsely chop ¼ cup cilantro. With food processor on using the steel blade, put jalapeño through the feed tube with ¼ cup chopped cilantro. Turn processor off and add tomatoes. Process only until tomatoes are in chunks.

2 Coarsely chop red onion; squeeze 1 teaspoon lime juice over and combine with tomato mixture and pepper to taste.

3 Spoon half of the salsa into a heavy skillet (*not* cast iron) large enough to hold fish. Arrange fish on top of salsa and spread with yogurt. Top with remaining salsa. Cover and simmer 7 to 10 minutes, until fish is cooked through.

4 Chop remaining 3 tablespoons cilantro. Cut remaining lime half into two wedges.

5 Arrange fish on dinner plates and spoon salsa over, reserving some for potatoes. Sprinkle each with cilantro and garnish with lime wedge.

**Yield:** 2 servings

## BOILED NEW POTATOES

12 ounces tiny new potatoes

1. Scrub but do not peel potatoes. If potatoes are no larger than golf balls, they may be cooked whole; otherwise, cut them in half.

2. Place in pot with water to cover. Cover and boil for about 18 minutes for whole potatoes, 10 minutes for halves.

3. Drain; cut whole potatoes into halves and place on dinner plates. Spoon the remaining salsa over potatoes.

**Yield:** 2 servings

### ◆ Game Plan ◆

*Prepare and cook potatoes.*
*Follow fish recipe.*
*Serve fish and salsa with potatoes, cilantro and lime.*

### PANTRY

Whole black pepper
Plain low- or non-fat yogurt

### SHOPPING LIST

1 jalapeño chile
Fresh cilantro (¼ cup plus 3 tablespoons)
20–24 ounces ripe tomatoes
5 ounces whole red onion or 4 ounces sliced (ready-cut)

1 lime
12 ounces fish fillets (sole, snapper or flounder)
12 ounces tiny new potatoes

# ORIENTAL FISH ◆ PASTA WITH SPINACH–CHEESE SAUCE ◆ SWEET AND SOUR CUCUMBERS ◆ ◆

*This menu, including the cucumber salad, cannot be prepared in 20 minutes. Twenty-two minutes would be more accurate, but even that is rushing it. If you eliminate the salad, you'll come in under 20 minutes.*

*Note: Fresh linguine is preferred to dried but either can be used.*

---

## ORIENTAL FISH

12  ounces white fish fillets (scrod, sole or flounder)
1  tablespoon coarsely grated fresh ginger
2  tablespoons oyster sauce
2½  tablespoons dry vermouth
1  teaspoon sugar

1 Wash fish; cut each piece in half and place on a large piece of aluminum foil. Turn up the sides of the foil to make a container, but do not fold it over the top of the fish.

2 Bring water to boil in steamer.

3 Grate ginger and combine with oyster sauce, vermouth and sugar and pour over fish.

4 Place the foil containing fish and sauce in the top of steamer; cover and steam fish, allowing 8 to 10 minutes per inch of thickness.

**Yield:** 2 servings

---

## PASTA WITH SPINACH–CHEESE SAUCE

3  quarts water
16  ounces fresh loose spinach or 10-ounce package fresh spinach
¼  teaspoon minced garlic in oil
¼  cup plain low- or non-fat yogurt
5  tablespoons low- or non-fat cottage cheese
Few shakes nutmeg
Freshly ground black pepper to taste
2½  ounces freshly grated Parmesan cheese, preferably Parmigiano Reggiano
6  ounces fresh or dried linguine

1 Boil water for linguine in covered pot.

2 Wash spinach, trim the tough stems, and steam with the garlic in a pot only in the water clinging to its leaves, just until spinach wilts. Drain thoroughly and press dry.

3 Process yogurt, cottage cheese, nutmeg and black pepper in food processor until smooth. Add drained spinach and process to puree.

4 Grate Parmesan.

5 Cook linguine in boiling water, 1–2 minutes for fresh or according to package directions for dried. Drain and spoon into serving bowl; top with spinach–cheese sauce and serve sprinkled with Parmesan.

**Yield:** 2 servings

## SWEET AND SOUR CUCUMBERS

3 small Kirby cucumbers or
   1 regular cucumber
   (about 12 ounces)
3 scallions
¼ cup white vinegar
¼ cup water
1–2 tablespoons sugar

1  Wash Kirbys; peel regular cucumber; trim and slice, using the slicing blade, in food processor. Slice the scallions the same way.

2  Mix vinegar, water and sugar in serving bowl, and stir in cucumber slices and scallions.

**Yield:** 2 servings

---

### ◆ Game Plan ◆

Boil water for pasta.  Boil water for fish.
Wash spinach and steam with garlic.  Cut fish in half; place on foil.
Grate ginger and mix with sauce ingredients for fish. Top fish with sauce;
steam fish.  Drain spinach.  In food processor blend yogurt,
cottage cheese, nutmeg and pepper for the spinach–cheese sauce.
Add spinach and puree.  Slice cucumbers and scallions in food processor.
Cook linguine.  Prepare sweet and sour dressing and combine
with cucumbers and scallions.  Grate Parmesan.
Drain pasta and mix with spinach–cheese sauce. Top with grated cheese.

---

### PANTRY

Fresh ginger
Oyster sauce
Dry vermouth
Sugar
Minced garlic in oil

Plain low- or non-fat
   yogurt
Nutmeg
Whole black pepper
White vinegar

Parmesan cheese
   (preferably Parmigiano
   Reggiano)
Dried linguine, if fresh not
   available

---

### SHOPPING LIST

12 ounces white fish fillets
   (scrod, sole or flounder)
16 ounces fresh loose
   spinach or 10-ounce
   package fresh spinach

Plain low- or non-fat
   cottage cheese (5
   tablespoons)
6 ounces fresh linguine

3 small Kirby cucumbers
   or 1 regular cucumber
Bunch scallions (3)
   (12 ounces)

# SAGE-BRUSHED BLUEFISH ◆ CHINESE NOODLES IN SESAME SAUCE ◆ ◆ ◆ ◆ ◆ ◆ ◆ ◆ ◆ ◆ ◆

*At some salad bars the broccoli is already cooked and the snow peas blanched; at others they are raw. The noodle recipe can be used with either. If fresh noodles are available they are preferable.*

## SAGE-BRUSHED BLUEFISH

12 ounces bluefish fillets
1 tablespoon fresh lemon juice
¼ teaspoon dried, crumbled sage

1. Heat broiler; cover broiler pan with double thickness of aluminum foil.

2. Arrange bluefish on broiler pan and rub both sides with lemon juice and sage.

3. Measure fish at thickest part and broil, allowing 8–10 minutes for each inch of thickness.

**Yield:** 2 servings

## CHINESE NOODLES IN SESAME SAUCE

3 quarts water
8 ounces whole broccoli or 4 ounces broccoli flowerettes (ready-cut) (1½–2 cups)
4 ounces snow peas
8 ounces very fine Italian or Chinese egg noodles, preferably fresh
½-inch cube fresh ginger
2 teaspoons sesame seeds
3 tablespoons water
2 tablespoons reduced-sodium soy sauce
2 tablespoons Oriental sesame paste, well mixed (see Note below)

1. Bring water to boil in covered pot. If broccoli and snow peas are whole and uncooked, trim stems from broccoli and cut tops into flowerettes; string snow peas. Cook the flowerettes in boiling water for 3 minutes, snow peas for 1 minute. Remove with slotted spoon. Return water to boil. Add the noodles to the water. Cook fresh noodles in boiling water 30–60 seconds after water returns to boil. Cook dried noodles according to package directions. Rinse under cold water and drain.

2. Turn on food processor; with the steel blade, process ginger through feed tube. Turn off processor and add sesame seeds, water, soy sauce, sesame paste, sherry, vinegar, sugar and garlic. Process to a paste.

1 tablespoon dry sherry
1 tablespoon red wine vinegar
1 teaspoon sugar
1 teaspoon minced garlic in oil
2 tablespoons chopped scallion

3 Spoon the sauce into serving dish and mix in noodles, broccoli and snow peas.

4 Chop scallions and sprinkle over noodles and vegetables.

**Yield:** 2 servings

**Note:** Keep sesame paste turned upside down in its jar so that the oil will mix with the paste; stir before measuring.

---

## ◆ Game Plan ◆

Boil water for noodles.   Heat broiler.   Prepare fish and broil.
Cook raw broccoli and snow peas in boiling noodle water.
Mince ginger in food processor.
Add remaining ingredients to food processor and finish preparing sesame sauce.
Remove vegetables from water and drain.
Cook noodles in same water.
Chop scallions and sprinkle on noodles.
Drain noodles and combine with vegetables and sauce.

---

### PANTRY

Lemon
Dried sage
Very thin dried egg noodles, if fresh not available
Fresh ginger
Sesame seeds

Reduced-sodium soy sauce
Oriental sesame paste
Dry sherry
Red wine vinegar
Sugar
Minced garlic in oil

---

### SHOPPING LIST

12 ounces bluefish fillets
8 ounces whole broccoli or 4 ounces broccoli flowerettes (ready-cut)
4 ounces snow peas

8 ounces very fine Italian or Chinese egg noodles, preferably fresh
Bunch scallions (2 tablespoons)

# MONKFISH ON CABBAGE AU BERNARDIN ◆ CURRIED POTATOES AND PEAS ◆ ◆ ◆ ◆ ◆

*This is a much simplified variation of a fabulous dish served at Le Bernardin, one of New York's very best restaurants, which specializes in seafood.*

## MONKFISH ON CABBAGE AU BERNARDIN

16 ounces Savoy cabbage
 2 tablespoons chopped or
   cut-up boiled or baked
   ham
12 ounces monkfish
 1 teaspoon plus 1½
   tablespoons unsalted
   butter
 3 tablespoons chicken
   stock
   Freshly ground black
   pepper to taste

1. Heat broiler. Cover broiler pan with double thickness of aluminum foil.

2. Shred cabbage in food processor.

3. Chop or cut up ham.

4. Wash and dry fish, and rub on both sides with 1 teaspoon of butter. Place on broiler pan and broil several inches from source of heat, allowing 8 to 10 minutes for each inch of thickness.

5. Cook cabbage and ham in pot with chicken stock, 1½ tablespoons butter and pepper for about 10 minutes.

6. Arrange cabbage on dinner plates and top with monkfish.

**Yield:** 2 servings

## CURRIED POTATOES AND PEAS

16 ounces tiny new potatoes
2 tablespoons unsalted
  butter
1–1½ teaspoons curry
  powder
2 tablespoons chicken
  stock
8 ounces frozen peas

1. Scrub potatoes but do not peel; quarter and bring to boil in covered pot with water to cover. Cook for 10 minutes. Drain.

2. Add butter to pot with curry powder and sauté potatoes to coat.

3. Stir in stock and peas; cover and cook over medium heat 2–3 minutes to heat peas through.

**Yield:** 2 servings

◆ *Game Plan* ◆

*Heat broiler.*
*Scrub and quarter potatoes and cook.*
*Shred cabbage and chop ham.*
*Rub fish with butter and broil.*
*Cook cabbage and ham with chicken stock, butter and black pepper.*
*Drain potatoes; add butter and curry powder and sauté; add chicken stock and peas and cook.*

---

### PANTRY

Unsalted butter                    Chicken stock
Curry powder                       Whole black pepper

---

### SHOPPING LIST

16 ounces Savoy cabbage            16 ounces tiny new potatoes
1 ounce ham (2 tablespoons)        8 ounces frozen peas
12 ounces monkfish

# SALMON HASH ◆ GREEN OR RED SALSA ◆ FLOUR TORTILLAS ◆ ◆

*With thanks and apologies to Jeremiah Tower and his wonderful salmon hash at Stars, in San Francisco.*

*Tomatillos are small green tomatolike vegetables with papery skins but if they are not available use plum tomatoes for a red salsa.*

## SALMON HASH

15½-ounce can salmon
  ½ serrano or other hot
      chile
  4 ounces whole red onion
      or 3 ounces sliced
      (ready-cut) (1 cup)
  2 tablespoons bread
      crumbs, approx.
  ½ teaspoon cinnamon
  1 teaspoon cumin
  ⅛ teaspoon cloves
  ½ teaspoon ground
      coriander
  2 tablespoons corn,
      safflower or canola oil
  2 tablespoons fresh
      cilantro leaves
      Green or red salsa
      (recipe follows)
  4 flour tortillas (recipe
      follows)
  4 tablespoons plain low-
      or non-fat yogurt

1. Rinse salmon and remove skin.

2. Cut chile in half and remove seeds. Reserve other half for salsa.

3. Turn on food processor; through the feed tube, add chunks of onion and half the chile; process just until coarsely minced.

4. Add salmon, bread crumbs, cinnamon, cumin, cloves and coriander and process until paste is formed. If necessary, add more crumbs to make patty that will hold its shape.

5. Shape mixture into 4 patties.

6. Heat oil in skillet and over medium heat sauté patties on both sides until browned.

7. Remove cilantro leaves from stems.

8. Serve patties on warm tortillas with salsa, garnished with yogurt and cilantro leaves.

**Yield:** 2 servings

## GREEN OR RED SALSA

  ½ of serrano or other hot
      chile (see hash recipe)
  2 ounces red onion (⅓ cup
      finely chopped)

1. Turn on food processor; through feed tube, add cut-up chile half and mince.

2. Add onion and mince coarsely.

| | |
|---|---|
| 12 ounces tomatillos or plum tomatoes<br>2 tablespoons cilantro leaves<br>1 teaspoon lime juice | $\overline{3}$ If tomatillos are available, remove husks, wash and coarsely chop in food processor. Otherwise, chop plum tomatoes.<br><br>$\overline{4}$ Remove cilantro leaves from stems.<br><br>$\overline{5}$ Squeeze lime juice into salsa; stir in cilantro leaves and serve over salmon patties.<br>**Yield:** 2 servings |

## FLOUR TORTILLAS

| | |
|---|---|
| 4 8-inch flour tortillas | $\overline{1}$ Heat oven or toaster oven to 400 degrees.<br><br>$\overline{2}$ Wrap tortillas in aluminum foil.<br><br>$\overline{3}$ Heat tortillas for 10–15 minutes. Serve warm.<br>**Yield:** 2 servings |

## ◆ *Game Plan* ◆

*Drain salmon.    Heat oven for tortillas.*
*Chop onion and chile for salmon.*
*Add salmon, bread crumbs, spices and process; shape into patties and*
*sauté in hot oil.    Heat tortillas.    Make salsa.*
*Wash, dry and remove cilantro leaves from stems.*
*Assemble salmon hash, salsa, yogurt on tortillas.*

### PANTRY

| | | |
|---|---|---|
| Bread crumbs<br>Cinnamon<br>Cumin | Cloves<br>Ground coriander | Corn, safflower or canola oil<br>Plain low- or non-fat yogurt |

### SHOPPING LIST

| | | |
|---|---|---|
| 15½-ounce can salmon<br>1 serrano or other hot chile<br>5 or 6 ounces red onion | Fresh cilantro<br>  (4 tablespoons)<br>4 8-inch flour tortillas | 12 ounces tomatillos or<br>  plum tomatoes<br>Lime |

# POACHED SALMON WITH GINGER AND CILANTRO ◆ TURKISH CARROT PILAF ◆ ◆ ◆ ◆ ◆ ◆ ◆ ◆ ◆

*The salmon recipe is the kind that gives low-fat recipes a good name.*

## POACHED SALMON WITH GINGER AND CILANTRO

12 ounces salmon fillets
1-inch piece fresh ginger
4 tablespoons coarsely chopped fresh cilantro
1 teaspoon minced garlic in oil
¼ cup dry white wine
2 tablespoons water

1 Place salmon, skin side down, in small heavy-bottomed pan.

2 Grate ginger.

3 Chop cilantro coarsely; add 2 tablespoons of cilantro with ginger and garlic to salmon; add wine and water.

4 Cover and simmer, cooking according to size of salmon at its thickest point, allowing 8 to 10 minutes per inch.

5 Serve salmon with remaining pan juices and top with remaining cilantro.

**Yield:** 2 servings

## TURKISH CARROT PILAF

14 ounces whole carrots or 12 ounces sliced (ready-cut) (2½ cups)
½ cup long-grain rice
Freshly ground black pepper to taste
1 teaspoon cumin
1 cup chicken stock

1 Scrape whole carrots. Grate carrots in food processor.

2 Bring rice, carrots, pepper and cumin to boil in chicken stock. Reduce heat to low; cover and cook over low heat for about 17 minutes, until rice is tender but firm and stock has been completely absorbed.

**2–3 tablespoons toasted pine nuts (about 1 ounce)**

3 Toast pine nuts. When rice is cooked stir in pine nuts and serve.

**Yield:** 2 servings

---

◆ *Game Plan* ◆

*Grate carrots.*
*Cook rice with carrots, pepper and cumin in stock.*
*Arrange salmon in skillet.*
*Process ginger; coarsely chop cilantro and combine with ginger and garlic and add to salmon; add wine and water; cook.*
*Toast pine nuts.*
*Sprinkle salmon with remaining cilantro and serve.*

---

### PANTRY

*Fresh ginger*
*Minced garlic in oil*
*Dry white wine*
*Long-grain rice*

*Whole black pepper*
*Cumin*
*Chicken stock*

---

### SHOPPING LIST

*12 ounces salmon fillets*
*Fresh cilantro (4 tablespoons)*
*14 ounces whole carrots or 12 ounces sliced (ready-cut)*

*1 ounce pine nuts (2–3 tablespoons)*

# SALMON "CAPONATA" ◆ FRESH ANGEL HAIR PASTA ◆ ◆ ◆ ◆ ◆

*Whether you use four or six ounces of pasta depends on how hungry the people who eat this meal are.*

## SALMON "CAPONATA"

2 tablespoons fresh thyme or 2 teaspoons dried
16 ounces ripe tomatoes
9 ounces whole onion or 8 ounces sliced (ready-cut) (1¾ cups)
9 ounces whole red or yellow bell pepper or 8 ounces sliced (ready-cut) (1¾ cups)
2 tablespoons capers
1 teaspoon minced garlic in oil
¼ cup red wine vinegar
Freshly ground black pepper to taste
12 ounces salmon fillets

1 Remove leaves from stems of fresh thyme.

2 Coarsely chop tomatoes.

3 Slice onion and bell pepper, if whole. Rinse capers.

4 Cook tomatoes and capers with onion, bell pepper, garlic, vinegar, thyme and black pepper in covered skillet over high heat for about 10 minutes.

5 Wash and drain fish. Place fish on the vegetables in the skillet. Cover with some of the vegetable mixture. Measure fish at thickest point. Cover skillet and cook fish, allowing 8 to 10 minutes per inch of thickness.

6 Remove cooked fish to a serving platter; reserve vegetables and pan juices for pasta.

**Yield:** 2 servings

## ANGEL HAIR PASTA

3 quarts water
4–6 ounces fresh angel hair pasta or other very thin fresh pasta or similar thin dried pasta

Bring water to boil in covered pot. Add fresh angel hair pasta and cook about 1 minute after water returns to boil. Cook dried pasta according to package directions. Drain. Pour vegetable mixture from fish over pasta. Serve.

**Yield:** 2 servings

## ◆ Game Plan ◆

Boil water for pasta in covered pot.

Remove leaves from thyme.

Cook tomatoes, onion, bell pepper, capers, garlic, vinegar, thyme and black pepper.

Prepare fish and cook.

Cook pasta and drain.

### PANTRY

Dried thyme, if fresh not available
Capers
Minced garlic in oil
Red wine vinegar

Whole black pepper
Angel hair or other very thin dried pasta, if fresh not available

### SHOPPING LIST

Fresh thyme
16 ounces ripe tomatoes
9 ounces whole onion or 8 ounces sliced (ready-cut)
9 ounces whole red or yellow bell pepper or 8 ounces sliced (ready-cut)

12 ounces salmon fillets
4–6 ounces fresh angel hair pasta or other fresh very thin pasta

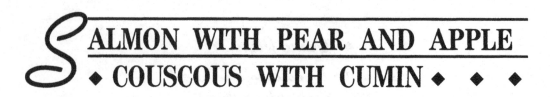

# SALMON WITH PEAR AND APPLE
## ♦ COUSCOUS WITH CUMIN ♦ ♦ ♦

### SALMON WITH PEAR AND APPLE

2 large apples
2 large ripe pears
1 lime
1 tablespoon unsalted butter
  Freshly ground black pepper
12 ounces salmon fillets

1 Heat broiler and cover broiler pan with double thickness of aluminum foil.

2 Quarter, core and slice apples and pears.

3 Cut lime in half.

4 Using thin slicer of food processor, slice apples, pears and one lime half.

5 Heat butter in small skillet and add apple, pear and lime slices. Season with pepper. Sauté until fruit begins to soften, about 5 minutes.

6 Sprinkle juice from remaining lime half over salmon slices. Measure fish at thickest point. Broil salmon 2 inches from source of heat until browned on both sides, allowing 8 to 10 minutes per each inch of thickness.

7 Sprinkle again with lime juice and serve with fruit.

**Yield:** 2 servings

### COUSCOUS WITH CUMIN

  Chicken stock (1⅛–1½ cups)
¾ teaspoons cumin
2 tablespoons tomato paste
1 cup corn niblets
½ cup couscous (precooked)

1 Following directions on couscous package, bring chicken stock with cumin to boil. Add tomato paste and corn. Cover and cook 30 seconds.

2 Stir in couscous. Remove from heat and cover. Set aside for 3 to 5 minutes, until liquid has been absorbed.

**Yield:** 2 servings

## ◆ Game Plan ◆

Heat broiler.

Prepare and cook fruit.

Sprinkle fish with lime juice and cook.

Boil stock and cumin for couscous; add tomato paste and corn.

Cook couscous.

Sprinkle fish with lime juice; serve with fruit.

---

### PANTRY

Chicken stock

Unsalted butter

Cumin

Tomato paste

Couscous

Whole black pepper

---

### SHOPPING LIST

2 large apples

2 large pears

1 lime

12 ounces salmon fillets

Corn niblets (1 cup)

# LINGUINE WITH SALMON IN TOMATO SAUCE ◆ BROCCOLI WITH MUSTARD DRESSING ◆ ◆ ◆ ◆

*Swordfish steak may be substituted for the salmon.*

## LINGUINE WITH SALMON IN TOMATO SAUCE

3 quarts water
½ cup chopped fresh cilantro
1 tablespoon olive oil
1½ teaspoons minced garlic in oil
1 tablespoon lemon juice
2 cups canned or fresh tomato sauce
16 ounces salmon fillets
8 ounces fresh or dried linguine
¼ cup French, Italian or Greek pitted black olives, packed in brine or oil

1. Boil water for linguine in covered pot.

2. Chop cilantro and sauté in hot oil with garlic for about 30 seconds over low heat.

3. Stir in lemon juice and tomato sauce and cook another 3–4 minutes over low heat.

4. Wash, skin and cut salmon fillets into bite-size chunks. Add to tomato sauce and cook about 5 minutes, until fish has lost its opaqueness but is still moist.

5. Cook fresh linguine for about 1 minute; cook dried linguine according to package directions. Drain linguine.

6. Pit olives; add to sauce just before serving. Stir the linguine into the tomato sauce.

**Yield:** 3 servings

## BROCCOLI WITH MUSTARD DRESSING

28 ounces whole broccoli or 16 ounces broccoli flowerettes (ready-cut) (6–7 cups)

1. Cut off flowerettes from whole broccoli and wash. Steam the flowerettes for 5–7 minutes, until tender but firm.

1½ tablespoons olive oil
1 tablespoon lemon juice
1 tablespoon balsamic vinegar
1 teaspoon grainy mustard

2 Meanwhile, in serving dish, whisk remaining ingredients for dressing. When broccoli is cooked, drain and stir into dish, coating thoroughly.

**Yield:** 3 servings

---

### ◆ Game Plan ◆

Boil water for linguine.
Chop cilantro and sauté with garlic in oil.
Boil water for broccoli.
Add tomato sauce and lemon juice to cilantro.
Cut up salmon.
Cook broccoli.
Make dressing for broccoli.
Add salmon to tomato sauce.
Cook pasta.
Drain broccoli and mix with dressing.
Drain pasta and mix with tomato sauce.

---

### PANTRY

Dried linguine, if fresh not available
Olive oil
Minced garlic in oil
Lemon

Tomato sauce
French, Italian or Greek black olives, packed in brine or oil
Balsamic vinegar
Grainy mustard

---

### SHOPPING LIST

8 ounces fresh linguine
Fresh cilantro (½ cup)
16 ounces salmon fillets

28 ounces whole broccoli or 16 ounces broccoli flowerettes (ready-cut)

# SALMON FLOATING ON WINE ◆ NEW POTATOES AND CILANTRO ◆ TOMATOES WITH SCALLIONS ◆ ◆

*My former colleague at* The New York Times, *Nancy Harmon Jenkins, discovered this dish at Michael Tong's Shun Lee West restaurant in Manhattan. Not only is it healthful, but it is quick and breathtakingly delicious. A few small changes have made this a very summery meal.*

## SALMON FLOATING ON WINE

| | |
|---|---|
| 12 | ounces salmon fillets |
| 1 | egg white |
| 1 | teaspoon cornstarch |
| 4 | ounces snow peas |
| 1 | teaspoon finely minced scallion, white part only (reserve green part for the Tomatoes with Scallions recipe, which follows) |
| ½ | teaspoon finely minced hot green chile, such as jalapeño or serrano |
| 1 | tablespoon corn oil |
| ½ | teaspoon minced garlic in oil |
| ½ | teaspoon hot Oriental chili paste |
| 3 | tablespoons dry sherry or dry vermouth |
| 6 | tablespoons chicken or fish stock |
| ¼ | teaspoon Oriental sesame oil |

1. Wash and slice salmon on diagonal into ½-inch-thick pieces. Place in bowl with egg white. Mix well but gently, using your hands to coat salmon. Add cornstarch and mix well again with hands to coat. Place in colander in sink and allow excess egg white to drain off.

2. Wash and cut snow peas into thirds.

3. Mince scallion and green chile.

4. Heat wok or skillet, large enough to hold salmon, over high heat. Add corn oil. When oil is very hot, quickly sauté the scallion, green chile and garlic, stirring until ingredients just begin to brown.

5. Add chili paste, sherry and stock; bring to rolling boil.

6. Add salmon pieces in single layer and cook quickly on both sides, about 2 minutes total.

7. Add snow peas to pan after 1 minute and stir. Sprinkle with sesame oil and serve.

**Yield:** 2 servings

---

## NEW POTATOES AND CILANTRO

| | |
|---|---|
| 10 | ounces tiny new potatoes |

1. Scrub potatoes but do not peel. Place in pot with water to cover. Cover and bring to boil.

| | |
|---|---|
| 2 tablespoons fresh cilantro | $\underline{2}$ Boil potatoes until they are tender, 18–20 minutes. |
| | $\underline{3}$ Coarsely cut up cilantro. |
| | $\underline{4}$ Drain potatoes and cut into halves or quarters, depending on size. Sprinkle with cilantro. |
| | **Yield:** 2 servings |

---

## TOMATOES WITH SCALLIONS

| | |
|---|---|
| 1 large ripe tomato<br>2 scallions, green part only | $\underline{1}$ Wash and slice tomato. |
| | $\underline{2}$ Chop scallions and sprinkle over tomato slices. |
| | **Yield:** 2 servings |

---

### ◆ Game Plan ◆

Scrub potatoes and cook.   Prepare salmon with egg white and cornstarch.
Prepare snow peas.   Mince scallion and hot chile.
Slice tomato; chop green part of scallion and sprinkle over tomatoes. Chop
cilantro.   Heat oil and cook scallion, chile and garlic.
Add chili paste, sherry and stock and bring to boil.
Add salmon to stock mixture and cook quickly.
Drain potatoes and mix with cilantro.
Add snow peas to salmon.   Top with sesame oil.

---

#### PANTRY

| | | |
|---|---|---|
| Egg | Minced garlic in oil | Chicken or fish stock |
| Cornstarch | Hot Oriental chile paste | Oriental sesame oil |
| Corn oil | Dry sherry or dry vermouth | |

---

#### SHOPPING LIST

| | | |
|---|---|---|
| 12 ounces salmon fillets | 1 hot green chile, such as | Fresh cilantro |
| 4 ounces snow peas | jalapeño or serrano | (2 tablespoons) |
| Bunch scallions (2) | 10 ounces tiny new potatoes | 1 large ripe tomato |

# SCROD PROVENÇAL ◆ GREEN BEANS AND CORN ◆ RICE ◆ ◆

*A quickie. So quick, in fact, that you will have time to clean up before dinner is ready. There is no oil in the fish dish. In fact, the only fat in the menu is in the Green Beans and Corn recipe.*

## SCROD PROVENÇAL

2 ripe medium tomatoes
10 small or 6 large Italian, French or Greek pitted black olives, packed in oil or brine
1 tablespoon fresh oregano or 1 teaspoon dried
½ cup dry white wine
Freshly ground black pepper to taste
12 ounces scrod or other white fish fillets

1 Slice tomatoes and pit olives.

2 Chop fresh oregano; place it in skillet with tomatoes, olives, wine, pepper and scrod.

3 Cover and cook over medium-high heat 6–8 minutes, until fish loses its translucency; do not overcook.

**Yield:** 2 servings

## GREEN BEANS AND CORN

4 ounces green beans
10-ounce package frozen corn kernels (2 cups)
⅓ cup low-fat milk
1 tablespoon unsalted butter
½ teaspoon ground cumin
Freshly ground black pepper to taste

1 If green beans are not already trimmed, wash and cut off the tips, then cut them into 1-inch lengths.

2 Combine beans with remaining ingredients and bring to boil. Cook, uncovered, over high heat 5–7 minutes, until milk is almost evaporated.

**Yield:** 2 servings

## RICE

½ cup rice
1 cup water

Combine water and rice and bring to boil. Reduce heat and cook, covered, for about 17 minutes total, until rice is tender and water has evaporated.

**Yield:** 2 servings

## ◆ Game Plan ◆

Cook rice.
Prepare fish ingredients.
Prepare vegetable ingredients.
Cook fish.
Cook vegetables.

### PANTRY

Italian, French or Greek black
    olives, packed in oil or brine
Dried oregano, if fresh not
    available
Dry white wine

Whole black pepper
Low-fat milk
Unsalted butter
Ground cumin
Rice

### SHOPPING LIST

2 ripe medium tomatoes
Fresh oregano (1 tablespoon)
12 ounces scrod or other white fish
    fillets

4 ounces green beans
10-ounce package frozen corn
    kernels

# $\mathcal{S}$AUTÉED SHAD ROE ◆ ASPARAGUS ◆ NEW POTATO SALAD WITH MUSTARD AND CHIVE DRESSING ◆ ◆ ◆ ◆ ◆ ◆ ◆ ◆ ◆

*Along the East Coast, nothing says spring as clearly as a meal of shad roe and asparagus.*

*There is little that could be simpler, but what else could be more festive?*

## SAUTÉED SHAD ROE

2 sets shad roe
3 tablespoons unsalted butter

1. Wash roe; cover with water and parboil in covered skillet for 5 minutes. Drain.

2. Wipe out skillet, then melt butter in it. Sauté roe on both sides in hot butter over medium heat for about 10 minutes, until roe is golden brown on both sides.

**Yield:** 2 servings

## ASPARAGUS

14–16 asparagus

1. Bring water to boil in bottom of steamer.

2. Wash asparagus and break off tough end at point where it snaps naturally.

3. Steam about 7 minutes, until bright green and tender but not soft.

**Yield:** 2 servings

## NEW POTATO SALAD WITH MUSTARD AND CHIVE DRESSING

9 ounces tiny new
   potatoes
⅔ cup low- or non-fat
   cottage cheese
⅔ cup plain low- or non-fat
   yogurt
2 teaspoons chopped fresh
   chives
1½ teaspoons Dijon
   mustard
2 teaspoons capers
   Freshly ground black
   pepper to taste

1. Scrub potatoes but do not peel. Cover with water and cook in covered pot, about 18 minutes.

2. Beat cottage cheese and yogurt with wire whisk.

3. Chop chives and add to cottage cheese mixture with mustard, capers and pepper.

4. When potatoes are cooked, drain and cut into halves or quarters. Add to dressing, mix and serve.

**Yield:** 2 servings

---

◆ *Game Plan* ◆

*Cook potatoes.*
*Parboil shad roe.*
*Bring water to boil for asparagus.*
*Prepare asparagus.*
*Sauté shad roe.*
*Steam asparagus.*
*Make dressing for potatoes.*
*Mix potatoes with dressing.*

---

*PANTRY*

*Unsalted butter*
*Plain low- or non-fat yogurt*
*Dijon mustard*

*Capers*
*Whole black pepper*

---

*SHOPPING LIST*

*2 sets shad roe*
*14–16 asparagus*
*9 ounces tiny new potatoes*

*Low- or non-fat cottage cheese (⅔ cup)*
*Fresh chives (2 tablespoons)*

# ƑUSILLI WITH TUNA, BROCCOLI AND TOMATOES WITH CRUSTY WHOLE WHEAT BREAD ♦ ♦ ♦ ♦ ♦

*Salad bars have either cooked, blanched or raw broccoli flowerettes; the recipe will work with any of them. Without the ripe tomatoes of summer and early fall, this recipe really won't work. Fusilli look like corkscrews; any similar type of dried pasta, including shells, is equally good. Serve this with a crusty, whole wheat bread.*

### FUSILLI WITH TUNA, BROCCOLI AND TOMATOES WITH CRUSTY WHOLE WHEAT BREAD

3 quarts water
16 ounces whole broccoli or 8 ounces broccoli flowerettes (ready-cut) (3½–4 cups)
8 ounces fresh tuna or 6½-ounce can of tuna packed in water
3 medium tomatoes
4 ounces fusilli
2 heaping tablespoons chopped fresh basil or 2 teaspoons dried basil
2 teaspoons chopped fresh oregano or ¾ teaspoon dried oregano
2 slices red onion
4 tablespoons olive oil
4 tablespoons red wine vinegar
Freshly ground black pepper to taste
2 ounces sharp cheese, such as Cheddar, Provolone or Parmesan
Crusty whole wheat bread

1. If using fresh tuna, heat broiler and cover broiler pan with aluminum foil.

2. Boil water for fusilli.

3. If broccoli is whole, trim off stems and cut heads into flowerettes.

4. If using canned tuna, drain and rinse.

5. Cut tomatoes into large chunks.

6. If using fresh tuna, broil for about 3–5 minutes on each side, depending on thickness, turning once. Cut into small chunks.

7. Cook fusilli about 7 minutes.

8. Chop fresh basil, oregano and sliced onion.

9. Cook raw broccoli flowerettes by adding to pot of fusilli for the final 2–3 minutes of cooking time. Drain fusilli and broccoli.

10. Beat together oil and vinegar, and stir in herbs and onion; add pepper to taste.

<u>11</u> Combine dressing with fusilli, tuna, broccoli and tomatoes.

<u>12</u> Cut cheese into small cubes and add. Serve with crusty whole wheat bread.

**Yield:** 3 servings

---

### ◆ *Game Plan* ◆

*Follow recipe directions.*

---

#### PANTRY

6½-ounce can of tuna packed in water, if fresh tuna not used
Fusilli
Dried basil, if fresh not available
Dried oregano, if fresh not available

Olive oil
Red wine vinegar
Whole black pepper
Sharp cheese, such as Cheddar, Provolone or Parmesan

---

#### SHOPPING LIST

8 ounces fresh tuna (about 2 slices)
3 medium tomatoes
16 ounces whole broccoli or 8 ounces broccoli flowerettes (ready-cut)

Red onion (2 slices)
Fresh basil
Fresh oregano
Crusty whole wheat bread

# FRESH TUNA WITH CAPERS AND LEMON JUICE ◆ VEGETABLE RICE SALAD WITH PARMESAN DRESSING ◆ ◆ ◆ ◆ ◆ ◆ ◆ ◆ ◆

## FRESH TUNA WITH CAPERS AND LEMON JUICE

2 teaspoons capers
½ lemon
12 ounces fresh tuna
    Olive oil for brushing
    tuna

1 Heat broiler and cover broiler pan with double thickness of aluminum foil.

2 Drain and rinse capers.

3 Dice lemon, leaving peel on, and mix with capers.

4 Brush fish with oil. Measure fish at thickest point. Broil about 2 inches from source of heat, allowing 8 to 10 minutes per inch of thickness.

5 When fish is cooked, sprinkle with capers and lemon and serve.

**Yield:** 2 servings

## VEGETABLE RICE SALAD WITH PARMESAN DRESSING

½ cup long-grain rice
1 cup water
1 Kirby cucumber
5 ounces whole red bell
    pepper or 4 ounces sliced
    (ready-cut) (1 cup)
2 scallions
¼ cup freshly grated
    Parmesan cheese,
    preferably Parmigiano
    Reggiano (about 2
    ounces)
1 tablespoon minced fresh
    basil or 1 teaspoon dried

1 Place rice and water in saucepan and bring to boil. Reduce heat, cover and simmer 17 minutes total, until water has been absorbed.

2 Wash and thinly slice cucumber but do not peel.

3 Coarsely dice pepper.

4 Wash, trim and slice scallions.

5 Coarsely grate Parmesan cheese; mince fresh basil and combine with oil, vinegar, yogurt, mustard and

2 tablespoons olive oil
2 tablespoons cider vinegar
2 tablespoons plain low- or
  non-fat yogurt
½ teaspoon Dijon mustard
  Freshly ground black
  pepper to taste

black pepper. Mix well; stir in cucumber, red pepper and scallions.

6 When rice is cooked combine with vegetables and dressing.

**Yield:** 2 servings

---

## ◆ Game Plan ◆

*Heat broiler.*

*Cook rice.*

*Dice lemon and mix with capers.*

*Broil fish.*

*Prepare vegetables.*

*Grate cheese; mince basil.*

*Prepare salad dressing.*

*Mix vegetables and dressing.*

*Add rice to salad.*

*Sprinkle caper–lemon mixture over fish.*

---

### PANTRY

Capers
Lemon
Olive oil
Long-grain rice
Parmesan cheese, preferably
  Parmigiano Reggiano

Dried basil, if fresh is not available
Cider vinegar
Plain low- or non-fat yogurt
Dijon mustard
Whole black pepper

---

### SHOPPING LIST

12 ounces fresh tuna
1 Kirby cucumber
5 ounces whole red bell pepper or 4
  ounces sliced (ready-cut)

Bunch scallions (2)
Fresh basil (1 tablespoon)

# MARINATED TUNA ON BED OF SAUTÉED SNOW PEAS ◆ CHINESE NOODLES WITH GINGER–SESAME SAUCE ◆ ◆ ◆ ◆ ◆ ◆ ◆

*Elegant and simple. I got the idea for the main dish from a restaurant, to which I would be happy to give credit if only I could remember which one it was!*

## MARINATED TUNA ON BED OF SAUTÉED SNOW PEAS

1 tablespoon coarsely grated ginger
1 tablespoon reduced-sodium soy sauce
2 tuna steaks (12 ounces)
4 ounces snow peas
1 teaspoon plus 1 tablespoon corn, safflower or canola oil

1. Heat broiler. Cover broiler pan with double thickness of aluminum foil.

2. Grate ginger; mix with soy sauce in dish large enough to hold tuna.

3. Wash tuna; dry and coat with marinade.

4. Wash and trim snow peas; cut each in half.

5. Remove tuna from marinade; rub ½ teaspoon of oil on each side and broil 2 inches from source of heat for about 4 minutes; turn and broil on second side about 2 minutes longer.

6. Heat 1 tablespoon oil in skillet and sauté snow peas for 2 minutes, until slightly softened but still firm. Arrange peas on 2 dinner plates and place tuna steaks on top.

**Yield:** 2 servings

## CHINESE NOODLES WITH GINGER–SESAME SAUCE

3 quarts water

1. Bring water to boil in covered pot.

1 large scallion
1 tablespoon coarsely
grated ginger
1 teaspoon reduced-sodium
soy sauce
2 teaspoons Chinese black
vinegar or red wine
vinegar
½ teaspoon sugar
2 teaspoons Oriental
sesame oil
4 ounces fresh thin Chinese
noodles or fresh thin
(angel hair) Italian
noodles

2  Slice scallion; grate ginger. Place in bowl large enough to hold noodles.

3  Stir in soy sauce, vinegar, sugar and sesame oil.

4  Cook noodles for 1–2 minutes, depending on thickness. Drain and stir into sauce.

**Yield:** 2 servings

---

◆ *Game Plan* ◆

*Boil water for noodles.*
*Heat broiler.*
*Marinate tuna.*
*Prepare snow peas.*
*Make sauce for noodles.*
*Broil tuna.*
*Cook noodles.*
*Sauté snow peas*

---

*PANTRY*

*Ginger*
*Reduced-sodium soy sauce*
*Corn, safflower or canola oil*

*Chinese black vinegar or red wine*
  *vinegar*
*Sugar*
*Oriental sesame oil*

---

*SHOPPING LIST*

*2 tuna steaks (12 ounces)*
*4 ounces snow peas*

*4 ounces fresh thin Chinese noodles*
  *or fresh angel hair pasta*
*Bunch scallions (1 large)*

# OYSTERS WITH ITALIAN TOMATO SAUCE ◆ RICE ◆ ◆ ◆ ◆ ◆ ◆

*Granted, not everyone has easy access to shucked fresh oysters, but for the lucky ones of us who do, this is a delicious dish and very quick to execute.*

## OYSTERS WITH ITALIAN TOMATO SAUCE

8 ounces whole red bell pepper or 7 ounces sliced (ready cut) (1½ cups)
4 ounces whole onion or 3 ounces sliced (ready-cut) (1 cup)
1 stalk celery or 2 ounces sliced (ready cut) (⅓ cup)
1–2 tablespoons olive oil
1 teaspoon minced garlic in oil
1 pint shucked oysters, with their liquor
4 teaspoons Greek, Italian or French black olives, packed in oil or brine (10–12 small; 6–8 large)
2 tablespoons flour
16-ounce can tomatoes
½ cup dry white wine or dry vermouth
Freshly ground black pepper to taste
½ teaspoon dried oregano
½ teaspoon dried basil
½ teaspoon dried thyme

1. Coarsely chop red pepper, onion and celery, and sauté in hot oil with garlic until slightly soft.

2. Drain oysters, reserving liquor; you should have ½ cup.

3. While vegetables are cooking, cut up olives and add.

4. When vegetables are soft, stir in flour.

5. Crush tomatoes with fingers and add to vegetables along with wine, oyster liquor, pepper and herbs. Stir and cook until mixture begins to thicken, 1–2 minutes.

6. Stir in oysters and cook over medium heat, about 4 minutes for large oysters. Do not boil or overcook oysters or they will toughen. Serve over rice.

**Yield:** 2 servings

## RICE

½–¾ cup long-grain rice
1–1½ cups water

1  Combine rice and water in saucepan and bring to boil.

2  Reduce heat, cover and cook about 17 minutes total, until rice is soft and liquid has been absorbed.

**Yield:** 2 servings

◆ *Game Plan* ◆

*Cook rice.*
*Follow directions for oyster recipe.*

### PANTRY

Olive oil
Minced garlic in oil
Greek, Italian or French black
    olives, packed in oil or brine
Flour

Dry white wine or dry vermouth
Whole black pepper
Dried oregano
Dried basil
Dried thyme
Long-grain rice

### SHOPPING LIST

8 ounces whole red pepper or
    7 ounces sliced (ready-cut)
4 ounces whole onion or 3 ounces
    sliced (ready-cut)

2 ounces sliced (ready-cut) celery
    or 1 stalk
1 pint shucked oysters with their
    liquor
16-ounce can tomatoes

# OYSTERS WITH LINGUINE ◆
# CUCUMBERS WITH ALMONDS ◆

*The oyster recipe is adapted from one developed by Clare Vanderbeek, of the National Fisheries Institute.*

*The salad of cucumbers and almonds may seem like an unlikely combination, but the toasted almonds add a marvelous extra crunch to the already crunchy cucumbers.*

## OYSTERS WITH LINGUINE

3 quarts water
3 scallions
1 tablespoon chopped fresh parsley
1–2 tablespoons olive oil
1 tablespoon minced garlic in oil
Freshly ground black pepper to taste
Crushed hot red pepper to taste
1 teaspoon Dijon mustard
⅓ cup dry white wine
1 pint shucked oysters, with their liquor
1½ tablespoons flour
12-ounce can corn niblets
6–8 ounces fresh linguine or dried
6 tablespoons grated Cheddar cheese (about 3 ounces)

1. Boil water for linguine in covered pot.

2. Clean and chop scallions.

3. Chop parsley.

4. Heat oil in skillet and sauté scallions, parsley and garlic over medium heat until softened.

5. Season with black and red pepper and add mustard and wine; reduce heat and cook slowly for 1–2 minutes.

6. Drain liquor from oysters; mix 1½ tablespoons of liquor with flour to make a paste. Add to pan along with remaining liquor and cook for 1–2 minutes, stirring until mixture thickens a little.

7. Add oysters and corn, with the liquid from the can; cook 3–4 minutes over moderate heat, just until oysters begin to curl.

8. Cook linguine, about 2 minutes if fresh, 6–7 minutes for dried, depending on brand.

9. Grate cheese.

10. Serve oyster sauce over linguine, sprinkled with cheese.

**Yield:** 2 servings

## CUCUMBERS WITH ALMONDS

2 tablespoons slivered
  almonds (about 1 ounce)
2 scallions
4 small Kirby cucumbers
2 tablespoons olive oil
1 tablespoon red wine
  vinegar
½ teaspoon ground cumin

1 Toast almonds to golden brown in toaster oven.

2 Chop scallions (this can be done at the same time as you are chopping scallions for the oyster dish).

3 Scrub cucumbers—do not peel—and slice into ¼-inch thick rounds.

4 Combine oil, vinegar and cumin in bowl large enough to hold salad and mix well.

5 Add cucumbers, scallions and almonds to dressing and toss to coat well.

**Yield:** 2 servings

---

## ◆ *Game Plan* ◆

*Boil water for pasta.    Toast almonds.*
*Chop scallions and parsley; sauté with garlic in oil.*
*Wash and slice cucumbers.*
*Add seasonings and wine to scallion mixture for oysters.*
*Prepare salad dressing.*
*Drain oysters and make paste; add to scallion mixture.*
*Cook oysters and corn.   Cook pasta.   Grate cheese.   Finish salad.*

---

### PANTRY

*Olive oil*
*Minced garlic in oil*
*Whole black pepper*

*Crushed hot red pepper*
*Dijon mustard*
*Dry white wine*
*Flour*

*Dried linguine, if fresh*
  *not available*
*Red wine vinegar*
*Cumin*

---

### SHOPPING LIST

*Bunch scallions (5)*
*Fresh parsley (1 tablespoon)*
*1 pint shucked oysters, with*
  *their liquor*

*12-ounce can corn niblets*
*3 ounces Cheddar cheese*
  *(6 tablespoons)*
*6–8 ounces fresh linguine*

*1 ounce slivered almonds*
  *(2 tablespoons)*
*4 small Kirby cucumbers*

# OYSTER CEVICHE ◆ RICE SALAD WITH FENNEL, MUSHROOMS AND PARMESAN ◆ ◆ ◆ ◆ ◆ ◆

*This ceviche is an adaptation of a recipe that won first prize at the annual National Oyster Cooking Contest, held each October in St. Mary's County, Maryland. I've been one of the judges ever since the contest began, and it is always a delightful experience.*

*This was one of the most delicious dishes ever entered, though it is misnamed. The oysters are poached in hot chicken broth, whereas a true ceviche calls for "cooking" ingredients in lemon or lime juice, without heat.*

## OYSTER CEVICHE

1 cup chicken stock
24 fresh shucked oysters, with their liquor
2 tablespoons chopped green bell pepper
2 tablespoons chopped red bell pepper
1 lime
4 tablespoons chopped red onion
1 tablespoon chopped fresh parsley
1 ripe avocado
2 ripe medium tomatoes
½ cup catsup
2 teaspoons prepared horseradish

1. Bring chicken stock to boil; reduce heat to simmer and add oysters and their liquor. Poach gently for 2–3 minutes. Drain and place in serving bowl.

2. Finely chop the green and red pepper.

3. Squeeze lime juice over oysters and refrigerate while preparing rest of menu.

4. Finely chop the red onion and parsley.

5. Cut avocado and tomatoes into small chunks. Add with vegetables to oysters.

6. Carefully stir in catsup and horseradish.

**Yield: 2 large or 3 small servings**

## RICE SALAD WITH FENNEL, MUSHROOMS AND PARMESAN

½ cup long-grain rice
1 cup water
14 ounces whole fennel bulb or 7 ounces trimmed (2 cups)
4 ounces fresh whole mushrooms or 3 ounces sliced (ready cut)

1. Bring rice and water to boil in heavy-bottomed pot. Reduce heat, cover and simmer until water has evaporated, 17 minutes total cooking time.

2. Trim fennel so that only the bulb remains; remove tough or badly scarred outer layer. Trim bottom. Cut into halves or quarters if the bulb is large and

2 ounces Parmigiano
  Reggiano
1½ tablespoons olive oil
2 tablespoons balsamic
  vinegar
Freshly ground black
  pepper to taste

slice on thinnest slicing blade of food processor. Measure out 2 cups into serving bowl. Reserve extra for another occasion.

3̄ Wash mushrooms and trim off stems. Slice in food processor, using thinnest slicing blade. Add to fennel.

4̄ Slice cheese in food processor.

5̄ Whisk oil and vinegar and add with cheese to fennel.

6̄ When rice is cooked stir into vegetables and mix well. Season with pepper.

**Yield:** 2 large or 3 small servings

---

## ◆ Game Plan ◆

Cook rice.   Heat stock and poach oysters.   Chop peppers.
Drain oysters and sprinkle with lime juice; refrigerate.
Chop onion and parsley.
Cut up avocado and tomatoes and add with vegetables to oysters.
Stir catsup and horseradish into oysters.   Prepare fennel and slice.
Prepare mushrooms and slice.   Slice cheese.
Dress with oil and vinegar; stir in rice.   Season with pepper.

---

### PANTRY

| | | |
|---|---|---|
| Chicken stock | Long-grain rice | Balsamic vinegar |
| Catsup | Parmigiano Reggiano | Whole black pepper |
| Horseradish | Olive oil | |

---

### SHOPPING LIST

24 shucked oysters, with their
  liquor
Green bell pepper (2 tablespoons)
Red bell pepper (2 tablespoons)
1 lime
Red onion (4 tablespoons)

Fresh parsley (1 tablespoon)
1 ripe avocado
2 ripe medium tomatoes
14 ounces whole fennel bulb
4 ounces fresh whole mushrooms
  or 3 ounces sliced (ready-cut)

# GERMAINE'S SCALLOPS AND RICE ◆

*Germaine Swanson owns Germaine's Pan-Asian restaurant in Washington, D.C. Her signature dish is a scallop salad that calls for marinating the scallops two hours or more. That automatically eliminated it from a book of 20-minute meals until I thought of a way to accomplish what the marinating does, but in less time—cooking the scallops about 60 seconds in lemon juice.*

*So this is an adaptation of Germaine's delectable dish.*

*The meal also needed starch, so I added some rice—perfect—then surrounded the dish with cherry tomatoes for color and balance.*

*There was some discussion as to whether this dinner provides enough food for a man. The answer: Add a Dove bar!*

## GERMAINE'S SCALLOPS AND RICE

½ cup long-grain rice
1 cup water
16 ounces scallops (bay, calico or sea)
⅓ cup fresh lemon juice
20 snow peas
1 teaspoon minced garlic in oil
2–3 tablespoons chopped or sliced (ready-cut) onion (1 ounce)
1 tablespoon chopped fresh dill
2 tablespoons rice vinegar
3 tablespoons corn, safflower or canola oil
1½ teaspoons Dijon mustard
White pepper to taste
10 cherry tomatoes
2 cups shredded iceberg lettuce
1 tablespoon pine nuts

1. Bring rice and water to boil; reduce heat and cover. Cook for a total of 17 minutes.

2. Rinse scallops. If sea scallops are used, cut them in half; leave other types of scallops whole.

3. Squeeze lemon juice and add to a skillet large enough to hold scallops. Bring to boil; add scallops; reduce heat and cook about 60 seconds, just until scallops become white. Drain immediately and set aside.

4. Meanwhile, wash and trim snow peas.

5. Rinse out skillet in which scallops were cooked and bring enough water to cover the snow peas to boil, covered. Add snow peas and blanch for 30 seconds. Drain and rinse to stop cooking. Cut in halves or thirds, depending on size.

6. Turn on food processor and through the feed tube, process garlic and onion to puree.

$\underline{7}$ Chop dill, and with vinegar, oil, mustard and pepper, add to processor and process to creamy mixture.

$\underline{8}$ Wash cherry tomatoes.

$\underline{9}$ Shred lettuce and combine with snow peas; arrange on serving plate.

$\underline{10}$ When rice is cooked, gently mix it with scallops and spoon over greens. Spoon on dressing. Sprinkle with pine nuts.

$\underline{11}$ Arrange cherry tomatoes around edge of dish and serve.

**Yield:** 2 servings

---

## ◆ *Game Plan* ◆

*Follow recipe directions.*

---

### PANTRY

Long-grain rice
Lemon
Minced garlic in oil
Rice vinegar

Corn, safflower or canola oil
Dijon mustard
White pepper

---

### SHOPPING LIST

16 ounces scallops (bay, calico or
    sea)
20 snow peas
1 ounce chopped or sliced (ready-
    cut) onion (2–3 tablespoons)

Fresh dill (1 tablespoon)
10 cherry tomatoes
Shredded iceberg lettuce (2 cups)
1 ounce pine nuts (1 tablespoon)

# CURRIED SCALLOPS ◆ CARROTS IN CUMIN–MUSTARD SAUCE ◆ RICE ◆ ◆ ◆ ◆ ◆ ◆ ◆ ◆ ◆ ◆

*There is nothing called "curry powder" in this recipe, just a typical combination of the spices traditionally used in curried dishes—though there are literally thousands of curry variations.*

## CURRIED SCALLOPS

1½–3 teaspoons unsalted butter
1½–3 teaspoons corn, safflower or canola oil
½ teaspoon ground cumin
¼ teaspoon ground coriander
⅛ teaspoon ground turmeric
12 ounces scallops (sea, bay or calico)
1 teaspoon cornstarch
¼ cup dry vermouth
2 teaspoons lemon juice
1 teaspoon chopped fresh parsley

1 Heat butter and oil in medium-sized skillet.

2 Stir in cumin, coriander and turmeric, and cook for 30 seconds.

3 Wash and dry scallops and add to pan. Cook 1–3 minutes, depending on size, stirring. If scallops are large, cook 1–2 minutes longer. Remove the scallops from pan with a slotted spoon and keep warm.

4 Mix cornstarch with vermouth and lemon juice and add to skillet. Cook to thicken and return scallops just to heat through.

5 Chop parsley. Serve scallops and sauce over rice, sprinkled with parsley.

**Yield:** 2 servings

## CARROTS IN CUMIN–MUSTARD SAUCE

11 ounces whole carrots or 10 ounces sliced (ready-cut) (2 cups)
2 teaspoons unsalted butter, softened
2 teaspoons lemon juice
2 teaspoons coarse-grained mustard
½ teaspoon cumin

1 Bring water to boil in steamer.

2 Scrape and slice whole carrots. Place carrots in steamer over boiling water and steam about 7 minutes.

3 Put butter, lemon juice, mustard and cumin in serving dish and mix thoroughly.

$\overline{4}$ When carrots are cooked, drain and place in dish. Mix well to coat carrots with sauce. Serve immediately.

**Yield:** 2 servings

---

## RICE

¾ cup long-grain rice
1½ cups water

$\overline{1}$ Combine rice and water and bring to boil.

$\overline{2}$ Reduce heat, cover and simmer for 17 minutes, until rice is tender and water has been absorbed.

**Yield:** 2 servings

---

### ◆ *Game Plan* ◆

*Cook rice. Steam carrots. Mix ingredients for carrot sauce.
Cook spices and add scallops.
Set scallops aside and mix cornstarch with vermouth and lemon juice.
Add vermouth mixture to scallop pan and cook until thick; return
scallops to pan to heat through.
Chop parsley.
Drain carrots and mix with sauce.*

---

### PANTRY

Unsalted butter
Corn, safflower or canola oil
Cumin
Coriander
Turmeric

Cornstarch
Dry vermouth
Lemon
Coarse-grained mustard
Long-grain rice

---

### SHOPPING LIST

12 ounces scallops (sea, bay or
   calico)
Fresh parsley (1 teaspoon)

11 ounces whole carrots or 10
   ounces sliced (ready-cut)

# SCALLOPS IN ORANGE JUICE AND GINGER ◆ RICE ◆ BRUSSELS SPROUTS WITH MUSTARD–LEMON SAUCE ◆ ◆ ◆ ◆ ◆ ◆ ◆ ◆ ◆ ◆

*The scallop recipe is adapted from a dish served at The Back Porch, in Rehobeth, Delaware. The mustard–lemon sauce for the Brussels sprouts is equally good over broccoli, green beans or cauliflower.*

## SCALLOPS IN ORANGE JUICE AND GINGER

2½ teaspoons coarsely grated fresh ginger
½ cup fresh orange juice
½ cup dry white wine
1 tablespoon honey
1–2 tablespoons unsalted butter
1 teaspoon minced garlic in oil
2 tablespoons slivered almonds (about 1 ounce)
12 ounces scallops (bay, calico or sea)

1. Grate ginger.

2. Mix orange juice with wine, honey and 1 teaspoon ginger; set aside.

3. Heat butter in skillet with garlic. Add almonds and sauté 2–3 minutes, until they begin to turn golden.

4. Wash and dry scallops and add to almonds with remaining ginger; cook just until scallops lose opaqueness, about 1 minute for calicos or bays, 3–4 minutes for sea scallops.

5. Remove scallops and almonds to heated dish and pour off liquid in pan.

6. Add orange juice mixture to pan and cook over medium-high heat until mixture boils; reduce heat and cook at high simmer until it is reduced by half.

7. Return scallops to pan and heat through; serve with sauce over rice.

**Yield:** 2 servings

## RICE

¾ cup long-grain rice

1. Combine rice and water in pot and bring to boil, uncovered.

1½ cups water

$\underline{2}$ Reduce heat, cover and simmer until water has been absorbed, a total of 17 minutes.

**Yield:** 2 servings

## BRUSSELS SPROUTS WITH MUSTARD–LEMON SAUCE

10 ounces Brussels sprouts
2 teaspoons softened
   unsalted butter
2 teaspoons lemon juice
2 teaspoons grainy mustard

$\underline{1}$ Boil water in steamer.

$\underline{2}$ Wash and trim sprouts and steam about 10 minutes.

$\underline{3}$ Mix butter, lemon juice and mustard in serving dish.

$\underline{4}$ When sprouts are cooked, drain and spoon into serving dish. Mix until butter melts and sprouts are coated.

**Yield:** 2 servings

◆ *Game Plan* ◆

*Cook rice.*
*Boil water for steaming sprouts and trim sprouts.*
*Grate ginger and mix with orange juice, wine and honey for scallops;*
*sauté almonds.*
*Steam sprouts.    Prepare sauce for sprouts.    Cook scallops.*

### PANTRY

| | | |
|---|---|---|
| *Fresh ginger* | *Honey* | *Long-grain rice* |
| *Fresh orange juice* | *Unsalted butter* | *Lemon* |
| *Dry white wine* | *Minced garlic in oil* | *Grainy mustard* |

### SHOPPING LIST

| | | |
|---|---|---|
| *1 ounce slivered almonds* | *12 ounces scallops* | *10 ounces Brussels sprouts* |
| *(2 tablespoons)* | *(bay, calico or sea)* | |

# GINGER SOFT SHELL CRABS ◆ CORN ON THE COB ◆ SLICED TOMATOES ◆ ◆ ◆ ◆ ◆ ◆ ◆ ◆

*This meal is not for everyone, I know. It is not easy to find soft shell crabs in some parts of the country, and they are often very costly as well.*

*But if they are available, there is no simpler meal. And for those who live in Maryland there is no better treat. Have the fishmonger clean the crabs for you if you don't know how to clean them yourself.*

*You can substitute scallops for the crabs if you need to. Simply flour them lightly and sauté—delicious!*

*Good, very sweet corn really does not need butter, but it is up to you.*

## GINGER SOFT SHELL CRABS

4 large soft shell crabs, cleaned
Flour
1 tablespoon coarsely grated ginger
3 tablespoons unsalted butter
4 tablespoons sliced scallions

1 Wash and dry crabs. Flour lightly.

2 Grate ginger.

3 Heat butter and ginger in skillet large enough to hold crabs. Sauté crabs on top side for several minutes, until they are golden brown and are beginning to turn red.

4 While crabs are cooking, slice scallions.

5 Turn and brown crabs on the other side. Total cooking time is 7–8 minutes. Drain on paper towels.

6 Serve crabs sprinkled with scallions.

**Yield:** 2 servings

## CORN ON THE COB

2–4 ears of very fresh corn

1 Bring water to boil in steamer.

$\underline{2}$ Shuck corn and cook about 5 minutes, only until tender. Remove and place in serving dish, covered with cloth.

**Yield:** 2 servings

---

## SLICED TOMATOES

2 ripe medium tomatoes
  Balsamic or raspberry
  vinegar
1–2 sprigs fresh basil
  (optional)

$\underline{1}$ Wash and slice tomatoes and arrange on 2 salad plates.

$\underline{2}$ Sprinkle with vinegar.

$\underline{3}$ Wash and dry basil and place leaves on top of tomatoes, if desired.

**Yield:** 2 servings

---

## ◆ *Game Plan* ◆

*Boil water for corn.*
*Wash, dry and dredge crabs in flour.*
*Grate ginger.   Shuck corn.*
*Heat butter and ginger; sauté crabs.*
*Slice scallions.   Cook corn.*
*Slice tomatoes and sprinkle with vinegar.*
*Turn crabs and sauté.*
*Add basil to tomatoes, if desired.*
*Sprinkle crabs with scallions.*

---

### PANTRY

*Flour*
*Fresh ginger*

*Unsalted butter*
*Balsamic or raspberry vinegar*

---

### SHOPPING LIST

*4 large soft shell crabs*
*Bunch scallions (4 tablespoons)*
*2–4 fresh ears corn*

*2 ripe medium tomatoes*
*Fresh basil, optional (1–2 sprigs)*

# MARYLAND CRAB CAKES ◆ POTATOES WITH BASIL– TOMATO DRESSING ◆ ◆ ◆ ◆ ◆ ◆

*Ask any Maryland cook—the secret to a good crab cake is the presence of lots of crabmeat and the absence of a lot of filler.*

*And if you have a choice between fresh and pasteurized crabmeat, choose the fresh.*

## MARYLAND CRAB CAKES

| | |
|---|---|
| 1 beaten egg | 1 Beat egg lightly. |
| 1 tablespoon chopped fresh parsley | |
| 1½ tablespoons mayonnaise | 2 Chop parsley and combine with mayonnaise, mustard, Worcestershire sauce and egg. |
| 2 teaspoons prepared mustard | |
| ½ teaspoon Worcestershire sauce | 3 Pick over crabmeat and discard cartilage and shell. |
| 12 ounces backfin or lump crabmeat | 4 Mix crabmeat with cracker crumbs and egg mixture. |
| ⅓ cup cracker crumbs | |
| 2 tablespoons unsalted butter | 5 Shape crabmeat into 4 patties and sauté in butter until golden, about 4 minutes on each side. |

**Yield:** 2 servings

## POTATOES WITH BASIL–TOMATO DRESSING

| | |
|---|---|
| 12 ounces tiny new potatoes | 1 Scrub potatoes but do not peel. Bring to boil in water to cover in covered pot and boil for about 17 minutes, until tender. |
| 1¼ cups lightly packed fresh basil leaves | |
| 1 teaspoon minced garlic in oil | 2 Wash, dry and trim basil. Place in food processor with garlic, cottage cheese and Gorgonzola. Process until mixture is completely blended. |
| ¾ cup low-fat cottage cheese | |

1 ounce Gorgonzola or
  other good-quality blue
  cheese
5 ounces ripe tomato
  Freshly ground black
  pepper to taste

3 Wash, trim and cut tomato into large chunks; add to processor and process until tomato is diced.

4 When potatoes are cooked, drain, place in serving bowl and cut into halves or quarters, depending on size of potatoes.

5 Spoon on basil sauce and mix; season with black pepper.

**Yield:** 2 servings

---

### ◆ *Game Plan* ◆

*Scrub and cook potatoes.*
*Beat egg and mix with other ingredients for the crab cakes.*
*Pick over crabmeat and mix with cracker crumbs and egg mixture; shape into 4 patties.*
*Sauté crab cakes in hot butter.*
*Prepare dressing for potatoes.*
*Mix potatoes with dressing.*

---

### PANTRY

Egg
Mayonnaise
Prepared mustard
Worcestershire sauce

Cracker crumbs
Unsalted butter
Minced garlic in oil
Whole black pepper

---

### SHOPPING LIST

Fresh parsley (1 tablespoon)
12 ounces backfin or lump
  crabmeat
12 ounces tiny new potatoes
Fresh basil leaves (1¼ cups lightly
  packed)

Low-fat cottage cheese (¾ cup)
1 ounce Gorgonzola or other good-
  quality blue cheese
5 ounces ripe tomato

# MIXED SEAFOOD WITH AGNOLOTTI ◆ STEAMED ASPARAGUS ◆ SESAME BREAD STICKS

*Make this seafood dish with whatever seafood you can find in your part of the country: clams, oysters, shrimp, scallops, even lobster if you are so inclined.*

*Note: Cheese-stuffed tortellini or other small stuffed pasta can be substituted for the agnolotti.*

*Needless to say, this meal is worthy of being served to guests.*

## MIXED SEAFOOD WITH AGNOLOTTI

4 quarts water
6 ounces whole onion or 5 ounces sliced (ready-cut) (1⅓ cups)
1 teaspoon minced garlic in oil
1–2 tablespoons olive oil
2 teaspoons minced fresh oregano or 1 teaspoon dried
¼ cup dry white wine
1 teaspoon anchovy paste or mashed whole anchovy
1¼ cups canned plum tomatoes
9 ounces ready-made agnolotti stuffed with pesto (see Note)
4 ounces large raw shrimp, shelled and deveined
8 ounces shucked oysters
8 ounces scallops (bay, calico or sea)
Sesame breadsticks

1. Boil water for agnolotti in covered pot.

2. Mince onion and sauté with garlic in hot oil over medium heat until onion begins to soften.

3. Mince fresh oregano and add to onion along with wine and anchovy paste. Cook about 30 seconds.

4. Stir in tomatoes; cover and simmer 5 minutes.

5. Cook agnolotti, according to package directions, about 7 minutes.

6. Wash shrimp and add to tomatoes. Cover and cook 4 minutes.

7. Add oysters; cover and cook 1 minute.

8. Wash scallops; cut sea scallops in halves or quarters. Add scallops; cover and cook an additional minute.

9. Drain agnolotti and mix with seafood sauce. Serve with sesame bread sticks.

**Yield:** 3 servings

## STEAMED ASPARAGUS

24 ounces asparagus

$\overline{1}$ Bring water to boil in steamer.

$\overline{2}$ Soak asparagus and break off tough stems at point where they bend naturally.

$\overline{3}$ Steam 5–7 minutes, until tender but still firm.

**Yield:** 3 servings

---

### ◆ Game Plan ◆

Boil water for agnolotti.
Sauté onion and garlic; stir in oregano, wine and anchovy paste.
Boil water for asparagus.
Add tomatoes to sauce for seafood and simmer.
Cook agnolotti.
Prepare asparagus and steam.
Add seafood to tomato sauce.
Drain agnolotti and mix with seafood sauce.

---

### PANTRY

Minced garlic in oil
Olive oil
Dried oregano, if fresh not
  available

Dry white wine
Anchovy paste or whole anchovies
Canned plum tomatoes

---

### SHOPPING LIST

6 ounces whole onion or 5 ounces
  sliced (ready-cut)
Fresh oregano (2 teaspoons)
9 ounces ready-made agnolotti
  stuffed with pesto
4 ounces large raw shrimp, shelled
  and deveined

8 ounces scallops (bay, calico or
  sea)
8 ounces shucked oysters
Sesame bread sticks
24 ounces asparagus

# PAD THAI ◆ BROCCOLI WITH SESAME OIL ◆ ◆ ◆ ◆ ◆ ◆ ◆

*I experimented with Pad Thai five or six times. After a trip to Thailand, where it is practically the national dish, I found that it should not contain catsup, even though two Thai cookbooks I had used called for it. So I went back to ground zero and this is the result. It is not absolutely authentic, but it comes close.*

*Obviously you must have access to a grocery store that sells Thai ingredients.*

*Note: If the flat rice noodles are not available, buy the thin Chinese rice noodles, sometimes called vermicelli. Even Italian linguine will do in a pinch.*

---

### PAD THAI

- 6 ounces flat rice noodles (see Note)
- 1 tablespoon sugar
- 2 tablespoons *nam pla* (Thai fish sauce)
- 1 egg
- 2 egg whites
- 1½ cups trimmed bean sprouts (about 4½ ounces)
- 2 tablespoons unsalted peanuts, chopped and roasted
- 2 scallions
- 2 tablespoons chopped fresh cilantro
- 1 teaspoon minced garlic in oil
- 2 tablespoons corn oil
- 10 small shrimp, cooked and peeled
- 2 teaspoons shrimp powder (optional)
- 1 small lime

1. Break noodles and soak in very hot tap water to cover for 15 minutes.

2. Make sauce of sugar and *nam pla*.

3. Beat egg and egg whites slightly; rinse bean sprouts.

4. With food processor running put peanuts through feed tube and chop. Remove and set aside.

5. Clean scallions and cut in thirds; with processor running put scallions through feed tube. Set aside.

6. With processor running put cilantro through feed tube. Set aside.

7. In large skillet, sauté garlic in hot oil for about 15 seconds over high heat. Stir in shrimp and sauté about 1 minute longer. Stir in *nam pla* mixture.

8. Pour eggs into skillet and allow to sit 30–60 seconds until they begin to firm up, then scramble them.

9. Drain noodles and stir into skillet with 1 cup bean sprouts. Stir and cook briefly over low heat to coat noodles and warm.

10. Arrange noodle–shrimp mixture on serving platter. Sprinkle with remaining bean sprouts, scallions, peanuts, shrimp powder (if desired) and cilantro.

11. Quarter lime and serve with Pad Thai.

**Yield:** 2 servings

## BROCCOLI WITH SESAME OIL

8 ounces whole broccoli or 4
ounces broccoli
flowerettes (ready-cut)
(1½–2 cups)
2 teaspoons Oriental sesame
oil

__1__ Bring water to boil in steamer.

__2__ Cut off tough stems and bottoms from broccoli and slice remaining stems thinly. Cut broccoli heads into flowerettes. Steam slices and flowerettes about 7 minutes.

__3__ Drain and sprinkle with sesame oil.

**Yield:** 2 servings

## ◆ Game Plan ◆

*Break noodles and soak.*
*Prepare broccoli and bring water to boil in steamer.*
*Mix sugar and nam pla.   Beat egg and egg whites and stir in.*
*Rinse bean sprouts and drain.   Cook broccoli.   Process peanuts.*
*Process scallions.   Process cilantro.   Sauté garlic in oil; add shrimp.*
*Stir in nam pla mixture; stir in eggs.*
*Drain noodles and add with 1 cup bean sprouts to skillet.*
*Arrange Pad Thai on serving plate; decorate with bean sprouts, scallions, peanuts, shrimp powder (if desired), cilantro and quartered lime.*
*Drain broccoli and drizzle with sesame oil.*

### PANTRY

Sugar
Nam pla *(Thai fish sauce)*
Eggs

Unsalted peanuts
Minced garlic in oil

Corn oil
Oriental sesame oil

### SHOPPING LIST

Package of flat rice noodles
(6 ounces)
4½ ounces trimmed bean
sprouts (1½ cups)
Bunch scallions (2)

Fresh cilantro (2
tablespoons)
10 small shrimp, cooked
and peeled

Shrimp powder (optional)
Small lime
8 ounces whole broccoli or
4 ounces broccoli
flowerettes (ready-cut)

# CURRIED SHRIMP, PEAS AND POTATOES ◆ TOASTED PITAS ◆

*If you can, use whole wheat pitas, which provide the fiber missing from white flour pitas.*

## CURRIED SHRIMP, PEAS AND POTATOES

12 ounces tiny new potatoes
13 ounces whole onion or 12 ounces sliced (ready-cut) (2½–3 cups)
 2 tablespoons corn, safflower or canola oil
 1 teaspoon ground cumin
 1 teaspoon ground coriander
½ teaspoon turmeric
⅛–¼ teaspoon cayenne pepper
   Freshly ground black pepper to taste
10 ounces frozen peas
 8 ounces fresh shrimp, cooked and peeled
1–1½ cups plain low- or non-fat yogurt
 2 tablespoons minced fresh mint or cilantro leaves (optional)

1. Scrub and halve potatoes but do not peel. Cook with water to cover in covered pot, about 17 minutes total.

2. Slice whole onion. Heat oil and sauté onion, cumin, coriander, turmeric, cayenne pepper and black pepper in hot oil.

3. When onion begins to soften, stir in peas.

4. When potatoes are cooked, drain and quarter; add to peas and onion along with shrimp and yogurt. Heat shrimp and yogurt through but do not allow to boil or yogurt will curdle.

5. Chop fresh mint or cilantro and sprinkle over shrimp mixture.

**Yield:** 2 servings

## TOASTED PITAS

2–4 small whole wheat pitas
   Unsalted butter (optional)

1. Set oven at 400 degrees.

$\overline{2}$ Split pitas into 2 rounds. Butter lightly, if desired.

$\overline{3}$ Toast for 4–6 minutes, until crisp.

**Yield:** 2 servings

---

## ◆ *Game Plan* ◆

*Prepare potatoes and boil.*
*Heat oven.*
*Cook onion with spices.*
*Toast pitas.*
*Add peas to onion.*
*Drain and quarter potatoes and add to peas and onion with*
*shrimp and yogurt.*
*Chop mint or cilantro and sprinkle over shrimp.*

---

### PANTRY

Corn, safflower or canola oil
Ground cumin
Ground coriander
Turmeric

Cayenne pepper
Whole black pepper
Plain low- or non-fat yogurt
Unsalted butter (optional)

---

### SHOPPING LIST

*12 ounces tiny new potatoes*
*13 ounces whole onion or 12*
*  ounces sliced (ready-cut)*
*10 ounces frozen peas*

*8 ounces fresh shrimp, cooked and*
*  peeled*
*Fresh mint or cilantro (2*
*  tablespoons)*
*Small whole wheat pitas (2–4)*

# SHRIMP, TOMATO AND FETA CHEESE WITH PASTA ◆ CUMIN-SCENTED CUCUMBER AND PEPPER SALAD ◆ ◆ ◆ ◆ ◆ ◆ ◆ ◆ ◆ ◆

*Note: If regular tomatoes are not in season, you can substitute fresh plum tomatoes if they are flavorful and ripe; otherwise, serve this dish only in tomato season.*

## SHRIMP, TOMATO AND FETA CHEESE WITH PASTA

3 quarts water
4 scallions
1 tablespoon fresh thyme or 1 teaspoon dried
6 ounces feta cheese
9 ounces low- or non-fat cottage cheese
12 ounces raw, shelled shrimp
12 ounces ripe tomatoes (see Note)
Freshly ground black pepper
9 ounces fresh angel hair or other fresh pasta

1. Boil water for pasta in covered pot.

2. Clean scallions and cut into thirds.

3. With food processor running put fresh thyme and scallions through feed tube and chop.

4. Add feta cheese and cottage cheese and process to make creamy sauce.

5. When pasta water boils add shrimp and cook 1–2 minutes, depending on size of shrimp.

6. Wash tomatoes and coarsely chop. Combine with sauce in serving bowl. Season with pepper.

7. When shrimp are cooked, remove from water with slotted spoon. Keep water at simmer in pot. Combine shrimp with cheese sauce.

8. Return water to hard boil and cook pasta 1–2 minutes. Drain and stir into sauce.

**Yield:** 3 servings

## CUMIN-SCENTED CUCUMBER AND PEPPER SALAD

8 ounces Kirby cucumbers
6 ounces whole red pepper or 5 ounces sliced (ready cut)
¼ teaspoon ground cumin
2 tablespoons olive oil
2 tablespoons balsamic vinegar

1 Wash and trim cucumbers but do not peel.

2 Wash, seed and cut pepper into quarters. Slice whole pepper and cucumbers in food processor with slicing blade; drain excess liquid.

3 Measure cumin into serving bowl; whisk oil and vinegar with cumin.

4 Mix in sliced vegetables.

**Yield:** 3 servings

♦ *Game Plan* ♦

*Boil water for shrimp and pasta.    Process scallions and thyme.*
*Add cheeses and process.    Boil shrimp.*
*Wash and coarsely chop tomatoes; mix with cheese sauce.*
*Drain shrimp; add to sauce; keep cooking water at simmer.*
*Slice salad ingredients.    Cook pasta.*
*Make salad dressing; mix with vegetables.*
*Drain pasta and mix with sauce.*

### PANTRY

*Dried thyme, if fresh not available*
*Whole black pepper*
*Ground cumin*

*Olive oil*
*Balsamic vinegar*

### SHOPPING LIST

*Bunch scallions (4)*
*Fresh thyme*
*6 ounces feta cheese*
*Low- or non-fat cottage cheese (9 ounces)*
*12 ounces raw, shelled shrimp*

*12 ounces ripe tomatoes*
*9 ounces fresh angel hair pasta or other fresh pasta*
*8 ounces Kirby cucumbers*
*6 ounces whole red pepper or 5 ounces sliced (ready cut)*

# $S$USHI SALAD WITH CILANTRO ◆

*I have had a crisis in conscience over this dish. I don't recommend eating raw fish because of the health hazards—mainly the parasites that live in the fish—unless the fish comes from a fish farm or has been frozen.*

*Since sushi is sliced very thin, I think you can check for parasites yourself. Hold the fish slices under a very strong light and look for small curled-up wormlike substances.*

*Well, with those caveats in mind, here is a recipe for sushi, a one-dish meal modeled on the Japanese specialty. You need a source for Japanese ingredients to make this dish.*

*Short-grain rice is used for authentic sushi, but most American kitchens have long-grain rice on hand; it can be used by non-purists.*

*Note: Wasabi powder and rice wine or mirin are usually available in Oriental markets or some large supermarkets. If rice wine is not available, use dry sherry.*

## SUSHI SALAD WITH CILANTRO

1 cup rice, short- or long-grain
2 cups water
1 carrot
1 regular cucumber or 2 Kirby cucumbers
2 scallions
1 avocado
8 ounces very fresh raw fish, such as tuna, salmon, flounder or any combination of raw, saltwater fish that suits your taste
4 tablespoons coarsely cut fresh cilantro
2 teaspoons *wasabi* powder (see Note)
8 ounces cooked shrimp or crabmeat
1–2 tablespoons pickled ginger slices, as desired

1. Bring rice and water to boil. Stir; reduce heat, cover and simmer until rice is cooked, about 17 minutes total.

2. Peel carrot and shred in food processor using julienne blade.

3. Peel regular cucumber; scrub Kirbys. Slice in food processor, using slicing blade.

4. Wash and trim scallions and slice in food processor using slicing blade.

5. Peel, seed and cut avocado in chunks.

6. Wash, dry and slice raw fish very thinly.

7. Coarsely cut cilantro.

8. Make *wasabi* by combining equal parts water and *wasabi* powder.

1 tablespoon rice wine or mirin (see Note)
¼ cup rice vinegar

9 Arrange fish, shrimp or crabmeat, carrot, cucumber, avocado, pickled ginger and 1¼ teaspoons *wasabi* around edge of large serving plate, leaving the center for the rice.

10 When rice is cooked, spoon into strainer and run under cold water. Press to drain.

11 Combine remaining *wasabi* with rice wine and rice vinegar and mix with cooked rice. Place in center of plate and top with scallions and cilantro.

**Yield:** 2 servings

## ◆ Game Plan ◆

*Follow recipe directions.*

### PANTRY

Long- or short-grain rice
Pickled ginger

Rice wine (mirin) or dry sherry
Rice vinegar

### SHOPPING LIST

1 carrot
1 regular cucumber or 2 Kirby cucumbers
Bunch scallions (2)
1 avocado

8 ounces very fresh raw fish such as salmon, tuna or flounder
Fresh cilantro (4 tablespoons)
Wasabi *powder*
8 ounces cooked shrimp or crabmeat

# ANGEL HAIR PASTA WITH VEGETABLES AND CHEESES ◆ ◆

*This became a one-dish meal one night when I was too tired to prepare more than one thing to eat. It has everything for a balanced meal: the carbohydrates in the pasta, the protein in the cheese and yogurt, and the vitamins and fiber in the vegetables. But if you and your family or friends have Paul Bunyan-type appetites, add some bread.*

*You can substitute any kind of fresh pasta for the angel hair, including tortellini for an even more filling dish.*

## ANGEL HAIR PASTA WITH VEGETABLES AND CHEESES

| | |
|---|---|
| 3 quarts water | 1 Bring water to boil in covered pot. |
| 4 ounces fresh whole or sliced mushrooms (⅔ cup sliced) | 2 Wash and trim mushrooms and slice. |
| 16 ounces whole broccoli or 8 ounces broccoli flowerettes (ready-cut) (3½–4 cups) | 3 Wash and remove tough stems from whole broccoli and cut remaining stems into thin slices and break heads into bite-size flowerettes. |
| 1–2 tablespoons olive oil ¾ cup low-fat cottage cheese | 4 Heat oil in skillet large enough to hold vegetables; sauté mushrooms and broccoli in covered skillet over medium-high heat for 5 minutes. |
| ¾ cup plain low- or non-fat yogurt | 5 Process cottage cheese and yogurt in food processor to make smooth. |
| 1½ cups canned Italian plum tomatoes ½ teaspoon dried oregano ½ teaspoon dried basil ¼ cup freshly grated Parmesan cheese, preferably Parmigiano Reggiano (2 ounces) | 6 Break up tomatoes with your fingers and add to broccoli with oregano and basil. Cover and continue cooking over medium heat until broccoli is tender but still crisp. |
| 8 ounces fresh angel hair or other fresh pasta Freshly ground black pepper to taste | 7 Grate Parmesan. |
| | 8 Cook pasta; drain. |

$\overline{9}$ Remove vegetables from heat; stir in cottage cheese mixture and pour over pasta. Season with black pepper.

$\overline{10}$ Serve with grated cheese.

**Yield:** 2 servings

---

### ◆ Game Plan ◆

*Follow recipe directions.*

---

#### PANTRY

Olive oil
Plain low- or non-fat yogurt
Dried oregano
Dried basil

Parmesan cheese, preferably
    Parmigiano Reggiano
Whole black pepper

---

#### SHOPPING LIST

4 ounces fresh whole or sliced
    mushrooms
16 ounces whole broccoli or 8
    ounces flowerettes (ready-cut)
Low-fat cottage cheese (¾ cup)

16-ounce can Italian plum
    tomatoes (1½ cups)
8 ounces fresh angel hair or other
    fresh pasta

# FETTUCINE WITH ASPARAGUS AND GINGER CREAM SAUCE ◆
# ORANGE–OLIVE SALAD ◆ ◆ ◆ ◆

*In this, the simplest of meals for spring, the ginger highlights the subtle taste of the asparagus.*

## FETTUCINE WITH ASPARAGUS AND GINGER CREAM SAUCE

3 quarts water
3 large shallots
2 tablespoons coarsely grated ginger
16 ounces asparagus
1–2 tablespoons olive oil
¾ cup low-fat ricotta cheese
¾ cup plain low- or non-fat yogurt
6 ounces fresh fettucine
2 ounces Parmigiano Reggiano (¼ cup)
Freshly ground black pepper to taste

1 Boil water for fettucine in covered pot.

2 Mince shallots.

3 Coarsely grate ginger.

4 Wash and trim asparagus, breaking off tough stem end at point where it bends easily. Cut asparagus on diagonal, starting just below tips, into ½-inch pieces.

5 Heat oil in skillet large enough to hold asparagus. Add shallots, ginger and asparagus and sauté for about 10 minutes, until asparagus are tender.

6 In food processor, thoroughly blend ricotta with yogurt.

7 Cook fettucine 2–2½ minutes in boiling water.

8 Coarsely grate Parmigiano Reggiano.

9 When asparagus are cooked, remove from heat and stir in yogurt mixture.

10 Drain fettucine; top with asparagus mixture and sprinkle with grated cheese. Pepper to taste.

**Yield:** 2 servings

## ORANGE–OLIVE SALAD

2 eating oranges
12 small or 6 large French,
Greek or Italian black
olives, packed in brine or
oil
Olive oil

1 Peel oranges with knife down to the pith. Section
and arrange on 2 salad plates.

2 Top with olives and sprinkle with a few drops of
oil.

**Yield:** 2 servings

◆ *Game Plan* ◆

*Boil water for fettucine.*
*Mince shallots; grate ginger.*
*Wash, trim and slice asparagus.*
*Sauté shallots, ginger and asparagus in hot oil.*
*Peel oranges and arrange with black olives. Drizzle on oil.*
*Process yogurt and ricotta.*
*Cook fettucine.*
*Grate Parmigiano Reggiano.*
*Add yogurt mixture to asparagus.*
*Top fettucine with sauce and cheese.*

*PANTRY*

*Shallots*
*Fresh ginger*
*Olive oil*
*Plain low- or non-fat yogurt*

*Parmigiano Reggiano*
*Whole black pepper*
*French, Greek or Italian black*
*olives, packed in brine or oil*

*SHOPPING LIST*

*16 ounces asparagus*
*Low-fat ricotta cheese (¾ cup)*

*6 ounces fresh fettucine*
*2 eating oranges*

# ANNIE'S SPICY NOODLES AND VEGGIES ◆ WHOLE-GRAIN BREAD ◆ ◆ ◆ ◆ ◆ ◆ ◆ ◆ ◆ ◆

*The vegetable and starch make up a one-dish meal with a Chinese accent, named for my daughter who loves it.*

3 quarts water
8 ounces whole carrots or 7 ounces sliced (ready-cut) (1⅓ cups)
16–20 ounces whole broccoli or 8–12 ounces broccoli flowerettes (3½–5 cups) or Brussels sprouts or asparagus
6 ounces spiral-shaped pasta, such as fusilli (about 2 cups)
3 scallions
1 tablespoon grated ginger
2 tablespoons creamy natural peanut butter
1 tablespoon reduced-sodium soy sauce
1½ tablespoons wine vinegar
1 tablespoon dry white wine or vermouth
1 teaspoon Oriental sesame oil
1 teaspoon dry mustard
Few grinds freshly ground black pepper
Few dashes cayenne pepper

1 Boil water for pasta in covered pot.

2 Boil water for vegetables in steamer.

3 Wash and prepare vegetables. Scrape carrots and cut into 2- or 3-inch pieces. Place in steamer when water boils. Cook 10–12 minutes.

4 Remove tough stems from broccoli and cut into flowerettes, or trim Brussels sprouts or trim tough ends of asparagus and cut remaining stalks into 2 or 3 pieces. Add to carrots. Cook broccoli about 8–10 minutes, Brussels sprouts about 10 minutes, asparagus about 5 minutes. The total cooking time for the carrots is 18–20 minutes.

5 Cook pasta according to package directions.

6 Trim and cut scallions into 3 pieces; put in food processor. Grate ginger on coarse side of grater and add ginger to processor. Add peanut butter, soy sauce, vinegar, wine, sesame oil, mustard, black pepper and cayenne pepper. Process to blend thoroughly.

7 When pasta is cooked, remove and reserve ½ cup of water; drain. Add the pasta water to sauce in food processor and blend briefly.

$\overline{8}$ Pour pasta into serving dish; toss with some of sauce. Top with vegetables and pour on remaining sauce. Stir gently to mix. Serve with whole-grain bread.

**Yield:** 2 servings.

---

## ◆ *Game Plan* ◆

*Follow recipe directions.*

---

### PANTRY

Ginger
Creamy natural peanut butter
Reduced-sodium soy sauce
Wine vinegar
Dry white wine or vermouth

Oriental sesame oil
Dry mustard
Whole black pepper
Cayenne pepper

---

### SHOPPING LIST

8 ounces whole carrots or 7 ounces
   sliced (ready-cut)
16–20 ounces whole broccoli or
   8–12 ounces broccoli flowerettes,
   Brussels sprouts or asparagus

6 ounces spiral-shaped pasta
Bunch scallions (3)
Whole-grain bread (2 slices)

# COLD TOMATO SALSA ON HOT PASTA ◆ BREAD AND GOAT CHEESE ◆ ◆ ◆ ◆ ◆ ◆ ◆ ◆ ◆

*This pasta dish is a southwestern variation of an old Italian favorite. The new merchandising has made it more current. There is a wonderful cold tomato sauce in Italian cooking: this has jalapeño and cilantro, not to mention goat cheese. Use same type of goat cheese for both the tomato sauce and the bread.*

## COLD TOMATO SALSA

1 serrano or jalapeño chile
⅓ cup tightly packed cilantro
32 ounces ripe tomatoes, regular or plum
3 tablespoons red wine vinegar
2 tablespoons well-flavored olive oil
3½ ounces fresh goat cheese (about 6 tablespoons), optional

1 Trim, seed and quarter chile and with food processor running, put through feed tube and mince.

2 Wash, dry and trim cilantro. With motor running add to food processor.

3 Wash, trim and cut tomatoes in half. Squeeze to extract juice and most of seeds. Add to processor and process to make a rough puree. Do not over-process.

4 Blend vinegar and oil into tomatoes.

5 Spoon over hot pasta and garnish with goat cheese.

**Yield:** 3 servings

## PASTA

3–4 quarts water
9 ounces fresh or dried linguine

1 Bring water to boil in covered pot.

2 Add pasta and return to boil. Cook fresh pasta about 1–2 minutes; cook dried pasta according to package directions. Drain and top immediately with cold salsa.

**Yield:** 3 servings

## BREAD AND GOAT CHEESE

3 slices whole-grain bread
1½ ounces goat cheese
    (about 3 tablespoons)

Spread bread with goat cheese and toast until cheese begins to brown, 3–5 minutes.

**Yield:** 3 servings

---

### ◆ Game Plan ◆

*Boil water for pasta.*
*Make tomato sauce.*
*If dried pasta is used, cook.*
*Spread bread with goat cheese and toast.*
*If fresh pasta is used, cook.*
*Crumble optional goat cheese for pasta.*
*Drain pasta and top with tomato sauce;*
*garnish with optional goat cheese.*

---

#### PANTRY

Red wine vinegar
Olive oil

Dried linguine, if fresh not
    available

---

#### SHOPPING LIST

1 serrano or jalapeño chile
Fresh cilantro (⅓ cup)
32 ounces ripe tomatoes, regular or
    plum

1½–5 ounces fresh goat cheese
9 ounces fresh linguine
Whole-grain bread (3 slices)

# LINGUINE WITH BROCCOLI DI RAPE ◆ ARUGULA AND TOMATOES ◆ ◆ ◆ ◆ ◆ ◆ ◆ ◆

*This recipe for linguine with* broccoli di rape *is adapted from one served at Dieci, an Italian restaurant in New York where broccoli di rape, the bitter Italian green, now outsells fried zucchini.*

*It is only in the last few years that this distinctively Italian vegetable has begun moving outside of the Italian community into ordinary supermarkets.*

*Anyone familiar with other greens like mustard and dandelion will find broccoli di rape's intense flavor and bitter quality similar to those greens.*

*When buying broccoli di rape—sometimes called* cima di rape, *sometimes* rapini—*look for crisp, green, fresh-looking leaves. Avoid wilted or yellowing leaves, although yellow flowers are fine.*

## LINGUINE WITH BROCCOLI DI RAPE

3 quarts water
12 ounces broccoli di rape
1–2 tablespoons olive oil
1 teaspoon minced garlic in oil
8 ounces fresh or dried linguine
½ cup low-fat ricotta
Freshly ground black pepper to taste
1–1½ ounces freshly grated Parmigiano Reggiano (⅓–½ cup)

1 Bring water to boil in covered pot.

2 Wash broccoli di rape and trim off thick stems; discard. Cut each piece into 2 or 3 pieces.

3 Heat oil in skillet large enough to hold greens. Add garlic and cook 30 seconds. Add greens, stir, cover and cook over medium heat for 7–10 minutes, until greens are softened but still firm.

4 Cook fresh linguine in boiling water until it is al dente, 60–90 seconds; follow package directions for dried linguine. Remove and reserve about ⅓ cup cooking water; drain pasta. Stir some of the water and the ricotta into the greens to make a thick sauce; mix well. Add more water if needed. Season with pepper.

5 Grate cheese.

6 Stir broccoli di rape mixture into linguine and place in serving dish. Serve, sprinkled with cheese.

**Yield:** 2 servings

## ARUGULA AND TOMATOES

1 small bunch arugula
3 large or 4 small ripe plum
   tomatoes or 2 ripe medium
   regular tomatoes
1 tablespoon balsamic
   vinegar
1 tablespoon olive oil
   Freshly ground black
   pepper

$\underline{1}$ Wash and trim stems from arugula. Pat dry on paper towels.

$\underline{2}$ Wash, trim and cut tomatoes into bite-size pieces.

$\underline{3}$ In salad bowl beat vinegar with olive oil; add arugula and tomatoes and toss to coat. Season with pepper.

**Yield:** 2 servings

◆ *Game Plan* ◆

*Boil water for linguine.*
*Prepare broccoli di rape.*
*Prepare arugula and tomatoes.*
*Sauté garlic.*
*Add greens to garlic.   Cook dried linguine.*
*Make salad dressing and toss salad.*
*Cook fresh linguine.   Grate cheese.*
*Mix ricotta and water with greens.*
*Drain linguine and stir in greens mixture; top with Parmigiano Reggiano.*

### PANTRY

*Olive oil*
*Minced garlic in oil*
*Dried linguine, if fresh not*
   *available*

*Whole black pepper*
*Parmigiano Reggiano*
*Balsamic vinegar*

### SHOPPING LIST

*12 ounces broccoli di rape*
*8 ounces fresh linguine*
*Low-fat ricotta (½ cup)*
*Small bunch arugula*

*3 medium or 4 small plum*
   *tomatoes or 2 medium regular*
   *tomatoes*

# TORTELLINI AND CREAMY VEGETABLES ◆
# GREEN SALAD ◆ ◆ ◆ ◆ ◆ ◆ ◆ ◆

*If you don't want this to be a vegetarian meal, purchase tortellini or capelletti that are filled with meat or chicken.*

## TORTELLINI AND CREAMY VEGETABLES

4 quarts water
8 ounces whole carrots or 7 ounces sliced (ready-cut) (1⅓ cups)
8 ounces whole or sliced (ready-cut) zucchini (1⅔ cups)
9 ounces whole onion or 8 ounces sliced (ready-cut) (1⅔ cups)
6 ounces sliced or whole mushrooms (2 cups)
1 tablespoon chopped fresh basil or 1 teaspoon dried
1–2 tablespoons olive oil
1 teaspoon minced garlic in oil
Freshly ground black pepper to taste
9 ounces fresh cheese-filled tortellini
¾ cup plain low- or non-fat yogurt
¾ cup non-fat cottage cheese

1. Boil water for tortellini in covered pot.

2. Scrape whole carrots; shred carrots in food processor with shredding blade.

3. Wash whole zucchini; slice in processor with thin slicing blade.

4. Peel whole onion; slice in processor.

5. Wash and trim whole mushrooms; slice in processor.

6. If using fresh basil, mince in food processor.

7. Heat oil and sauté garlic for about 30 seconds. Add vegetables, basil and pepper and sauté until vegetables are tender-crisp.

8. Cook tortellini in boiling water, about 6 minutes or until tender.

9. Blend yogurt and cottage cheese in food processor until smooth.

10. Drain tortellini and stir into vegetables. Remove from heat. Arrange on plates and spoon on yogurt–cheese mixture.

**Yield:** 2 large servings

## GREEN SALAD

6 or 8 large soft lettuce
leaves
1 tablespoon good-quality
olive oil
1 tablespoon balsamic
vinegar
Freshly ground black
pepper to taste

1 Wash and dry lettuce leaves and arrange on 2 salad
plates.

2 Beat together oil and vinegar and drizzle over lettuce.

3 Sprinkle with freshly ground black pepper.

**Yield:** 2 servings

## ◆ Game Plan ◆

Boil water for tortellini.
Shred and slice vegetables; mince fresh basil in food processor.
Sauté garlic; add vegetables and basil.
Cook tortellini.
Blend cottage cheese and yogurt in food processor.
Wash and dry lettuce; arrange on plates.
Make salad dressing and drizzle over lettuce.
Drain tortellini and stir into vegetables.
Serve with yogurt–cheese mixture spooned over.

### PANTRY

Dried basil, if fresh not available
Olive oil
Minced garlic in oil

Whole black pepper
Plain low- or non-fat yogurt
Balsamic vinegar

### SHOPPING LIST

8 ounces whole carrots or 7 ounces
sliced (ready-cut)
8 ounces whole or sliced (ready-
cut) zucchini
9 ounces whole onion or 8 ounces
sliced (ready-cut)

6 ounces sliced or whole
mushrooms
Fresh basil (1 tablespoon)
9 ounces fresh cheese-filled
tortellini
Non-fat cottage cheese (¾ cup)
Head soft lettuce (6 or 8 leaves)

# MEATLESS AND NOODLELESS LASAGNA ◆ SNOW PEAS AND PEPPER SALAD ◆ ◆ ◆ ◆ ◆ ◆ ◆ ◆

*This lasagna has neither meat nor noodles. The tofu provides a meatlike consistency and also stands in for the lasagna noodles.*

## MEATLESS AND NOODLELESS LASAGNA

1 teaspoon minced garlic in oil
16 ounces whole mushrooms or 15 ounces sliced (ready-cut) (5 cups)
1 large sprig fresh basil or 1½ teaspoons dried basil
29-ounce can tomato puree
16 ounces soft tofu
6 ounces loose spinach leaves or 4 ounces fresh packaged spinach leaves
8 ounces low-fat cottage cheese
Freshly ground black pepper to taste
2 ounces thinly sliced Parmesan, preferably Parmigiano Reggiano, or other strong hard cheese

1. In large skillet, briefly sauté minced garlic in its own oil. Wash, trim and slice mushrooms, if they are whole. Wash, dry and remove basil leaves from stems. Add mushrooms and basil to skillet with tomato puree. Cook over low heat while preparing tofu.

2. Wash tofu and slice into 8 equal pieces.

3. Wash and trim spinach leaves; dry.

4. Arrange 4 slices of tofu on tomato sauce in skillet. Top with cottage cheese and spinach leaves, and then top with remaining 4 slices of tofu. Sprinkle with pepper and spoon over some of the tomato sauce.

5. Slice cheese and arrange on top of tofu.

6. Cover and cook 10–15 minutes over medium heat. Check once or twice to see if sauce is becoming too thick; if it is, add 2–3 tablespoons water.

**Yield:** 3 large or 4 small servings

## SNOW PEAS AND PEPPER SALAD

2 tablespoons olive oil
2 tablespoons balsamic vinegar

1. Beat oil with vinegar and mustard in salad bowl.

1 tablespoon Dijon mustard
9 ounces whole red, yellow, green or purple pepper or 8 ounces sliced (ready-cut) (1¾ cups)
8 ounces raw or blanched snow peas (ready-cut)

2 Wash and cut whole pepper into strips, using slicing blade of food processor; drain excess moisture.

3 If snow peas are raw, wash and trim. Cut them in half and add to dressing with peppers; mix to coat well.

**Yield:** 3 large or 4 small servings

---

## ◆ *Game Plan* ◆

*Sauté garlic; prepare whole mushrooms and fresh basil; add with puree to garlic and cook.*
*Prepare tofu.*
*Prepare spinach leaves.*
*Arrange 4 slices of tofu on sauce; top with cottage cheese, spinach leaves and remaining tofu.*
*Slice cheese and place on tofu.*
*Prepare salad dressing.*
*Prepare whole pepper and snow peas. Stir snow peas and pepper into dressing.*

---

### PANTRY

*Minced garlic in oil*
*Dried basil, if fresh not available*
*Tomato puree*
*Whole black pepper*
*Parmigiano Reggiano or other strong hard cheese*

*Olive oil*
*Balsamic vinegar*
*Dijon mustard*

---

### SHOPPING LIST

*16 ounces whole mushrooms or 15 ounces sliced (ready-cut)*
*Fresh basil (1 sprig)*
*16 ounces soft tofu*
*6 ounces loose spinach leaves or 4 ounces fresh packaged spinach leaves*

*8 ounces low-fat cottage cheese*
*9 ounces whole red, yellow, green or purple pepper or 8 ounces sliced (ready-cut)*
*8 ounces raw or blanched snow peas (ready-cut)*

# BULGUR AND VEGETABLES ◆
## TOMATOES WITH SCALLIONS ◆ ◆

*This began as a simple recipe that I developed and served at Thanksgiving to my vegetarian son. Everyone tried it and said it did not have enough flavor: Why didn't I try adding a little of this and that?*

*Well, this and that resulted in this recipe. It is now a big success.*

## BULGUR AND VEGETABLES

1 cup bulgur
8 ounces whole red onion or 7 ounces sliced (ready-cut) (1½ cups)
2 tablespoons corn, safflower or canola oil
1 teaspoon minced garlic in oil
16 ounces whole red and yellow bell peppers or 14 ounces sliced (ready-cut) (4 cups)
8 ounces snow peas, raw or blanched (ready-cut)
2 tablespoons hoisin sauce
2 teaspoons hot chili paste with garlic
1 tablespoon reduced-sodium soy sauce
Freshly ground black pepper to taste
½ cup unsalted peanuts, roasted or blanched

1. Boil 2 to 3 cups water and pour over bulgur; let soak while finishing rest of recipe.

2. Chop onion in food processor. In large skillet, sauté onion in hot oil with garlic until onion begins to soften, about 5 minutes.

3. Wash and seed whole peppers and slice in food processor with thin slicing blade.

4. Cut snow peas into thirds.

5. Add peppers to onions and cook over medium heat, about 4 minutes.

6. Add hoisin sauce, chili paste, soy sauce and black pepper. Cook another 3 minutes.

7. Drain bulgur and squeeze out excess liquid; add bulgur to vegetables with snow peas and peanuts. Stir and cook 1–2 minutes, until bulgur is heated through and snow peas are tender.

**Yield:** 3 large or 4 smaller servings

## TOMATOES WITH SCALLIONS

3–4 ripe medium tomatoes
4 scallions

1 Wash and slice tomatoes into thick pieces and arrange on 2 salad plates.

2 Wash and cut scallions into rings and sprinkle over tomatoes.

**Yield:** 3 large or 4 smaller servings

---

## ◆ *Game Plan* ◆

*Boil water and soak bulgur.*
*Chop onion and sauté in oil with garlic.*
*Slice peppers and add to onion.*
*Cut snow peas.*
*Add hoisin sauce, chili paste, soy sauce and pepper to vegetables.*
*Drain bulgur and stir into vegetables with snow peas and peanuts.*
*Slice tomatoes; arrange on plates.*
*Slice scallions and sprinkle over tomatoes.*

---

### PANTRY

*Bulgur*
*Corn, safflower or canola oil*
*Minced garlic in oil*
*Hoisin sauce*

*Hot chili paste with garlic*
*Reduced-sodium soy sauce*
*Whole black pepper*

---

### SHOPPING LIST

*8 ounces whole red onion or 7*
*    ounces sliced (ready-cut)*
*16 ounces whole red and yellow*
*    bell peppers or 14 ounces sliced*
*    (ready-cut)*

*8 ounces raw or blanched snow*
*    peas (ready-cut)*
*½ cup unsalted peanuts, blanched*
*    or roasted*
*3–4 ripe, medium tomatoes*
*Bunch scallions (4)*

# CURRIED LENTILS AND
## VEGETABLES ◆ RICE ◆ ◆ ◆ ◆ ◆

*This is an easy one, and gives you lots of time to clean up while dinner is cooking.*

*Strictly speaking, this is not a vegetarian dish because chicken stock is used, but you could substitute vegetable broth or water to make it truly vegetarian.*

*Note: Red lentils are available at natural food stores and Indian markets. Keep a supply on hand, as they cook in half the time it takes for regular lentils to cook.*

## CURRIED LENTILS AND VEGETABLES

8 ounces (1 heaping cup) red lentils (see Note)

8 ounces whole onion or 7 ounces sliced (ready-cut) (1⅔ cups)

1 teaspoon minced garlic in oil

2 tablespoons olive oil

1 teaspoon ground coriander

1 teaspoon ground cumin

1 teaspoon turmeric

½ teaspoon mild to hot chile powder, depending on degree of hotness desired

¼ teaspoon ground cardamom

⅛ teaspoon ground cloves

¼ teaspoon ground cinnamon

1 small to medium head cauliflower or 12 ounces flowerettes (ready-cut) (4½ cups)

1 cup chicken stock

3 ounces tomato paste (½ of 6-ounce can)

½ cup unsalted, roasted cashews

½ cup plain low- or non-fat yogurt

1. In covered pot, bring lentils to boil in plenty of water to cover. Cook about 10 minutes, until soft.

2. Coarsely chop whole onion. Sauté onion and garlic in hot oil until soft.

3. Reduce heat and add coriander, cumin, turmeric, chile powder, cardamom, cloves and cinnamon. Stir well.

4. Add flowerettes to pan with chicken stock and tomato paste. Stir well to mix. Cover and cook until cauliflower is tender, about 8–10 minutes.

5. Drain and stir in lentils, adding some liquid from the pot to thin the sauce if necessary.

6. Stir in cashews and serve with yogurt on the side.

**Yield:** 2 servings

## RICE

½ cup long-grain rice
1 cup water

<u>1</u> Place rice and water in heavy-bottomed pot; bring to boil.

<u>2</u> Reduce heat, cover and cook for a total of 17 minutes, until water has been absorbed and rice is tender.

**Yield:** 2 servings

---

## ◆ *Game Plan* ◆

*Cook rice.*
*Follow lentil recipe directions.*

---

### PANTRY

Red lentils
Minced garlic in oil
Olive oil
Ground coriander
Ground cumin
Turmeric
Mild to hot chile powder

Ground cardamom
Ground cloves
Ground cinnamon
Chicken stock
Tomato paste
Plain low- or nonfat yogurt
Rice

---

### SHOPPING LIST

8 ounces whole onion or 7 ounces
    sliced (ready-cut)

1 small to medium head
    cauliflower or 12 ounces
    flowerettes (ready-cut)
Unsalted, roasted cashews (½ cup)

# CHILI ◆ TORTILLAS ◆ CUCUMBERS WITH YOGURT AND WALNUTS ◆

*No, this chili does not need to be simmered for four hours, but it still tastes delicious and makes for a satisfying meal.*

## CHILI

8 ounces whole onion or 7 ounces sliced (ready-cut) (1½ cups)
8 ounces whole red bell pepper or 7 ounces sliced (ready-cut) (1½ cups)
½ jalapeño chile
1 tablespoon corn, safflower or canola oil
1 teaspoon minced garlic in oil
¼ teaspoon ground coriander
1½ teaspoons mild chile powder
1 teaspoon cumin
28- or 29-ounce can tomato puree with tomato bits or plain tomato puree
15-ounce can pinto, navy or Great Northern beans

1 Coarsely chop onion and red pepper.

2 Trim, seed and finely chop ½ of jalapeño chile. Reserve the other half for another purpose.

3 Heat oil in skillet and sauté onion, pepper, jalapeño, garlic, coriander, chile powder and cumin until onion softens, 4–5 minutes.

4 Add tomato puree and beans, with liquid from can. Cover and cook over low heat until ready to serve, 12–15 minutes. Serve with tortillas.

**Yield:** 2 servings

## CUCUMBERS WITH YOGURT AND WALNUTS

2 Kirby cucumbers
½ cup plain low- or non-fat yogurt
2 tablespoons dry vermouth
2 tablespoons broken walnut meats
Freshly ground black pepper to taste

1 Wash but do not peel the cucumbers; slice them.

2 Mix yogurt with vermouth, walnuts and pepper in serving bowl. Stir in cucumbers.

**Yield:** 2 servings

**TORTILLAS**

2–4 corn tortillas

$\underline{1}$ Heat oven or toaster oven to 500 degrees.

$\underline{2}$ Wrap tortillas in aluminum foil and heat for about 10 minutes.

**Yield:** 2 servings

◆ *Game Plan* ◆

*Heat oven or toaster oven.*
*Prepare onion, red pepper and jalapeño; sauté in oil with spices.*
*Add tomato puree and pinto beans.*
*Wrap tortillas in foil and heat.*
*Prepare cucumbers.*
*Prepare dressing for cucumbers and combine.*

*PANTRY*

*Corn, safflower or canola oil*
*Minced garlic in oil*
*Ground coriander*
*Mild chile powder*
*Cumin*

*Tomato puree with tomato bits or*
*    plain tomato puree*
*Plain low- or non-fat yogurt*
*Dry vermouth*
*Whole black pepper*

*SHOPPING LIST*

*8 ounces whole onion or 7 ounces*
*    sliced (ready-cut)*
*8 ounces whole red bell pepper or 7*
*    ounces sliced (ready-cut)*
*1 jalapeño chile*
*15-ounce can pinto, navy or Great*
*    Northern beans*

*Corn tortillas (2–4)*
*2 Kirby cucumbers*
*1 ounce walnut pieces*
*    (2 tablespoons)*

# VEGETABLE CURRY ◆ TOASTED PITAS ◆ ◆ ◆ ◆ ◆ ◆ ◆ ◆ ◆ ◆

Curry *doesn't* always *mean prepared curry powder; traditionally it refers to a combination of spices—fennel, cumin, coriander, cayenne, turmeric—that go into a curry.*

*The combination of potatoes and cauliflower or potatoes and peas is typically Indian.*

*If you can't find pitas, use any good bread.*

## VEGETABLE CURRY

16 ounces tiny new potatoes
1 small head cauliflower or 8 ounces flowerettes (ready-cut) (3 cups)
1½ tablespoons grated ginger
1–2 tablespoons olive oil
1 teaspoon minced garlic in oil
1½ teaspoons fennel seeds
2 teaspoons cumin
1 teaspoon ground coriander
¼ teaspoon cayenne pepper (or less, as desired)
½ teaspoon turmeric
4 tablespoons water
10 ounces frozen peas
½ pint plain low- or non-fat yogurt
Chutney (optional)

1 Scrub potatoes but do not peel. If potatoes are not small enough to cook whole in 15 minutes, cut into halves or quarters. Cook in water to cover in covered pot.

2 If using whole head of cauliflower, wash and break cauliflower into bite-size flowerettes.

3 Coarsely grate ginger.

4 Heat oil in skillet large enough to hold all the vegetables. Add the ginger, garlic, fennel, cumin, coriander, cayenne and turmeric and cook over medium heat for about 30 seconds, stirring. Stir in cauliflower and the water. Mix thoroughly to coat cauliflower with spice mixture. Cover and cook about 5 minutes, over low heat, until cauliflower is almost tender. Stir in peas and turn off heat.

5 When potatoes are cooked, drain them. If they are not already quartered or halved, cut them and add to skillet. Stir thoroughly to coat vegetables with spices and cook over medium heat just long enough to cook peas, 2–3 minutes.

$\overline{6}$ Top with yogurt or serve it on the side. Serve with chutney, if desired.

**Yield:** 2 servings

---

## TOASTED PITAS

4 small whole wheat pitas

Toast the pitas.

**Yield:** 2 servings

---

### ◆ *Game Plan* ◆

*Follow directions for the curry recipe.*
*When the vegetables are cooking with the spices, toast the pitas.*

---

### *PANTRY*

Fresh ginger
Olive oil
Minced garlic in oil
Fennel seeds
Cumin

Ground coriander
Cayenne pepper
Turmeric
Plain low- or non-fat yogurt

---

### *SHOPPING LIST*

16 ounces tiny new potatoes
1 small head cauliflower or 8
   ounces flowerettes (ready-cut)
10 ounces frozen peas

Chutney (optional)
Small whole wheat pitas (4)

# POTATOES SMOTHERED IN EVERYTHING WITH CRUSTY WHOLE-GRAIN BREAD ◆ ◆ ◆ ◆ ◆

*Very quick and easy to make, this is a one-dish meal that can be topped with any vegetables you have around. Serve with crusty whole-grain bread.*

## POTATOES SMOTHERED IN EVERYTHING

| | |
|---|---|
| 24 | ounces tiny new potatoes |
| 7 | ounces whole onion or 6 ounces (ready-cut) sliced (1¼ cups) |
| 6 | ounces whole mushrooms or 5 ounces sliced (ready-cut) (2 cups) |
| 1 | tablespoon corn, safflower or canola oil |
| 2½ | ounces firmly packed, coarsely grated Monterey Jack cheese (about ½ cup) |
| 1 | jalapeño or serrano chile |
| 2 | scallions |
| 2 | large ripe tomatoes or 14 cherry tomatoes |
| 3 | tablespoons coarsely chopped cilantro |
| 2–4 | tablespoons plain low- or non-fat yogurt Crusty whole-grain bread |

1. Scrub potatoes but do not peel. Depending on the size of potatoes, cut into halves or thirds and boil in water to cover in covered pot, about 12–15 minutes, until tender.

2. Slice whole onion; wash and slice whole mushrooms.

3. Break onion slices into rings; sauté in hot oil with mushrooms until tender.

4. Coarsely grate cheese.

5. Trim and seed jalapeño; quarter. With food processor running, process jalapeño through feed tube until minced.

6. Wash and trim scallions; repeat processing.

7. Wash and cut up tomatoes. Continue to run food processor; add cut-up tomatoes or cherry tomatoes and process until salsa is finely chopped.

8. Wash and dry cilantro. Coarsely chop and stir into salsa.

$\underline{9}$ When potatoes are cooked, drain and place in 2 bowls. Top each bowl with onion–mushroom mixture, cheese, salsa and finally with 1–2 tablespoons yogurt. Serve with crusty whole-grain bread.

**Yield:** 2 servings

---

### ◆ Game Plan ◆

*Follow recipe directions.*

---

### PANTRY

Corn, safflower or canola oil            Plain low- or non-fat yogurt

---

### SHOPPING LIST

24 ounces tiny new potatoes
7 ounces whole onion or 6 ounces
   sliced (ready-cut)
6 ounces whole mushrooms or 5
   ounces sliced (ready-cut)
2½ ounces grated Monterey Jack
   cheese

1 jalapeño or serrano chile
Bunch scallions (2)
2 large ripe tomatoes or 14 cherry
   tomatoes
Fresh cilantro (3 tablespoons)
Crusty whole-grain bread

# VEGETABLES WITH TOMATO–VINEGAR SAUCE ◆ CRUSTY WHOLE WHEAT BREAD ◆ ◆ ◆ ◆ ◆

*This Tunisian dish was inspired by one of cooking teacher and author Copeland Marks' recipes. Although his version is far more elaborate, this one is delicious in its own right as a one-dish meal, and perfect for the night you want a light supper.*

## VEGETABLES WITH TOMATO–VINEGAR SAUCE

16 ounces small new potatoes
16 ounces whole zucchini or 15 ounces sliced (ready-cut) (3½ cups)
12 ounces whole green bell pepper or 11 ounces sliced (ready-cut) (1¾ cups)
3–4 tablespoons olive oil
½ cup water
3 tablespoons tomato paste
½ teaspoon ground coriander
1 tablespoon red or white wine vinegar
Freshly ground black pepper to taste

1. Scrub but do not peel potatoes; scrub zucchini and cut off ends; wash, core and seed green pepper.

2. Using the fine slicer of the food processor, slice the potatoes.

3. Heat 2 tablespoons oil in skillet large enough to hold potatoes. Sauté potatoes until they are browned on both sides, about 15 minutes. Turn frequently.

4. Using same blade as before, slice whole zucchini and green pepper. In a second skillet heat remaining oil and sauté zucchini and green pepper until they are soft, about 10 minutes.

$\overline{5}$ Meanwhile, combine water, tomato paste, coriander, wine vinegar and black pepper in saucepan and cook over medium heat until mixture begins to thicken, about 5 minutes.

$\overline{6}$ Place potatoes in a shallow serving dish; top with zucchini and green pepper and spoon over the sauce. Season with pepper to taste. Serve with whole wheat bread.

**Yield:** 2 servings

---

### ◆ *Game Plan* ◆

*Follow recipe directions.*

---

#### PANTRY

Olive oil
Tomato paste
Ground coriander

Red or white wine vinegar
Whole black pepper

---

#### SHOPPING LIST

16 ounces small new potatoes
16 ounces whole zucchini or 15
    ounces sliced (ready-cut)

12 ounces whole green pepper or 11
    ounces sliced (ready-cut)
Crusty whole wheat bread

# BLACK BEAN SALAD ON TORTILLAS ◆ RICE WITH ONION AND CHEESE ◆ ◆ ◆ ◆ ◆ ◆ ◆

*Dean Fearing, executive chef at the Mansion on Turtle Creek, in Dallas, gave me a recipe several years ago, which I have served a number of times with great success. This vegetarian main dish is a version of that recipe.*

*In order to make the salad in 20 minutes, I have had to resort to canned beans; but I have found a variety packed in water and salt only—no sugar and no preservatives. If you rinse them off well, they do quite nicely.*

*The combination of beans and rice makes a complete protein. Nutritionally it is just as good as a piece of chicken.*

## BLACK BEAN SALAD ON TORTILLAS

4 ounces whole red bell pepper or 3 ounces sliced (ready-cut) (½ cup)
4 ounces whole yellow bell pepper or 3 ounces sliced (ready-cut) (½ cup)
2 16-ounce cans black beans
6 corn tortillas
1 jalapeño chile
1 teaspoon minced garlic in oil
3 tablespoons white wine vinegar

1. Heat oven or toaster oven to 400 degrees.

2. If red and yellow peppers are whole, wash, trim, seed and put them in the food processor with the thin slicing blade; drain. Place peppers in serving bowl.

3. Place beans in colander and rinse under running water.

4. Wrap tortillas in aluminum foil and heat in oven for about 10 minutes.

5. Wash, seed and mince jalapeño and add to serving bowl.

6. Add black beans, garlic and vinegar and stir well to mix.

7. Spoon some of pepper mixture into the center of each tortilla and roll up, if desired, or eat with fork and knife.

**Yield:** 3 servings

## RICE WITH ONION AND CHEESE

14 ounces whole onion or 12 ounces sliced (ready-cut) (2½ cups)
3 tablespoons corn, safflower or canola oil
¾ cup rice
1½ cups chicken stock
6 ounces Monterey Jack cheese

1 Trim and quarter whole onion; chop in food processor.

2 Heat oil in skillet large enough to hold onion and rice. Sauté onion and rice for 2–3 minutes.

3 Add chicken stock and bring to boil; reduce heat, cover and simmer until rice is done, about 15 minutes.

4 Coarsely grate cheese. When liquid has been absorbed into the rice, sprinkle cheese over; cover and let melt.

**Yield:** 3 servings

## ◆ Game Plan ◆

Heat oven to 400 degrees.    Chop onion and sauté in hot oil with rice.
Slice red and yellow peppers; place in serving bowl.    Rinse beans.
Add chicken stock to rice; cover and simmer.
Wrap tortillas and heat.    Grate cheese; add to rice.
Chop jalapeño and add to serving bowl; add beans, garlic and vinegar
and stir.

### PANTRY

Minced garlic in oil
White wine vinegar
Corn, safflower or canola oil

Rice
Chicken stock

### SHOPPING LIST

4 ounces whole red bell pepper or 3 ounces sliced (ready-cut)
4 ounces whole yellow bell pepper or 3 ounces sliced (ready-cut)
2 16-ounce cans black beans

1 jalapeño chile
Package corn tortillas (6)
14 ounces whole onion or 12 ounces sliced (ready-cut)
6 ounces Monterey Jack cheese

# CHEESE AND VEGETABLE ENCHILADAS ◆ AVOCADO AND PEPPERS ◆ ◆ ◆ ◆ ◆ ◆ ◆ ◆

*It will take more than 20 minutes to make these savory enchiladas—as much as 5 minutes longer—but they are well worth the extra time when you want something quite hearty and satisfying.*

## CHEESE AND VEGETABLE ENCHILADAS

16-ounce combination of chopped or sliced (ready-cut) carrots, celery, onion, bell pepper (red, yellow or green) and mushrooms, or 20 ounces whole vegetables (about 4 cups)
¼ cup dry white wine or dry vermouth
16 ounces ripe tomatoes, regular or plum
1 tablespoon ground cumin
2 teaspoons ground coriander
1 teaspoon mild to hot pure chile powder, depending on degree of hotness desired
1 teaspoon minced garlic in oil
28-ounce can tomato puree
4–6 ounces Gouda or other hard cheese
4 10-inch white or whole wheat flour tortillas

1 Heat broiler. Line broiler pan with double thickness of aluminum foil.

2 Combine the carrots, celery, onion, bell pepper and mushrooms with wine and simmer in large pan, covered, for 2 minutes.

3 Chop tomatoes in food processor and add to vegetables, along with cumin, coriander, chile powder, garlic and tomato puree. Simmer over medium-high heat for about 7 minutes longer.

4 Grate cheese in food processor.

5 With slotted spoon, remove about 3½ cups of the vegetables from sauce and set aside. Place remaining sauce and vegetables in processor and puree coarsely.

6 Return puree to skillet. Dip each tortilla in sauce to moisten. Place heaping cooking spoon of reserved vegetables in center of tortilla and roll. Place rolled tortilla, seam side down, on foil-lined pan; repeat until all tortillas are in pan. Sprinkle cheese over tortillas.

7 Place pan in broiler 2 inches from source of heat. Broil 2–4 minutes, until cheese begins to brown.

**Yield:** 2 servings

## AVOCADO WITH PEPPERS

½–1 jalapeño or serrano
   chile
5 ounces whole red or
   green bell pepper or 4
   ounces sliced (ready-cut)
   (1 cup)
1 small ripe avocado
1–2 tablespoons lime juice

1  With food processor running, put seeded jalapeño through feed tube; set aside.

2  Coarsely chop bell pepper; set aside.

3  Peel avocado and cut up. Add to processor with lime juice and process until mixture is coarsely mashed. Mix with jalapeño and bell pepper.

**Yield:** 2 servings

---

### ◆ *Game Plan* ◆

*Heat broiler.   Cook vegetables in wine.*
*Chop tomatoes and add to vegetables with cumin, coriander,*
*chile powder, garlic and tomato puree.*
*Grate cheese.   Mince jalapeño chile.   Coarsely chop bell pepper.*
*Finish enchilada preparation and broil.*
*Coarsely mash avocado with lime juice; mix with jalapeño and bell pepper.*

---

### PANTRY

*Dry white wine or dry vermouth*
*Ground cumin*
*Ground coriander*

*Pure chile powder, mild to hot*
*Minced garlic in oil*
*Tomato puree*

---

### SHOPPING LIST

*16-ounce combination of chopped*
*  or sliced (ready-cut) carrots,*
*  celery, onion, bell pepper (red,*
*  yellow or green) and*
*  mushrooms, or 20 ounces whole*
*  vegetables*
*16 ounces ripe tomatoes, regular or*
*  plum*
*4–6 ounces Gouda or other hard*
*  cheese*

*Package 10-inch white or whole*
*  wheat flour tortillas (4)*
*1 jalapeño or serrano chile*
*5 ounces whole red or green bell*
*  pepper or 4 ounces sliced*
*  (ready-cut)*
*1 small ripe avocado*
*1 lime*

# INDIAN RICE AND RED PEPPERS WITH PAPAYA ◆ TOMATOES WITH GOAT CHEESE DRESSING ◆ ◆ ◆ ◆

*Green, yellow or purple peppers can be substituted for the red peppers. And plum tomatoes can be used in the salad if tomatoes are not in season. If you can't find pecans use almonds, raw cashews or whatever nuts you prefer.*

## INDIAN RICE AND RED PEPPERS WITH PAPAYA

1 cup long-grain rice
2 cups water
8–12 ounces whole red bell pepper or 7–11 ounces sliced (ready-cut) (1½– 2¼ cups)
¼ cup pecan pieces
2 tablespoons chopped fresh parsley
3 large scallions
1–2 tablespoons olive oil
3 tablespoons red wine vinegar
½ teaspoon minced garlic in oil
1 teaspoon ground cumin
1 teaspoon ground coriander
¼ cup raisins
1 ripe papaya
Freshly ground black pepper to taste

1 Combine rice with water and cook over high heat until water boils. Reduce heat, cover and simmer until water has been absorbed, 17 minutes total.

2 Wash and seed whole red pepper; chop medium-fine.

3 Toast pecans until light brown.

4 Wash, dry and chop parsley and scallions.

5 In serving bowl combine oil, vinegar, garlic, cumin and coriander. Stir in red pepper, pecans, parsley, scallions and raisins.

6 Cut papaya into large cubes and add to mixture.

7 When rice is cooked, stir into mixture and season with black pepper.

**Yield:** 2 servings

## TOMATOES WITH GOAT CHEESE DRESSING

2 ripe medium tomatoes
2 tablespoons fresh goat cheese

1 Wash tomatoes and cut into thick slices. Place on 2 serving plates.

**2–3 tablespoons milk**
**1 tablespoon fresh thyme, basil or marjoram**

$\underline{2}$ Mix goat cheese with milk and fresh herb, and spoon over tomato slices.

**Yield:** 2 servings

---

## ◆ Game Plan ◆

*Cook rice.*
*Chop red pepper.*
*Toast pecans.*
*Chop parsley and scallions.*
*Combine ingredients for rice mixture; add papaya.*
*Slice tomatoes and prepare dressing.*
*Mix rice with red pepper mixture.*
*Spoon dressing over tomatoes.*

---

### PANTRY

*Long-grain rice*
*Olive oil*
*Red wine vinegar*
*Minced garlic in oil*
*Ground cumin*

*Ground coriander*
*Raisins*
*Whole black pepper*
*Milk*

---

### SHOPPING LIST

*8–12 ounces whole red bell pepper or 7–11 ounces sliced (ready-cut)*
*¼ cup pecans*
*Fresh parsley (2 tablespoons)*
*Bunch scallions (3)*

*1 papaya*
*2 ripe medium tomatoes*
*2 ounces fresh goat cheese (2 tablespoons)*
*Fresh thyme, basil or marjoram (1 tablespoon)*

# TEX-MEX PIZZA ◆ ◆ ◆ ◆ ◆ ◆

*It took seven tries to figure out how to get a crispy pizza crust and cooked vegetables at the same time. The first five attempts produced either a soggy crust or half-raw vegetables. The sixth worked but was too complicated. This method, the seventh try, was the simplest and most successful.*

*When I wanted to make the pizza an eighth time, the store had no zucchini so I substituted yellow squash. With meals like these you have to be flexible.*

*This is a light meal, so fruit salad or some other dessert is suggested. Or you could use three tortillas for each serving instead of two, and increase the topping ingredients by half.*

*If you want to add a green salad, add another 5 minutes to the preparation time.*

## TEX-MEX PIZZA

4 10-inch flour tortillas (see Note)
6 ounces whole red onion or 5 ounces sliced (ready-cut) (1¼ cups)
1–2 tablespoons olive oil
12–16 ounces whole zucchini or 11–15 ounces sliced (ready-cut) (3–3½ cups)
16 ounces whole red pepper or 14 ounces sliced (ready-cut) (4 cups)
6 large shiitake or other wild mushrooms, or ordinary white mushrooms.
1⅓ cups tomato puree
4 ounces grated Parmigiano Reggiano

1. Heat broiler. Cover broiler pan with double thickness of aluminum foil.

2. Arrange 2 tortillas on broiler pan and heat 2 inches from heat source for 1–2 minutes, just until puffy and beginning to brown—the time depends on how hot the broiler is. Remove and repeat with remaining 2 tortillas.

3. Meanwhile, slice whole onion on slicing blade of food processor.

4. Heat oil and sauté onion.

5. Wash zucchini and red pepper and slice if they are whole. Add to onion and continue to sauté.

6. Wash, stem and slice mushrooms; add to vegetables and cover pan. Continue cooking until vegetables are tender, about 10–12 minutes total.

$\underline{7}$ Using a paintbrush, spread tomato puree evenly over top of each tortilla.

$\underline{8}$ Arrange vegetables on top of each tortilla.

$\underline{9}$ Grate cheese and sprinkle over vegetables.

$\underline{10}$ Broil pizzas 2 inches from heat source for about 1 minute or less, just enough to melt cheese. Watch carefully, as the pizzas burn quickly. (Most broiler pans cannot hold more than 2 tortillas at a time. While you are eating the first 2 pizzas, the others can be broiling.) Serve fruit salad for dessert.

**Yield:** 2 servings

**Note:** If you cannot find 10-inch tortillas, buy the next size down and make one or two extra.

---

## ◆ *Game Plan* ◆

*Follow recipe directions.*

---

### PANTRY

Olive oil
Tomato puree

Parmigiano Reggiano

---

### SHOPPING LIST

10-inch flour tortillas (4)
6 ounces whole red onion or 5
  ounces sliced (ready-cut)
12–16 ounces whole zucchini or
  11–15 ounces sliced (ready-cut)

16 ounces whole red pepper or
  14 ounces sliced (ready-cut)
6 large shiitake or other wild
  mushrooms, or ordinary white
  mushrooms
Fruit salad for dessert

# RISOTTO WITH RADICCHIO ◆ ◆ ◆

*You probably won't be able to make this risotto recipe in 20 minutes, but it shouldn't take you longer than 23. Risotto can be a pretty speedy dish when you are working with flavorings that do not require additional cooking.*

*Several good recipes give different cooking times for risotto: one recipe says 17 minutes, another says 25. I suspect it depends on the rice. Not all arborio rice, which is essential for a good risotto, cooks in the same amount of time.*

*To make the dish in 23 minutes, you will have to purchase chopped onion from a salad bar; otherwise, you will have to add another minute or two of chopping time.*

*Some will say that this dish is not authentic because the amount of oil has been reduced, the butter has been eliminated, and the radicchio has not been cooked from the very beginning but added part way through instead. But, authenticity aside, the dish is wonderful and you don't need anything else for a complete meal.*

## RISOTTO WITH RADICCHIO

1 tablespoon olive oil
4–5 cups chicken broth or stock
½ cup chopped onion
12 ounces radicchio
1 cup arborio rice
½ cup dry white wine
2 ounces freshly grated Parmigiano Reggiano (½ cup)
Freshly ground black pepper to taste

1. Heat the oil in a heavy-bottomed pot.

2. Heat the broth in a separate pot.

3. Sauté the onion in the oil until it takes on a little color.

4. Meanwhile, wash the radicchio and cut out core.

5. Add the rice to the onion and stir until well coated.

6. Add the wine and stir; let the wine cook away, about 2 minutes.

$\overline{7}$ While the wine is cooking, shred the radicchio with a knife.

$\overline{8}$ Add about a cup of simmering chicken broth to rice and cook over high heat, stirring very often until broth has been absorbed. Repeat the procedure, this time adding the shredded radicchio. Continue adding broth as it is absorbed into the rice, while stirring almost continuously. You may not need all the broth to cook the rice.

$\overline{9}$ Meanwhile, finely grate the cheese.

$\overline{10}$ When rice is tender and there is still enough broth left in the rice to make it slightly runny, add the cheese, stirring well; season with pepper and serve.

**Yield:** 2 large servings

---

## ◆ Game Plan ◆

*Follow recipe directions.*

---

### PANTRY

Olive oil

Chicken broth or stock

Arborio rice

Dry white wine

Parmigiano Reggiano

Whole black pepper

---

### SHOPPING LIST

1 onion (½ cup chopped)

12 ounces radicchio

# SPICY PEANUT CHICKEN ♦
# ARBORIO RICE ♦ ASPARAGUS ♦ ♦

*This Italian rice is usually turned into risotto, but the short, fat grain makes a delicious ordinary dish of rice as well.*

## SPICY PEANUT CHICKEN

3 ounces whole or sliced (ready-cut) onion (1 cup)
12 ounces chicken breasts, skinless and boneless
1 teaspoon ground cumin
½ teaspoon ground cinnamon
1–2 tablespoons corn, safflower or canola oil
2 plum tomatoes
½ jalapeño or serrano chile
1 tablespoon lemon juice
2 tablespoons peanut butter
½ teaspoon minced garlic in oil
½ cup tomato puree
Fresh cilantro leaves (for garnish)

1 Slice onion.

2 Wash and dry chicken breasts and rub with cumin and cinnamon on both sides.

3 Heat oil in large skillet and sauté onion and chicken in hot oil, browning chicken on both sides.

4 Wash plum tomatoes and cut into large chunks. Halve jalapeño and remove seeds; reserve half for another use. Cut jalapeño into 2 or 3 pieces. Turn on food processor and add pepper through feed tube. Open processor and add plum tomatoes, lemon juice, peanut butter, garlic and puree. Process to blend well.

5 When chicken is browned on both sides, pour the sauce over. Cover, reduce heat and simmer about 5–7 minutes, until chicken is cooked.

6 Prepare cilantro leaves. Spoon some of sauce over rice and garnish with cilantro.

**Yield:** 2 servings

## ARBORIO RICE

½ cup arborio rice
1 cup water

Place rice and water in heavy-bottomed saucepan. Bring to boil. Reduce heat, stir, cover and simmer about 17 minutes, until water has been absorbed and rice is tender.

**Yield:** 2 servings

## ASPARAGUS

12–14 asparagus

1. Bring water to boil in steamer.

2. Wash asparagus and break off tough stems.

3. Steam asparagus about 7 minutes, until tender but firm.

   **Yield:** 2 servings

◆ *Game Plan* ◆

*Cook rice.*

*Slice onion.*

*Wash and dry chicken breasts and rub with cinnamon and cumin.*

*Sauté chicken in oil with onion.*

*Boil water for asparagus.*

*Prepare sauce for chicken.*

*Add sauce to chicken; cover and cook.*

*Clean asparagus.*

*Steam asparagus.*

*Garnish chicken with cilantro.*

### PANTRY

Ground cumin

Ground cinnamon

Corn, safflower or canola oil

Lemon

Peanut butter

Minced garlic in oil

Tomato puree

Arborio rice

### SHOPPING LIST

3 ounces onion whole or sliced
  (ready-cut) (1 cup)

12 ounces chicken breasts, skinless
  and boneless

2 plum tomatoes

1 jalapeño or serrano chile

Fresh cilantro leaves (for garnish)

12–14 asparagus

# SESAME CHICKEN NUGGETS ◆
# SWEET AND SHARP
# CUCUMBERS ◆ ◆ ◆ ◆ ◆ ◆ ◆ ◆ ◆

*My mother used to make the cucumber salad in the summer. She added thin, raw onion rings.*

## SESAME CHICKEN NUGGETS

16 ounces cubed white meat chicken nuggets (see page 18) or skinless and boneless chicken breasts
6 tablespoons sesame seeds
1–2 tablespoons corn, safflower or canola oil
16 ounces whole red bell pepper or 14 ounces sliced (ready-cut) (4 cups)
6 ounces snow peas
4 ounces bean sprouts
1 tablespoon coarsely grated fresh ginger
6 tablespoons dry sherry
4 teaspoons reduced-sodium soy sauce
¼–½ teaspoon Sichuan peppercorns (optional)

1. Cut up whole chicken breasts into large dice; wash chicken; drain on paper towels, pat dry and dip in sesame seeds to coat.

2. Heat oil and brown chicken pieces on both sides.

3. Cut up whole red pepper and string snow peas. Wash snow peas and sprouts and drain.

4. Grate ginger and add to chicken with sherry, soy sauce and peppercorns, if desired.

5. Add red pepper and cook for 3 minutes, covered. Add snow peas and cook for 1 minute longer. Add bean sprouts and stir, cooking just long enough to heat through.

**Yield:** 3 servings

## SWEET AND SHARP CUCUMBERS

4½ tablespoons rice vinegar
1½ tablespoons sugar
12 ounces Kirby cucumbers

1. Mix vinegar and sugar in serving bowl large enough to hold cucumbers.

$\underline{2}$ Scrub cucumbers but do not peel; slice in food processor on fine slicer. Stir into vinegar–sugar mixture.

**Yield:** 3 servings

---

## ◆ *Game Plan* ◆

*Prepare chicken and cook.*
*Prepare red pepper, snow peas and sprouts; grate ginger.*
*Add ginger, sherry, soy sauce, and optional peppercorns to chicken;*
*add red pepper.*
*Mix vinegar with sugar for cucumbers.*
*Prepare cucumbers and toss with vinegar–sugar mixture.*
*Add snow peas to chicken and cook; add bean sprouts and heat.*

---

### PANTRY

Sesame seeds
Corn, safflower or canola oil
Fresh ginger
Dry sherry

Reduced-sodium soy sauce
Sichuan peppercorns (optional)
Rice vinegar
Sugar

---

### SHOPPING LIST

16 ounces cubed white meat
  chicken nuggets or skinless and
  boneless chicken breasts
16 ounces whole red pepper or 14
  ounces sliced (ready-cut)

6 ounces snow peas
4 ounces bean sprouts
12 ounces Kirby cucumbers

# CHICKEN IN MUSTARD "CREAM" SAUCE ◆ PEPPER–RICE SALAD ◆

*No cream in this sauce—just the illusion, thanks to a mixture of ricotta and yogurt.*

## CHICKEN IN MUSTARD "CREAM" SAUCE

12 ounces chicken breasts, skinless and boneless
2 tablespoons flour
1–2 tablespoons olive oil
½ cup chicken stock
½–1 teaspoon dry mustard
1 teaspoon cornstarch
Freshly ground black pepper to taste
2 tablespoons chopped fresh parsley
3 tablespoons dry sherry
⅓ cup low-fat ricotta
⅓ cup plain low- or non-fat yogurt

1. Wash and dry chicken breasts and cut in half. Dredge in flour.

2. Heat oil in heavy pan and brown chicken on both sides, 7–10 minutes.

3. Stir a little chicken stock into dry mustard and cornstarch to make a paste. Then stir in rest of chicken stock; add pepper.

4. Chop parsley; set aside.

5. When chicken breasts are browned, remove and keep warm; deglaze pan with sherry. Add mustard mixture, return chicken to pan and cook until mixture thickens.

6. Process ricotta with yogurt until smooth.

7. Remove the chicken when cooked; turn heat to very low and quickly stir in ricotta mixture. Do not boil.

8. Serve sauce over chicken, sprinkled with parsley.

**Yield:** 2 servings

## PEPPER–RICE SALAD

½ cup long-grain rice
1 cup water
4 tablespoons chopped red onion (about 2 ounces)

1. Bring rice and water to boil. Reduce heat, cover and cook about 17 minutes over medium heat, until rice is tender and water has been absorbed.

2. Chop onion finely.

| | |
|---|---|
| 7 ounces whole green bell pepper or 6 ounces sliced (ready-cut) (1¼ cups) | $\underline{3}$ Slice green and red peppers into strips with fine slicing blade in food processor; drain. Spoon into serving bowl with onion. |
| 7 ounces whole red bell pepper or 6 ounces sliced (ready-cut) (1¼ cups) | $\underline{4}$ Toast sesame seeds. |
| 1 tablespoon sesame seeds | $\underline{5}$ Stir sugar and vinegar into serving bowl; add sesame seeds. |
| 1 teaspoon sugar | |
| 4 tablespoons balsamic vinegar | $\underline{6}$ When rice is cooked, stir into dressing mixture. |

**Yield:** 2 servings

---

◆ *Game Plan* ◆

*Cook rice.*
*Wash, flour and brown chicken.*
*Chop onion and prepare peppers for rice.   Make sauce for chicken.*
*Combine onion and peppers with dressing for salad.*
*Toast sesame seeds.   Chop parsley.*
*Remove chicken from pan and deglaze; return chicken to pan with*
*mustard mixture and cook until mixture thickens.*
*Process ricotta with yogurt.   Stir ricotta mixture into sauce for chicken.*
*Add rice to dressing mixture.*

---

*PANTRY*

| | | |
|---|---|---|
| *Flour* | *Plain low- or non-fat yogurt* | *Long-grain rice* |
| *Olive oil* | *Cornstarch* | *Sesame seeds* |
| *Chicken stock* | *Whole black pepper* | *Sugar* |
| *Dry mustard* | *Dry sherry* | *Balsamic vinegar* |

---

*SHOPPING LIST*

| | |
|---|---|
| *12 ounces chicken breasts, skinless and boneless* | *7 ounces whole green bell pepper or 6 ounces sliced (ready-cut)* |
| *Fresh parsley (2 tablespoons)* | *7 ounces whole red bell pepper or 6 ounces sliced (ready-cut)* |
| *Low-fat ricotta (⅓ cup)* | |
| *2 ounces chopped red onion (4 tablespoons)* | |

# MUSTARD-COATED CHICKEN ◆ BRUSSELS SPROUTS WITH CARAWAY ◆ ◆ ◆ ◆ ◆ ◆ ◆ ◆ ◆ ◆

*If heartier appetites demand more food, add some crusty whole-grain bread to this menu.*

## MUSTARD-COATED CHICKEN

3 tablespoons Dijon mustard
½ cup fine bread crumbs or cracker crumbs
1 tablespoon lemon juice
6 tablespoons water
12 ounces chicken breasts, skinless and boneless
2 tablespoons corn, safflower or canola oil
¼ cup dry white wine or dry sherry

1 Mix together mustard, bread crumbs, lemon juice and water to make a paste.

2 Wash and dry chicken breasts and pat half of the mustard coating on one side of each breast.

3 Heat oil in skillet large enough to hold breasts and place breasts in pan. While breasts are sautéing, spread remaining coating on top. When breasts are golden, turn and cook until golden on other side, about 8–10 minutes total cooking time.

4 Reduce heat and add wine; cook another 4–5 minutes, until breasts are cooked through. Do not cover. (Don't worry if the coating sticks to the pan; it will loosen up after the breasts are cooked in the wine.)

**Yield:** 2 servings

## BRUSSELS SPROUTS WITH CARAWAY

10 ounces Brussels sprouts
1 cup chicken stock or broth

1 Wash and trim Brussels sprouts.

1½ teaspoons unsalted
    butter
1 teaspoon caraway seeds
1 teaspoon lemon juice
    Freshly ground black
    pepper to taste

2. Bring stock to boil in skillet or pan large enough to hold sprouts in single layer. Add sprouts and simmer 3 minutes. Cover and cook until tender, about 5 minutes longer.

3. Drain and mix with butter, caraway seeds, lemon juice and black pepper to taste.

**Yield:** 2 servings

---

## ◆ *Game Plan* ◆

*Make mustard coating for chicken.*
*Sauté chicken.*
*Clean Brussels sprouts.*
*Heat stock for Brussels sprouts; add sprouts and cook.*
*Turn chicken.*
*When chicken is browned add wine.*
*Drain sprouts and mix with butter, caraway seeds,*
*lemon juice and black pepper.*

---

### PANTRY

Dijon mustard
Fine bread crumbs or cracker
    crumbs
Lemon
Corn, safflower or canola oil

Dry white wine or dry sherry
Chicken stock or broth
Unsalted butter
Caraway seeds
Whole black pepper

---

### SHOPPING LIST

12 ounces chicken breasts, skinless
    and boneless
10 ounces Brussels sprouts

Crusty whole-grain bread
    (optional)

# MARINATED CHICKEN WITH JIMMY SCHMIDT'S RELISH ◆ CHEESE-TOPPED TORTILLAS ◆ ◆ ◆

*The warm relish is a variation of the one Jimmy Schmidt makes at the Rattlesnake Club, in Denver, where southwestern flavors are given a sophisticated turn of great appeal.*

## MARINATED CHICKEN

12 ounces chicken breasts, skinless and boneless
2 tablespoons lime juice
1 teaspoon dried marjoram or oregano
1 tablespoon olive oil
1½ teaspoons hot chile oil
Jimmy Schmidt's relish (recipe follows)

1. Wash and dry chicken and cut into long strips about ¼-inch wide.

2. Squeeze lime juice over chicken in bowl. Sprinkle with herb and stir. Set aside to marinate until time to cook.

3. Heat oils in skillet. Drain chicken and sauté over high heat until golden. Serve atop the relish.

**Yield:** 2 servings

## JIMMY SCHMIDT'S RELISH

9 ounces whole red onion or 8 ounces sliced (ready-cut) (1¾ cups)
1–2 tablespoons olive oil
13 ounces whole zucchini or 12 ounces sliced (ready-cut) (2⅓ cups)
8 ounces ripe tomatoes
1 tablespoon chopped fresh marjoram or oregano or 1 teaspoon dried
2 tablespoons lemon juice
Freshly ground black pepper to taste

1. Dice sliced or whole onion and sauté over high heat in hot oil until softened, about 5 minutes.

2. Wash and trim whole zucchini. Dice zucchini and tomatoes. Chop fresh herb.

3. Add zucchini to onion and cook for 4 minutes.

4. Squeeze lemon and add juice with tomatoes and herb and cook another minute.

5. Season with pepper and cook 1 minute longer. Serve topped with chicken strips.

**Yield:** 2 servings

## CHEESE-TOPPED TORTILLAS

2–4 tablespoons coarsely
  grated Monterey Jack
  cheese
2–4 corn tortillas

$\frac{1}{\phantom{1}}$ Coarsely grate cheese and sprinkle over tortillas.

$\frac{2}{\phantom{2}}$ Toast in toaster oven or under broiler for about 1 minute, until cheese melts.

**Yield:** 2 servings

---

## ◆ *Game Plan* ◆

*Heat toaster oven or broiler.*
*Wash, dry and cut chicken into strips.*
*Marinate chicken in lime juice and herb.*
*Dice onion for relish and sauté in hot oil.*
*Dice zucchini and tomatoes and chop fresh herb.*
*Add zucchini to onion.   Heat oils for chicken.*
*Grate cheese for tortillas.   Drain and cook chicken.*
*Add tomatoes, herb and lemon juice to zucchini and onion.*
*Top tortillas with cheese and broil.*
*Season vegetables with pepper.   Top relish with chicken strips.*

---

### PANTRY

*Dried marjoram or oregano if*
  *fresh not available*
*Olive oil*

*Hot chile oil*
*Lemons*
*Whole black pepper*

---

### SHOPPING LIST

*12 ounces chicken breasts, skinless*
  *and boneless*
*1 lime (2 tablespoons)*
*9 ounces whole red onion or 8*
  *ounces sliced (ready-cut)*
*13 ounces whole zucchini or 12*
  *ounces sliced (ready-cut)*

*8 ounces ripe tomatoes*
*Fresh marjoram or oregano*
*1–2 ounces Monterey Jack cheese*
  *(2–4 tablespoons)*
*Corn tortillas (2–4)*

# SAUTÉED CHICKEN BREASTS WITH RED PEPPER PUREE ◆ YELLOW SQUASH WITH CUMIN ◆ CRUSTY ITALIAN OR FRENCH BREAD

*There's no time to roast red peppers when preparing a 20-minute meal, so these are sautéed before being pureed—not the same, but still quite good.*

## SAUTÉED CHICKEN BREASTS WITH RED PEPPER PUREE

7 ounces whole red bell pepper or 6 ounces sliced (ready-cut) (1¼ cups)
2–3 tablespoons olive oil
12 ounces chicken breasts, skinless and boneless
4 tablespoons sesame seeds
½ cup low-fat ricotta
1 teaspoon minced garlic in oil

1 Slice whole red pepper. Sauté pepper in 1 tablespoon oil until pepper begins to brown, about 3 minutes.

2 Wash and dry chicken breasts and coat with sesame seeds on both sides.

3 Remove red pepper from the pan and place in food processor. Add remaining oil to pan. Sauté chicken breasts in hot oil on both sides until brown, about 10–15 minutes depending on thickness of breasts.

4 Puree red pepper in food processor. Add ricotta and garlic and process until thoroughly blended.

5 When chicken is cooked, set aside. Add puree to skillet and reheat. Spoon some of puree onto plate; place breasts on top and spoon over remaining puree. Serve with crusty Italian or French bread.

**Yield:** 2 servings

## YELLOW SQUASH WITH CUMIN

9 ounces whole onion or 8 ounces sliced (ready-cut) (1¾ cups)

1 Slice whole onion. Sauté onion with cumin in hot oil over medium heat.

2 teaspoons ground cumin
2 tablespoons olive oil
12 ounces whole or sliced (ready-cut) yellow summer squash (2⅓ cups)
   Freshly ground black pepper to taste
2 teaspoons lemon juice

2 Meanwhile, scrub squash and slice on thin slicer in food processor. When onion begins to soften, add squash; season with black pepper and cook over medium heat, tightly covered, for about 10 minutes.

3 Squeeze lemon: when squash is tender, stir in lemon juice and serve.

**Yield:** 2 servings

---

### ◆ Game Plan ◆

*Sauté red pepper.*
*Prepare chicken.*
*Sauté onion and cumin for squash recipe.*
*Sauté chicken.*
*Prepare yellow squash.*
*Add squash and black pepper to onion.*
*Prepare red pepper puree.*
*Season squash with lemon.*

---

### PANTRY

*Olive oil*
*Sesame seeds*
*Minced garlic in oil*

*Ground cumin*
*Whole black pepper*
*Lemon*

---

### SHOPPING LIST

*7 ounces whole red bell pepper or 6 ounces sliced (ready-cut)*
*12 ounces chicken breasts, skinless and boneless*
*Low-fat ricotta (½ cup)*

*Crusty Italian or French bread*
*9 ounces whole onion or 8 ounces sliced (ready-cut)*
*12 ounces whole or sliced (ready-cut) yellow summer squash*

# CHICKEN AND ONIONS WITH BREAD DRESSING ◆ CABBAGE WITH RED ONION AND APPLE ◆ ◆

*The bread gives a pleasing, stuffing-like texture to the chicken dish. For a touch of color, add a bit of parsley to the chicken.*

## CHICKEN AND ONIONS WITH BREAD DRESSING

1–2 tablespoons olive oil
7 ounces whole onion or 6 ounces sliced (ready-cut) (1¼ cups)
12 ounces chicken breasts or thighs, skinless and boneless
1 teaspoon minced garlic in oil
1 teaspoon dried oregano
1 teaspoon dried basil
1 thick slice crusty bread
Freshly ground black pepper to taste
2 tablespoons red wine vinegar
½ cup water less 2 tablespoons (6 tablespoons)
Few sprigs fresh parsley for garnish

1. Heat oil in skillet.

2. Slice whole onion.

3. Wash and dry chicken and place in skillet with onion, browning chicken on both sides over medium-high heat.

4. Place garlic, oregano, basil and bread slice in food processor and process to make coarse crumbs.

5. When chicken is browned and onion is softened, add bread crumb mixture; reduce heat to low and cook for 1–2 minutes. Season with pepper.

6. Stir in vinegar and water; cover and cook until chicken is done, a few more minutes. Garnish with parsley.

**Yield:** 2 servings

## CABBAGE WITH RED ONION AND APPLE

1 large apple
2 medium carrots
10 ounces whole or shredded (ready-cut) cabbage

1. Wash and core apple but do not peel. Shred in food processor using shredder blade. Scrape and shred carrots. If cabbage is whole, also shred in processor. Shred onion in processor.

7 ounces whole red onion or 6 ounces sliced (ready-cut) (1¾ to 2 cups)
1 teaspoon ground cumin
¾ teaspoon ground coriander
Freshly ground black pepper to taste

**2** Place all ingredients in pot over medium-low heat. Stir, cover and cook about 6–8 minutes, until mixture is soft.

**Yield:** 2 servings

---

## ◆ Game Plan ◆

Sauté chicken and onion in hot oil.
Shred ingredients for cabbage dish and cook with herbs.
Process garlic, oregano, basil and bread slice.
Add bread mixture to chicken. Season with pepper.
Add vinegar and water to chicken; cover and finish cooking.

---

### PANTRY

Olive oil
Minced garlic in oil
Dried oregano
Dried basil
Crusty bread slice

Whole black pepper
Red wine vinegar
Ground cumin
Ground coriander

---

### SHOPPING LIST

7 ounces whole onion or 6 ounces sliced (ready-cut)
12 ounces chicken breasts or thighs, skinless and boneless
1 large apple
2 carrots

10 ounces whole or shredded (ready-cut) cabbage
7 ounces whole red onion or 6 ounces sliced (ready-cut)
Fresh parsley (few sprigs)

# GINGERED CHICKEN NUGGETS ◆ RICE WITH PINE NUTS, CARROTS AND ZUCCHINI ◆ ◆ ◆ ◆ ◆ ◆ ◆ ◆

*Using the same pan for these two recipes cuts down on cleanup.*

## GINGERED CHICKEN NUGGETS

8 ounces cut-up white meat chicken nuggets (see page 18) or skinless and boneless chicken breasts
1 tablespoon corn, safflower or canola oil
1 teaspoon Oriental sesame oil
4 scallions
2 teaspoons reduced-sodium soy sauce
2 tablespoons dry sherry
1½ tablespoons coarsely grated ginger

1. Cut up whole chicken breasts into large dice. Wash and dry chicken.

2. Using pan in which vegetables were cooked for rice dish (see Game Plan), heat oils. Sauté chicken in pan until golden.

3. Wash and trim scallions; cut into rings and add to chicken with soy sauce and sherry. Cook 1–2 minutes.

4. Grate ginger and add. Cook 1–2 minutes to soften ginger slightly.

**Yield:** 2 servings

## RICE WITH PINE NUTS, CARROTS AND ZUCCHINI

½ cup long-grain rice
1 cup water
5 ounces whole onion or 4 ounces sliced (ready-cut) (1¼ cups)
8 ounces whole carrots or 7 ounces sliced (ready-cut) (1⅓ cups)
13 ounces whole zucchini or 12 ounces sliced (ready-cut) (2⅓ cups)

1. Combine rice and water and bring to boil. Reduce heat, cover and cook over low heat for about 17 minutes, or until water has been absorbed and rice is tender.

2. Coarsely chop onion; chop whole carrots and whole zucchini; slice whole mushrooms.

5 ounces whole mushrooms or 4 ounces sliced (ready-cut) (1 cup)
1–2 tablespoons olive oil
Freshly ground black pepper
¼ cup coarsely chopped fresh cilantro
3 tablespoons pine nuts

3 In hot oil sauté onion, carrots, zucchini and mushrooms about 10 minutes. Add to rice, as it cooks, and season with black pepper.

4 Wash and dry cilantro and coarsely chop; add with pine nuts to cooked rice and vegetables.

**Yield:** 2 servings

---

## ◆ Game Plan ◆

Cook rice.
Chop vegetables and sauté 10 minutes.
Prepare chicken.
Cut up scallions.
Add vegetables to rice with pepper.
Brown chicken in corn and sesame oils in pan used to cook vegetables.
Add scallions, soy sauce and sherry to chicken and cook.
Grate ginger and add to chicken.
Chop cilantro and add to rice with pine nuts.

---

### PANTRY

Corn, safflower or canola oil
Oriental sesame oil
Reduced-sodium soy sauce
Dry sherry

Fresh ginger
Long-grain rice
Olive oil
Whole black pepper

---

### SHOPPING LIST

8 ounces cut-up white meat chicken nuggets or skinless and boneless chicken breasts
Bunch scallions (4)
5 ounces whole onion or 4 ounces sliced (ready-cut)
8 ounces whole carrots or 7 ounces sliced (ready-cut)

13 ounces whole zucchini or 12 ounces sliced (ready-cut)
5 ounces whole raw mushrooms or 4 ounces sliced (ready-cut)
Fresh cilantro (¼ cup)
2 ounces pine nuts (3 tablespoons)

# MIDDLE EASTERN CHICKEN AND VEGETABLES ◆ COUSCOUS ◆ ◆

*White meat chicken is now sometimes sold in small squares, called chicken nuggets. They cut down on preparation time but you pay for the service.*

## MIDDLE EASTERN CHICKEN AND VEGETABLES

16 ounces chicken nuggets or skinless and boneless chicken breasts

28 ounces whole onion or 24 ounces sliced (ready-cut) (about 5 cups)

2 tablespoons corn, safflower or canola oil

½ teaspoon ground coriander

1 teaspoon ground cumin

¼ teaspoon ground cinnamon

½ teaspoon ground turmeric
Freshly ground black pepper to taste

1 tablespoon coarsely grated fresh ginger

16 ounces ripe tomatoes

5 ounces whole red bell pepper or 4 ounces sliced (ready-cut) (¾ cup)

3 ounces whole or sliced (ready-cut) carrots (½ cup)

1 teaspoon minced garlic in oil

1 cup chicken stock

1. Wash and dry chicken. Cut up whole breasts into large dice.

2. Cut onion into large dice and sauté with chicken in hot oil. As chicken cooks add coriander, cumin, cinnamon, turmeric and black pepper and cook until chicken is white on all sides.

3. Coarsely grate ginger. Wash and cut tomatoes into medium chunks. Cut red pepper into medium dice. Cut carrots into large dice. Add ginger, garlic, vegetables and stock to chicken; cover and cook 12–15 minutes.

**Yield:** 3 servings

## COUSCOUS

2 teaspoons unsalted butter
1 cup couscous

1 Following the directions on the couscous package, bring water and butter to boil in covered pot.

2 Add couscous; cover and remove from heat. Allow to sit for 3–5 minutes, until water has been absorbed.

**Yield:** 3 servings

---

### ◆ *Game Plan* ◆

*Wash and dry chicken; dice whole chicken breasts.*
*Dice onion.*
*Sauté onion, chicken and spices.*
*Grate ginger; cut up tomatoes, red pepper and carrots and add to chicken with ginger, garlic and stock.*
*Boil water with butter for couscous.*
*Add couscous; remove from heat.*

---

#### PANTRY

Corn, safflower or canola oil
Ground coriander
Ground cumin
Ground cinnamon
Ground turmeric
Whole black pepper

Fresh ginger
Minced garlic in oil
Chicken stock
Unsalted butter
Couscous

---

#### SHOPPING LIST

16 ounces chicken nuggets or skinless and boneless chicken breasts
28 ounces whole onion or 24 ounces sliced (ready-cut)

16 ounces ripe tomatoes
5 ounces whole red bell pepper or 4 ounces sliced (ready-cut)
3 ounces whole or sliced (ready-cut) carrots

# CHICKEN FAJITAS WITH GUACAMOLE AND RED PEPPER ◆

*Fajitas, a simple Mexican border dish, has become so popular, particularly in Texas, and taken on so many permutations—such as chicken-fried fajitas with cream gravy or beef fajitas with soy sauce—that it's hard to tell what the original recipe was. In all likelihood it simply called for marinated and barbe-cued skirt steaks.*

*Here, chicken is the meat, served with guacamole in tacos.*

*Fajitas are a meal for an evening when you want something simple, quick, and delicious.*

## CHICKEN FAJITAS WITH GUACAMOLE AND RED PEPPER

12 ounces chicken breasts, skinless and boneless
1½ large limes
½ teaspoon minced garlic in oil
Freshly ground black pepper to taste
1 medium-large ripe avocado
1–2 serrano chiles, depending on degree of hotness desired
3 ounces whole red onion or sliced (ready-cut) (1 cup)
8 ounces whole red bell pepper or 7 ounces sliced (ready-cut) (1½ cups)
½ bunch cilantro
2 tablespoons olive oil
5–6 6- or 7-inch flour tortillas

1 Heat oven or toaster oven to 350 degrees.

2 Wash and dry chicken breasts and sprinkle with juice of ½ lime, garlic and black pepper on both sides.

3 Pit, peel and coarsely mash avocado into serving bowl.

4 Sprinkle juice of 1 lime over avocado.

5 Stem, seed and mince chiles in food processor.

6 Coarsely chop onion in food processor; drain. Add to avocado.

7 Coarsely chop red pepper in food processor and add to avocado.

8 Wash, dry and chop cilantro by hand; add to avocado.

9 Cut chicken breasts in half and brown in hot oil in skillet on both sides.

$\underline{10}$ Wrap tortillas in aluminum foil and steam for 10 minutes in oven. (See Note.)

$\underline{11}$ When chicken is ready, cut into strips.

$\underline{12}$ Spread avocado mixture generously over one side of tortilla and top with strips of chicken. Roll up tortilla. Repeat process for the other tortillas and serve.

**Yield:** 2 servings

**Note:** Another method for warming tortillas is to heat a heavy, ungreased skillet or griddle and heat the tortillas for 10–15 seconds on each side. The better quality tortillas will puff slightly. This method gives tortillas a more toasted taste than the oven steaming method, but it takes a bit longer.

---

### ◆ *Game Plan* ◆

*Follow recipe directions.*

---

#### PANTRY

Minced garlic in oil          Olive oil
Whole black pepper

---

#### SHOPPING LIST

12 ounces chicken breasts, skinless and boneless

Limes (1½)

1 medium-large ripe avocado

1–2 serrano chiles

3 ounces whole or sliced (ready-cut) red onion

8 ounces whole red bell pepper or 7 ounces sliced (ready-cut)

Fresh cilantro (½ bunch)

1 package 6- or 7-inch flour tortillas (5–6)

# CHICKEN BREASTS STUFFED WITH GOAT CHEESE ◆ CARROTS WITH CORIANDER ◆ FRENCH OR ITALIAN BREAD ◆ ◆ ◆ ◆ ◆ ◆ ◆

*This is a simplified variation of an elegant recipe in which the chicken breasts are carefully pounded. But I've learned that the dish is still delicious, though not quite as pretty, if the pounding is eliminated.*

*The entire meal can be easily made in 20 minutes, and there's even time to clean up before serving. The bread should be of good quality.*

## CHICKEN BREASTS STUFFED WITH GOAT CHEESE

3 ounces soft, sharp goat cheese
½ teaspoon minced garlic in oil
½ tablespoon chopped fresh basil
1 tablespoon lemon juice
Freshly ground black pepper to taste
12 ounces whole chicken breasts, skinless and boneless (4 breast halves)
1–2 tablespoons olive oil
6 tablespoons dry white wine or dry vermouth
Basil leaves for garnish

1 Process goat cheese, garlic, basil, lemon juice and pepper in food processor.

2 Wash and dry chicken breasts; divide goat cheese filling equally and spread on half of each breast. Fold over the other breast half and press edges together to seal.

3 Heat oil in skillet and brown breasts on both sides. Reduce heat; add wine and cover. Simmer about 10 minutes, until chicken is cooked. Decorate with basil leaves, and serve with sauce and French or Italian bread.

**Yield:** 2 servings

## CARROTS WITH CORIANDER

9 ounces whole carrots or 8 ounces sliced (ready-cut) (1½ cups)

1 If carrots are whole, scrape, trim and put through food processor with thinnest slicing disk.

1 teaspoon ground
  coriander
¼ cup dry sherry
  Freshly ground black
  pepper to taste
1 teaspoon lemon juice

2 In a heavy, covered pot cook carrots with coriander, sherry and pepper for 4–6 minutes, depending of size of carrots.

3 Sprinkle with lemon juice and serve.

**Yield:** 2 servings

---

## ◆ Game Plan ◆

*Process ingredients for goat cheese stuffing*
*Spread stuffing on chicken breasts and seal.*
*Sauté chicken in hot oil until brown.*
*Slice carrots if whole.*
*Add wine to chicken; cover and simmer.*
*Cook carrots with coriander, sherry and pepper.*

---

### PANTRY

*Minced garlic in oil*
*Lemon*
*Whole black pepper*
*Olive oil*

*Dry white wine or dry vermouth*
*Ground coriander*
*Dry sherry*

---

### SHOPPING LIST

*3 ounces soft, sharp goat cheese*
*Fresh basil (½ tablespoon plus a few leaves for garnish)*
*12 ounces whole chicken breasts, skinless and boneless*

*9 ounces whole carrots or 8 ounces sliced (ready-cut)*
*Good-quality French or Italian bread*

# TUNISIAN CHICKEN ◆ MINTED CARROT SALAD ◆ COUSCOUS ◆ ◆

*Copeland Marks, cookbook author, provided the inspiration for the carrot recipe.*

## TUNISIAN CHICKEN

12 ounces cut-up white meat chicken nuggets (see page 18) or skinless and boneless chicken breasts
1–2 tablespoons olive oil
12 ounces whole onion or 10 ounces sliced (ready-cut) (2 cups)
7 ounces whole green bell pepper or 6 ounces sliced (ready-cut) (1¼ cups)
1 teaspoon minced garlic in oil
2 teaspoons ground coriander
1 tablespoon chopped fresh mint
8 ounces plum tomatoes
4 tablespoons cider vinegar
Freshly ground black pepper to taste

1. Cut whole breasts into large dice. Wash and pat chicken dry.

2. Heat oil in large skillet and sauté chicken pieces until golden.

3. Slice whole onion and whole green pepper. Add vegetables to chicken with garlic and coriander; stir and cook 7–10 minutes, until vegetables are soft.

4. Chop mint.

5. Wash and slice tomatoes with slicing blade in food processor. Add to chicken with mint, vinegar and black pepper. Cook over medium-high heat a few minutes longer to soften tomatoes slightly and allow flavors to meld.

**Yield:** 2 servings

## MINTED CARROT SALAD

12 ounces whole carrots or 11 ounces sliced (ready-cut) (2 cups)
1½ cups water
2 tablespoons chopped fresh mint
½ teaspoon minced garlic in oil
1 tablespoon olive oil
2 tablespoons red wine vinegar
Freshly ground black pepper

1. Scrape and slice whole carrots. Bring water to boil in covered pot. Add carrots and cook about 4 minutes, until tender but still firm.

2. Chop mint. Add to serving bowl with garlic, oil, vinegar and pepper and whisk.

3. When carrots are cooked, drain and stir directly into dressing. Serve at room temperature.

**Yield:** 2 servings

## COUSCOUS

1 teaspoon unsalted butter
½ cup couscous

1 Following the directions on the couscous package, bring water to boil in covered pot with butter.

2 Stir in couscous; cover and remove from heat. Let sit for 3–5 minutes.

**Yield:** 2 servings

### ◆ *Game Plan* ◆

*Cut up whole breasts; wash chicken, dry and sauté in hot oil.*
*Scrape and slice carrots.   Boil water for carrots.*
*Slice whole onion and green pepper.*
*Add onion, green pepper, garlic and coriander to chicken.*
*Chop mint for chicken and carrots.*
*Cook carrots.*
*Boil water for couscous with butter.*
*Make dressing for carrot salad.*
*Slice tomatoes.*
*Add couscous to water.*
*Add tomatoes, mint, vinegar and black pepper to chicken.*
*Drain carrots and add to dressing.*

### PANTRY

Olive oil
Minced garlic in oil
Ground coriander

Cider vinegar
Whole black pepper
Red wine vinegar

Unsalted butter
Couscous

### SHOPPING LIST

12 ounces cut-up white meat
  chicken nuggets or
  skinless and boneless
  chicken breasts
12 ounces whole onion or 10
  ounces sliced (ready-cut)

7 ounces whole green bell
  pepper or 6 ounces
  sliced (ready-cut)
Fresh mint (3 tablespoons)

8 ounces plum tomatoes
12 ounces whole carrots or
  11 ounces sliced (ready-
  cut)

# CHICKEN NIÇOISE ◆ PASTA, BROCCOLI AND PINE NUTS ◆ ◆

## CHICKEN NIÇOISE

12 ounces chicken breasts, skinless and boneless
6 large Greek, Italian or French olives, packed in brine or oil
12–14 ounces ripe tomatoes, regular or plum
1½ teaspoons capers
2 tablespoons olive oil
Freshly ground black pepper
1 teaspoon anchovy paste or 1 anchovy fillet, mashed with a fork
½ teaspoon dried tarragon
1 teaspoon minced garlic in oil

1. Heat broiler. Line broiler pan with aluminum foil.

2. Wash and dry chicken breasts; place on broiler pan.

3. Pit olives. Add with tomatoes and capers to food processor. Process to make sauce.

4. In small bowl combine olive oil, pepper, anchovy paste, tarragon and garlic. Brush both sides of breasts with mixture. Broil 2–3 inches from source of heat for 3–4 minutes on one side; turn and broil another 3–5 minutes on other side.

5. When chicken is cooked, spoon sauce onto plates and place breasts on top.

**Yield:** 2 servings

---

## PASTA, BROCCOLI AND PINE NUTS

3 quarts water
1 cup small shells or other small-shaped pasta (2 ounces)
16 ounces whole broccoli or 8 ounces broccoli flowerettes (ready-cut) (3½–4 cups)
4 tablespoons raisins or currants
3 tablespoons pine nuts
1 cup plain low- or non-fat yogurt
1 tablespoon rice vinegar
Freshly ground black pepper to taste

1. Bring water to boil in covered pot that can hold a steamer basket. Add pasta and cook until it is al dente, 7–10 minutes.

2. If broccoli is whole, cut off tough stems and slice remaining stems thinly. Break broccoli heads into flowerettes and 5 minutes before pasta is cooked, add steamer basket and broccoli to steamer. Cook 5 minutes.

3. Meanwhile, combine raisins, pine nuts, yogurt, rice vinegar and black pepper in serving bowl. When pasta and broccoli are cooked, drain and add to

yogurt mixture. (If broccoli is parboiled, stir into pot with drained pasta and heat briefly; add to yogurt mixture.)

**Yield:** 2 servings

---

## ◆ Game Plan ◆

Heat broiler.

Boil water for pasta.

Line broiler pan with foil.

Wash chicken and dry.

Make coating for chicken and brush on.

If using whole broccoli, wash and cut up.

Make tomato sauce for chicken.

Cook pasta.

Broil chicken.

Add broccoli and steamer basket to pot and cook with pasta.

Make yogurt sauce for pasta and broccoli.

Arrange tomato sauce on plate and top with chicken.

Drain pasta and broccoli and mix with yogurt sauce.

---

### PANTRY

Olive oil

Whole black pepper

Anchovy paste or anchovy fillets

Dried tarragon

Minced garlic in oil

Greek, Italian or French olives, packed in brine or oil

Capers

Small shells or other small shaped pasta

Raisins or currants

Plain low- or non-fat yogurt

Rice vinegar

---

### SHOPPING LIST

12 ounces chicken breasts, skinless and boneless

12–14 ounces ripe tomatoes, regular or plum

16 ounces whole broccoli or 8 ounces broccoli flowerettes (ready-cut)

2 ounces pine nuts (3 tablespoons)

# CHICKEN AND PEAS WITH CURRIED YOGURT ◆ MASHED POTATOES AND FENNEL ◆ ◆ ◆ ◆

*It is normally not advisable to puree potatoes in a food processor, as it makes them gummy. But when they are combined with fennel, as in the second recipe below, the results are fine.*

## CHICKEN AND PEAS WITH CURRIED YOGURT

12 ounces chicken breasts, skinless and boneless
1½ tablespoons corn, safflower or canola oil
4 ounces whole onion or 3 ounces sliced (ready-cut) (1 cup)
1 teaspoon grated fresh ginger
1 cup plain low- or non-fat yogurt
1 teaspoon minced garlic in oil
3 tablespoons unsulphured dark molasses
1 teaspoon cornstarch
1½ teaspoons curry powder
5 ounces frozen peas (½ of 10-ounce box)

1. Wash and dry chicken breasts.

2. Heat oil in skillet large enough to hold all ingredients.

3. Chop onion coarsely and add it with the chicken to the oil, cooking over medium-high heat until chicken is brown on both sides.

4. Grate ginger coarsely and mix with yogurt, garlic, molasses, cornstarch and curry powder.

5. Stir the yogurt mixture into chicken with the peas; cover and cook over low heat about 5 minutes longer, until peas and sauce are heated through.

**Yield:** 2 servings

## MASHED POTATOES AND FENNEL

12–16 ounces potatoes
5 ounces whole fennel (about 1 cup)

1. Peel potatoes and slice into ¼-inch-thick slices.

1 tablespoon unsalted butter
  Freshly ground black
  pepper to taste
  Few shakes nutmeg

2 Trim off the fingers, feathery tops, root end and tough outer shell of the fennel. Cut into slices less than ¼-inch thick.

3 Boil potatoes and fennel in water to cover in covered pot until tender, about 10–13 minutes.

4 Drain and place in food processor with butter, pepper and nutmeg; puree.

**Yield:** 2 servings

---

### ◆ *Game Plan* ◆

*Prepare and cook potatoes and fennel.*
*Prepare chicken and onion and sauté.*
*Prepare yogurt sauce for chicken; add to chicken with peas.*
*Drain potatoes and fennel and puree with butter and seasonings.*

---

#### PANTRY

| | |
|---|---|
| Corn, safflower or canola oil | Cornstarch |
| Fresh ginger | Curry powder |
| Plain low- or non-fat yogurt | Unsalted butter |
| Minced garlic in oil | Whole black pepper |
| Unsulphured dark molasses | Nutmeg |

---

#### SHOPPING LIST

| | |
|---|---|
| 12 ounces chicken breasts, skinless and boneless | 5 ounces frozen peas (½ of 10-ounce box) |
| 4 ounces whole onion or 3 ounces sliced (ready-cut) | 12–16 ounces potatoes |
| | 5 ounces whole fennel |

# PIQUANT CHICKEN ◆ SPICY CHINESE NOODLES WITH CUCUMBERS ◆ ◆ ◆ ◆ ◆ ◆ ◆ ◆ ◆

## PIQUANT CHICKEN

1 tablespoon coarsely grated fresh ginger
1 tablespoon chopped fresh basil or 1 teaspoon dried
¾ cup dry red wine
1 tablespoon reduced-sodium soy sauce
½ teaspoon minced garlic in oil
1 tablespoon brown sugar
12 ounces chicken breasts, skinless and boneless
1–2 tablespoons corn, safflower or canola oil

1. Grate ginger; wash, dry and chop fresh basil.

2. Combine ginger and basil with wine, soy sauce, garlic and sugar.

3. Wash and dry chicken breasts.

4. Heat oil in large skillet; sauté chicken on both sides until golden brown, about 8 minutes total.

5. Spoon over ginger mixture; reduce heat to simmer and cover pot. Cook about 4 minutes longer, turning once.

**Yield:** 2 servings

## SPICY CHINESE NOODLES WITH CUCUMBERS

3 quarts water
1 small Kirby cucumber
4 scallions
1½ tablespoons Oriental sesame oil
1½–2 teaspoons reduced-sodium soy sauce
1–2 teaspoons hot Oriental chili sauce

1. Boil water in covered pot.

2. Wash, trim and cut cucumber into medium dice.

3. Wash, trim and slice scallions coarsely.

4. Combine cucumber and scallions with sesame oil, soy sauce, chili sauce and vinegar in serving bowl.

2 tablespoons red wine
   vinegar
6 ounces very thin
   noodles, fresh or dried

$\overline{5}$ Cook fresh noodles in boiling water for 30–60 seconds; cook dried noodles according to package directions, until tender but still firm.

$\overline{6}$ Drain noodles and mix thoroughly with sauce.

**Yield:** 2 servings

---

## ◆ *Game Plan* ◆

*Boil water for noodles.*
*Make sauce for chicken.*
*Wash and dry chicken and sauté.*
*Prepare sauce for noodles.*
*Cook noodles.*
*Add sauce to chicken and cook.*
*Drain pasta and mix with sauce.*

---

### PANTRY

*Fresh ginger*
*Dried basil, if fresh not available*
*Dry red wine*
*Reduced-sodium soy sauce*
*Minced garlic in oil*
*Brown sugar*

*Corn, safflower or canola oil*
*Oriental sesame oil*
*Hot Oriental chili sauce*
*Red wine vinegar*
*Very thin dried noodles, if fresh not*
   *available*

---

### SHOPPING LIST

*Fresh basil (1 tablespoon)*
*12 ounces chicken breasts, skinless*
   *and boneless*

*1 small Kirby cucumber*
*Bunch scallions (4)*
*6 ounces very thin fresh noodles*

# TACO CHICKEN • ZUCCHINI RICE WITH LEMON • PLUM TOMATOES WITH BALSAMIC VINEGAR • • • •

## TACO CHICKEN

¾ cup tomato puree
½ teaspoon minced garlic in oil
½ teaspoon ground coriander
1 teaspoon ground cumin
½ teaspoon medium-hot or pure hot chile powder
2 teaspoons Dijon mustard
2 tablespoons lime juice
12 ounces chicken breasts, skinless and boneless
1½ tablespoons corn, safflower or canola oil
2 heaping tablespoons plain low- or non-fat yogurt

1 In medium bowl combine tomato puree with garlic, coriander, cumin, chile powder and mustard. Squeeze in lime juice.

2 Wash and dry chicken breasts and dip into sauce.

3 Heat oil in skillet large enough to hold chicken breasts. Remove chicken from sauce and sauté in hot oil over medium-high heat until golden brown on both sides, about 8 minutes. Spoon on sauce; reduce heat to simmer and cook about 5 minutes longer.

4 Place chicken and sauce on 2 dinner plates; top each with yogurt.

**Yield:** 2 servings

## ZUCCHINI RICE WITH LEMON

½ cup long-grain rice
1 cup less 1½ tablespoons chicken stock
1½ tablespoons lemon juice
¼ teaspoon grated lemon rind
8 ounces whole or sliced (ready-cut) zucchini (1⅔ cups)
1½ teaspoons fresh thyme or ½ teaspoon dried thyme
Freshly ground black pepper to taste

1 Combine rice, stock and lemon juice in heavy-bottomed saucepan. Grate in lemon rind. Bring to boil; reduce heat, cover and simmer for 10 minutes.

2 Scrub and trim zucchini and dice.

3 Add zucchini, thyme and pepper to rice and continue to cook until rice and zucchini are tender and water has been absorbed, a total of 17 minutes.

**Yield:** 2 servings

## PLUM TOMATOES WITH BALSAMIC VINEGAR

4 plum tomatoes
Balsamic vinegar

$\overline{1}$ Wash tomatoes and slice onto 2 salad plates.

$\overline{2}$ Sprinkle with balsamic vinegar.

**Yield:** 2 servings

---

### ◆ Game Plan ◆

Cook rice with stock, lemon juice and lemon rind.

Make tomato sauce for chicken.

Wash and dry chicken breasts and dip in sauce.

Brown chicken.

Chop zucchini and add to rice with thyme and pepper; cook.

Add tomato sauce to chicken.

Slice tomatoes; sprinkle with balsamic vinegar.

Serve chicken topped with yogurt.

---

### PANTRY

Tomato puree
Minced garlic in oil
Ground coriander
Ground cumin
Medium-hot or hot pure chile
  powder
Dijon mustard
Corn, safflower or canola oil

Plain low- or non-fat yogurt
Long-grain rice
Chicken stock
Lemon
Dried thyme, if fresh not available
Whole black pepper
Balsamic vinegar

---

### SHOPPING LIST

1 or 2 limes, depending on size
12 ounces chicken breasts, skinless
  and boneless

8 ounces whole or sliced (ready-
  cut) zucchini
Fresh thyme (1½ teaspoons)
4 plum tomatoes

# CHICKEN WITH SUN-DRIED TOMATOES ◆ POTATOES AND BROCCOLI WITH CARAWAY DRESSING ◆ ◆ ◆ ◆ ◆ ◆ ◆ ◆ ◆ ◆

*You can purchase sun-dried tomatoes that have not been packed in oil for much less than those that have been. You can then pack them in olive oil yourself. They will last indefinitely.*

## CHICKEN WITH SUN-DRIED TOMATOES

12 ounces chicken breasts, skinless and boneless
1½ tablespoons olive oil
1 large leek
¼ cup sun-dried tomatoes, packed in olive oil, drained
⅔ cup low-fat ricotta
¼ cup dry white wine or dry vermouth
¼ teaspoon dried oregano
Freshly ground black pepper to taste

1 Wash and dry chicken and cut each breast half into 3 pieces.

2 Heat oil in skillet and brown chicken on both sides.

3 Wash leek and slice; chop in food processor.

4 Add leek to chicken and sauté.

5 Meanwhile, chop tomatoes in processor. Add ricotta and wine and process until mixture is blended. Add to chicken in pan with oregano and pepper to taste. Cook over low heat just until sauce has been heated through. Do not boil.

**Yield:** 2 servings

## POTATOES AND BROCCOLI WITH CARAWAY DRESSING

8 ounces tiny new potatoes
16 ounces whole broccoli or 8 ounces broccoli flowerettes (ready-cut) (3½–4 cups)

1 Scrub potatoes. If they are too large to cook in 20 minutes, cut in half. Boil in water to cover in covered pot.

3 tablespoons red wine
   vinegar
2 teaspoons Dijon mustard
2 tablespoons olive oil
1 teaspoon caraway seeds
2–3 tablespoons chopped
   red onion (about 1
   ounce)
Freshly ground black
   pepper to taste

2. If broccoli is whole, cut flowerettes from stems and break up. Cook raw flowerettes in potato water for 2–3 minutes, just until al dente.

3. In serving bowl beat together vinegar, mustard and oil. Stir in caraway seeds.

4. Coarsely chop onion. Add to dressing and mix well.

5. Stir in broccoli.

6. Quarter potatoes and stir in. Season with pepper.

**Yield:** 2 servings

---

## ◆ *Game Plan* ◆

*Cook potatoes.*
*Cook broccoli, if raw.*
*Prepare chicken and sauté.*
*Prepare leek and add to chicken.*
*Process remaining ingredients for chicken dish.*
*Make dressing for potatoes and broccoli; coarsely chop onion and add.*
*Add sauce to chicken and heat through.*
*Add broccoli and potatoes to dressing and season.*

---

### PANTRY

*Olive oil*  
*Sun-dried tomatoes*  
*Dry white wine or dry vermouth*  
*Dried oregano*  

*Whole black pepper*  
*Red wine vinegar*  
*Dijon mustard*  
*Caraway seeds*  

---

### SHOPPING LIST

*12 ounces chicken breasts, skinless and boneless*  
*1 large leek*  
*Low-fat ricotta (⅔ cup)*  
*8 ounces tiny new potatoes*  

*16 ounces whole broccoli or 8 ounces broccoli flowerettes (ready-cut)*  
*1 ounce red onion (2–3 tablespoons)*

# SWEET-AND-SOUR CHICKEN WITH VEGETABLES ◆ RICE ◆ ◆ ◆ ◆ ◆

*A light, delicate and not-too-sweet version of the old Chinese favorite, this dish is a bit closer to what Cantonese food is supposed to taste like.*

## SWEET-AND-SOUR CHICKEN WITH VEGETABLES

12 ounces chicken breasts, skinless and boneless
 4 teaspoons reduced-sodium soy sauce
 1 teaspoon Oriental sesame oil
 1-inch piece fresh ginger
 ½ teaspoon minced garlic in oil
 2 tablespoons brown sugar
 2 tablespoons dry sherry
 2 tablespoons cider vinegar
 2 tablespoons catsup
 3 tablespoons water
 8 ounces whole green bell pepper or 7 ounces sliced (ready-cut) (1½ cups)
16 ounces whole red onion or 14 ounces sliced (ready-cut) (3½ cups)
16 ounces ripe tomatoes, regular or plum
 1 tablespoon cornstarch

1. Heat broiler. Line a rack or broiler pan with double thickness of aluminum foil.

2. Wash and dry chicken breasts and place on rack or in pan.

3. Mix together 1 teaspoon soy sauce and the sesame oil and apply to both sides of chicken with a pastry brush or a piece of crumpled wax paper. Broil chicken as close to heat source as possible, about 10 minutes, turning once.

4. Coarsely grate ginger and mix together with garlic, remaining 3 teaspoons soy sauce, brown sugar, sherry, vinegar, catsup and 2 tablespoons water in pot large enough to hold vegetables.

5. Clean, quarter and slice whole green pepper and whole onion in food processor using thin disc.

6. Bring soy–sugar mixture to boil.

7. Stir in green pepper and onion and cook over medium heat.

8. Meanwhile, wash and core tomatoes and cut into quarters; squeeze out seeds from regular tomatoes. Cut tomatoes into small pieces directly into onion and green pepper and cook for 3–5 minutes, until vegetables have softened.

9. Mix cornstarch with 1 tablespoon water to form a smooth paste. When vegetables are almost done,

stir in cornstarch mixture and cook until mixture thickens slightly.

10 While mixture is cooking, cut cooked chicken into small chunks. Stir into vegetable mixture to heat through. Serve over rice.

**Yield:** 2 servings

---

### RICE

½ cup long-grain rice
1 cup water

1 Bring rice and water to boil in heavy-bottomed pot.

2 Reduce heat to simmer, cover and cook a total of 17 minutes, until water has been absorbed and rice is tender.

**Yield:** 2 servings

---

## ◆ Game Plan ◆

*Cook rice.*
*Follow directions in chicken recipe.*
*Just before adding the vegetables to the sweet and sour sauce, check rice to make sure it is done. If it is, turn it off and keep it covered until serving time.*

---

### PANTRY

Reduced-sodium soy sauce
Oriental sesame oil
Fresh ginger
Minced garlic in oil
Brown sugar

Dry sherry
Cider vinegar
Catsup
Cornstarch
Long-grain rice

---

### SHOPPING LIST

12 ounces chicken breasts, skinless and boneless
8 ounces whole green pepper or 7 ounces sliced (ready-cut)

16 ounces whole red onion or 14 ounces sliced (ready-cut)
16 ounces ripe tomatoes, regular or plum

# SAUTÉED MUSTARD GREENS À LA DAVID K'S ◆ FRESH ANGEL HAIR PASTA ◆ ◆ ◆ ◆ ◆ ◆

*David Keh is a Chinese restaurateur extraordinaire. His newest restaurants, David K's and David K's Cafe, in New York, are excellent.*

*Note: Trimmed and cut-up broccoli di rape can be substituted for the mustard greens but will require a little longer cooking time. Shaoxing wine is available at Chinese grocery stores.*

## SAUTÉED MUSTARD GREENS À LA DAVID K'S

12 ounces mustard greens (see Note)

12 ounces white meat chicken

1–2 tablespoons corn, safflower or canola oil

10 ounces frozen baby lima beans
Minced dried hot red pepper to taste

4 tablespoons shaoxing wine (rice wine; see Note) or dry sherry

1 tablespoon reduced-sodium soy sauce

1 teaspoon sugar
Few drops Oriental sesame oil

1. Wash, dry and chop mustard greens.

2. Wash, dry and mince chicken.

3. Heat oil in wok or heavy skillet and stir-fry chicken until it turns white.

4. Add mustard greens, lima beans, red pepper and stir-fry until greens wilt.

5. Stir in wine, soy sauce and sugar.

6. Sprinkle with a few drops of sesame oil and spoon over pasta.

**Yield:** 2 servings

## FRESH ANGEL HAIR PASTA

3 quarts water

8 ounces fresh angel hair pasta

1. Bring water to boil in covered pot.

2. Cook pasta about 30 seconds; drain and serve with mustard greens.

**Yield:** 2 servings

## ◆ Game Plan ◆

Boil water for pasta in covered pot.
Prepare greens.
Mince chicken and cook.
Add mustard greens, lima beans, red pepper and stir-fry.
Cook pasta.
Add wine, soy sauce and sugar to mustard greens and stir.
Sprinkle sesame oil on greens.
Drain pasta.

---

### PANTRY

Corn, safflower or canola oil
Minced dried hot red pepper
Shaoxing wine (rice wine) or dry
   sherry, if shaoxing wine not
   available

Reduced-sodium soy sauce
Sugar
Oriental sesame oil

---

### SHOPPING LIST

12 ounces mustard greens
12 ounces white meat chicken

10-ounce package frozen baby lima
   beans
8 ounces fresh angel hair pasta

# CHICKEN WITH BULGUR AND PRUNES ◆ RED PEPPERS WITH SOY DRESSING ◆ ◆ ◆ ◆ ◆ ◆ ◆ ◆

*I have served this chicken dish, in a slightly more elaborate version, for many dinner parties. Either way it is delicious.*

## CHICKEN WITH BULGUR AND PRUNES

12 ounces cut-up white meat chicken nuggets (see page 18) or skinless and boneless chicken breasts
2 tablespoons corn, safflower or canola oil
2 scallions
2 teaspoons coarsely grated fresh ginger
1 teaspoon minced garlic in oil
8–10 pitted prunes, depending on size
½ cup bulgur
1½ cups orange juice
Freshly ground black pepper to taste

1. Cut up breast halves into large dice. Wash and pat chicken dry, and sauté in 1 tablespoon hot oil until golden on both sides. When chicken is browned remove and set aside.

2. Chop scallions; grate ginger.

3. Add remaining tablespoon oil to pan and sauté scallions, ginger and garlic for 1 minute.

4. Cut prunes in half and add with bulgur and orange juice to pan. Cover and cook over medium heat about 10 minutes. Add chicken, season with pepper and finish cooking, another 3–4 minutes.

**Yield:** 2 servings

## RED PEPPERS WITH SOY DRESSING

8 ounces whole red bell pepper or 7 ounces sliced (ready-cut) (1½ cups)
1 teaspoon reduced-sodium soy sauce
1 teaspoon water

1. Wash red pepper and slice thinly in food processor.

2. In salad bowl beat soy sauce, water, vinegar and oil. Add red pepper and mix to coat.

**Yield:** 2 servings

1½ teaspoons balsamic
   vinegar
2 teaspoons Oriental
   sesame oil

---

## ◆ *Game Plan* ◆

*Sauté chicken.*
*Chop scallions.*
*Grate ginger.*
*Remove chicken and set aside.*
*Sauté scallions, ginger and garlic.*
*Halve prunes and add to pan with bulgur and orange juice. Cover and*
*cook.*
*Wash and cut up red pepper.*
*Return chicken to pan and finish cooking.*
*Make salad dressing and combine with red pepper.*

---

### PANTRY

| | |
|---|---|
| *Corn, safflower or canola oil* | *Whole black pepper* |
| *Fresh ginger* | *Reduced-sodium soy sauce* |
| *Minced garlic in oil* | *Balsamic vinegar* |
| *Bulgur* | *Oriental sesame oil* |

---

### SHOPPING LIST

| | |
|---|---|
| *12 ounces chicken nuggets or skinless and boneless chicken breasts* | *8–10 pitted prunes* |
| | *Orange juice (1½ cups)* |
| *Bunch scallions (2)* | *8 ounces whole red bell pepper or 7 ounces sliced (ready-cut)* |

# GINGER–LEMON CHICKEN ◆ TEX-MEX RICE ◆ SLICED TOMATOES ◆

*This menu should be prepared at the height of the tomato season, when tomatoes need no further seasoning.*

## GINGER–LEMON CHICKEN

12 ounces chicken breasts, skinless and boneless
⅓ cup coarsely cut fresh cilantro
½-inch piece fresh ginger
  Grated peel of ½ lemon
1 teaspoon minced garlic in oil
  Juice from ½ lemon
2 teaspoons sherry vinegar
1 teaspoon olive oil

1 Heat broiler. Line broiler pan with foil.

2 Wash and dry chicken breasts and arrange on pan.

3 Wash and dry cilantro and place in food processor with steel blade.

4 Cut ginger into large dice and turn on processor. With feed tube open, add ginger to cilantro piece by piece, until each piece is ground.

5 Grate lemon and add to processor with garlic, lemon juice, vinegar and oil. Process to blend thoroughly.

6 Spoon half of ginger mixture over top of chicken breasts and broil close to source of heat, about 2 inches, for 6 minutes.

7 Turn chicken and spoon over remaining ginger mixture. Continue broiling until chicken is cooked, about 4–6 minutes longer.

**Yield:** 2 servings

## TEX-MEX RICE

¾ cup long-grain rice
1½ cups water
3 ounces whole or sliced (ready-cut) onion (1 cup)
1 tablespoon olive oil
½ jalapeño chile
1 large ripe tomato

1 Combine rice and water in heavy-bottomed pot and bring to boil; reduce heat to medium-low, cover and cook about 17 minutes total, until rice is tender and liquid has been absorbed.

2 Chop onion in food processor.

3 Heat oil in small skillet and sauté onion in oil for 2–3 minutes.

4 Wash, halve and remove seeds from jalapeño. With food processor on, add small pieces of half the jalapeño through feed tube to mince.

1 teaspoon ground cumin
   Freshly ground black
   pepper to taste
2 tablespoons chopped
   fresh cilantro

5 Wash tomato. Cut in half and squeeze out juice and seeds. Add chunks of tomato to food processor and process to dice. Stir tomato–jalapeño mixture into onion and continue cooking until mixture is blended. Then add to rice with cumin and black pepper.

6 Chop cilantro coarsely and sprinkle on top of rice to serve.

**Yield:** 2 servings

## SLICED TOMATOES

2 ripe medium red or yellow
   tomatoes

Wash, dry, trim and thickly slice tomatoes onto 2 salad plates.

**Yield:** 2 servings

## ◆ *Game Plan* ◆

*Cook rice.   Heat broiler.*
*Prepare chicken and coating.   Broil chicken.*
*Chop and sauté onion.   Prepare jalapeño and tomato.*
*Add tomato mixture to onion.   Turn chicken.*
*Mix tomato–onion mixture with rice, cumin and black pepper.*
*Chop cilantro for garnish.   Wash and slice tomatoes.*

### PANTRY

| | | |
|---|---|---|
| Fresh ginger | Sherry vinegar | Ground cumin |
| Lemon | Olive oil | Whole black pepper |
| Minced garlic in oil | Long-grain rice | |

### SHOPPING LIST

| | | |
|---|---|---|
| 12 ounces chicken breasts, skinless and boneless | 3 ounces whole or sliced (ready-cut) onion | 1 jalapeño chile |
| Fresh cilantro (⅓ cup plus 2 tablespoons) | | 1 large ripe tomato |
| | | 2 ripe medium red or yellow tomatoes |

# CHICKEN IN HOT SESAME VINAIGRETTE WITH SNOW PEAS AND SCALLIONS ◆ COUSCOUS ◆ ◆ ◆

*A very delicate, slightly sweetened vinaigrette with a spicy touch.*

## CHICKEN IN HOT SESAME VINAIGRETTE WITH SNOW PEAS AND SCALLIONS

12 ounces chicken breasts, skinless and boneless
2 tablespoons lime juice
   Few drops hot pepper sauce or a few hot pepper flakes
20 snow peas (about 4 ounces)
6 scallions
1 teaspoon minced garlic in oil
2 tablespoons Oriental sesame oil
2 tablespoons honey
2 tablespoons red wine vinegar
4 tablespoons rice vinegar
1 teaspoon cornstarch
2 tablespoons chopped fresh cilantro

1. Wash and dry chicken and cut into bite-size pieces; sprinkle with lime juice and hot pepper sauce or pepper flakes to taste. Marinate until ready to cook.

2. Wash and string snow peas and cut into thirds.

3. Wash and trim scallions and cut into ¼-inch lengths.

4. Sauté garlic in 1 tablespoon sesame oil in skillet large enough to hold all ingredients.

5. Remove chicken from marinade; reserve marinade. Add chicken to skillet and sauté until brown all over.

6. Combine honey and vinegars with cornstarch. Mix in remaining tablespoon sesame oil with marinade; add to chicken. Stir until mixture begins to thicken. Add snow peas and scallions, and cook about 1 minute, but no longer.

7. Wash, dry and chop cilantro and sprinkle over chicken. Serve over rice.

**Yield:** 2 servings

## COUSCOUS

¾ cup couscous

Following directions on couscous package, bring water to boil. Stir in couscous; cover and remove from heat. Allow to sit 3–5 minutes, until water has been absorbed.

**Yield:** 2 servings

## ◆ *Game Plan* ◆

*Wash, dry and cut up chicken and sprinkle with lime juice and hot pepper sauce or flakes.*
*Prepare snow peas and scallions.*
*Sauté garlic in oil.*
*Add chicken and sauté.*
*Boil water for couscous.*
*Add couscous to water; remove from heat.*
*Make sauce for chicken; add to chicken.*
*Add scallions and snow peas to chicken.*
*Chop cilantro and sprinkle over chicken.*

### PANTRY

| | |
|---|---|
| Hot pepper sauce or pepper flakes | Red wine vinegar |
| Minced garlic in oil | Rice vinegar |
| Oriental sesame oil | Cornstarch |
| Honey | Couscous |

### · SHOPPING LIST

| | |
|---|---|
| 12 ounces chicken breasts, skinless and boneless | 4 ounces snow peas (20) |
| 1 lime | Bunch scallions (6) |
| | Fresh cilantro (2 tablespoons) |

# BON BON CHICKEN WITH VEGETABLES ◆ WARM TORTILLAS OR WRAPPERS ◆ ◆ ◆ ◆ ◆ ◆ ◆ ◆

*This is a variation on a cold chicken recipe that is traditionally served on cucumber strips. To make it a full meal, I decided to treat it like moo shoo pork and wrap it in something. Since it is sometimes difficult to find Chinese mushi wrappers, I substituted flour tortillas, which work very well. Talk about cross-cultural!*

## BON BON CHICKEN WITH VEGETABLES

16 ounces whole broccoli or
    8 ounces flowerettes
    (ready-cut) (3½–4 cups)
10 ounces whole carrots
12 ounces chicken breasts,
    skinless and boneless
  1-inch piece fresh ginger
2 tablespoons Oriental
    sesame paste
½ teaspoon minced garlic in
    oil
1 or 2 teaspoons Oriental
    chili sauce or hot chili
    paste with garlic
3 or 4 tablespoons water
1 teaspoon sugar
2 tablespoons rice vinegar
5 teaspoons reduced-
    sodium soy sauce
  Hoisin sauce

1 Wash whole broccoli. Trim off tough ends and cut broccoli heads into small flowerettes.

2 Scrape whole carrots and slice on thin slicer in food processor.

3 Wash chicken breasts and place in skillet with just enough water to cover. Add broccoli and carrots. Cover and bring to boil. Reduce heat and simmer about 7 minutes, until chicken is tender and vegetables are cooked.

4 Meanwhile, process ginger; add sesame paste, garlic, chili sauce or paste, water, sugar, rice vinegar, and soy sauce. Process to smooth mixture and place in serving bowl large enough to hold chicken and vegetables.

5 When cooked, drain chicken; add vegetables to sauce; cut chicken into strips and add; mix well to coat with sauce. Serve on warm tortillas or Chinese wrappers with hoisin sauce.

**Yield:** 2 servings

## WARM TORTILLAS OR WRAPPERS

4–5 10-inch flour tortillas or
Chinese mushi wrappers

<u>1</u> Preheat toaster oven or regular oven to 400 degrees.

<u>2</u> Wrap tortillas or wrappers in foil, place in oven and heat for about 10 minutes. Serve warm.

**Yield:** 2 servings

---

## ◆ *Game Plan* ◆

*Preheat oven to 400 degrees.*
*Clean, slice and cook broccoli and carrots with chicken.*
*Warm tortillas.*
*Make sauce.*
*Drain chicken; add vegetables to sauce; cut chicken into strips and mix with vegetables and sauce.*

---

### PANTRY

Fresh ginger
Oriental sesame paste
Minced garlic in oil
Oriental chili sauce or hot chili
　paste with garlic

Sugar
Rice vinegar
Reduced-sodium soy sauce
Hoisin sauce

---

### SHOPPING LIST

16 ounces whole broccoli or 8
　ounces flowerettes (ready-cut)
10 ounces whole carrots

12 ounces chicken breasts, skinless
　and boneless
10-inch flour tortillas or Chinese
　mushi wrappers (4–5)

# CHILE–CORNMEAL-CRUSTED CHICKEN BREASTS ◆ MEXICAN RICE ◆ ◆ ◆ ◆ ◆ ◆ ◆ ◆ ◆ ◆ ◆

*The crusty, flavorful coating seals in the juiciness of the tender meat. The rice is a more elegant version of the Spanish rice we all probably remember from childhood. This is a generous amount of rice, so you may have leftovers.*

## CHILE–CORNMEAL-CRUSTED CHICKEN BREASTS

2 tablespoons finely ground cornmeal
1 tablespoon mild pure chile powder
½ teaspoon ground coriander
1 teaspoon ground cumin
1 teaspoon dried oregano
12 ounces chicken breasts, skinless and boneless
1–2 tablespoons corn, safflower or canola oil

1 Mix cornmeal with chile powder, coriander, cumin and oregano.

2 Wash and dry chicken breasts and dip into cornmeal mixture, making sure that both sides of breasts are well coated.

3 Heat oil in the same skillet used to sauté onion for rice (see Game Plan).

4 Brown chicken breasts on both sides, about 10 minutes.

**Yield:** 2 servings

## MEXICAN RICE

1 cup canned Italian plum tomatoes, drained (reserve 1 cup juice)
1 cup long-grain rice
1 cup chicken stock
½–1 jalapeño or serrano chile

1 Break up tomatoes with your fingers. Combine with rice, chicken stock and 1 cup juice from can in heavy-bottomed saucepan. Bring to boil; reduce heat, cover and cook for a total of 17 minutes.

2 Seed and chop chile and add to rice as it cooks.

8 ounces whole onion or 7 ounces sliced (ready-cut) (1½ cups)
1 teaspoon minced garlic in oil
1 tablespoon corn, safflower or canola oil
2 tablespoons chopped fresh cilantro or parsley

$\overline{3}$ Chop onion coarsely and sauté with garlic in hot oil in skillet large enough to accommodate the chicken later (see Game Plan).

$\overline{4}$ When onion begins to soften, add to rice and continue cooking, covered.

$\overline{5}$ Chop cilantro and sprinkle over rice.

**Yield:** 2 servings

---

## ◆ Game Plan ◆

*Cook rice with tomatoes, juice and stock.*
*Prepare jalapeño and add.*
*Chop onion and sauté with garlic; add to rice.*
*Heat oil in same skillet used to sauté onion for rice.*
*Mix cornmeal coating for chicken.*
*Wash and dry chicken and coat.*
*Sauté chicken in hot oil.*
*Chop coriander and sprinkle over rice.*

---

### PANTRY

| | |
|---|---|
| Cornmeal | Corn, safflower or canola oil |
| Mild chile powder | Long-grain rice |
| Ground coriander | Chicken stock |
| Ground cumin | Minced garlic in oil |
| Dried oregano | |

---

### SHOPPING LIST

| | |
|---|---|
| 12 ounces chicken breasts, skinless and boneless | 8 ounces whole onion or 7 ounces sliced (ready-cut) |
| 1 can Italian plum tomatoes (1 cup) | Fresh cilantro or parsley (2 tablespoons) |
| 1 jalapeño or serrano chile | |

# BROILED QUAIL WITH PANCETTA ♦ POLENTA WITH TOMATO AND WILD MUSHROOM SAUCE ♦ ♦ ♦ ♦

*This menu is not for an ordinary, everyday dinner, but, rather, for a special occasion when you still want to cook quickly, for a celebration when you want to have another couple in for dinner but have no time to prepare. Since it may not be easy to find some of the ingredients, you might have to purchase them by mail (see Mail Order Products on page 235 for places that carry johnnycake meal, which is made with cornmeal, and for quail).*

*You want semi-boneless quail, with breastbones removed. The menu is for two but can easily be doubled for four.*

*Note: Have butcher partially bone the quail. Many quail ordered by mail come semi-boneless, with metal frame inserted that hold the quail open.*

## BROILED QUAIL WITH PANCETTA

4 semi-boneless quail (see Note, above)
12 very thin slices pancetta

1 Heat broiler and cover broiler pan with double thickness of aluminum foil.

2 Wash and dry quail. Stuff each quail with one slice of pancetta and arrange another slice under the quail. Place quail, breast side up, in pan. Top each breast with remaining pancetta.

3 Broil quail about 4 inches from source of heat for about 5 minutes, breast side up. Turn and broil 5 minutes longer, breast side down.

4 If quail come with metal frame, remove it and serve.

**Yield:** 2 servings

## POLENTA WITH TOMATO AND WILD MUSHROOM SAUCE

2 heaping tablespoons dried porcini or other mushrooms

1 Cover mushrooms with hot water.

28-ounce can Italian plum
tomatoes
½ teaspoon dried thyme
½ teaspoon dried oregano
Freshly ground black
pepper to taste
2 tablespoons coarsely
grated Parmigiano
Reggiano
2 cups chicken stock
1 cup johnnycake meal or
instant polenta

2 Crush the plum tomatoes between your fingers and place in pot, without the juice, along with thyme, oregano and pepper. Cook over medium-high heat for 10 minutes, until most of liquid has been absorbed.

3 Grate cheese and set aside.

4 Bring chicken stock to boil (follow directions on instant polenta package for amount needed; use 2 cups for johnnycake meal).

5 Drain mushrooms and squeeze out liquid; chop coarsely and add to tomatoes. Add some mushroom liquid if tomatoes have become too dry.

6 When stock has boiled, slowly add polenta or johnnycake meal, stirring constantly, until mixture is thick and liquid has been absorbed.

7 Serve polenta topped with sauce.

**Yield:** 2 servings

---

## ◆ *Game Plan* ◆

*Heat broiler.   Soak mushrooms.   Cook tomatoes and seasonings.*
*Prepare quail.   Broil quail.   Grate cheese.   Boil stock for polenta.*
*Add mushrooms to tomato sauce.   Turn quail.   Cook polenta.*

---

### PANTRY

*Dried mushrooms, preferably
   porcini*
*Dried thyme*
*Dried oregano*
*Whole black pepper*

*Chicken stock*
*Parmigiano Reggiano*
*Instant polenta or johnnycake
   meal (see Mail Order Products,
   page 235)*

---

### SHOPPING LIST

*4 semi-boneless quail (if not
   available at butcher, see Mail
   Order Products, page 235).*

*12 very thin slices pancetta*
*28-ounce can Italian plum
   tomatoes*

# GOLDEN FLOWER TURKEY WITH BAMBOO SHOOTS AND CHILI ◆ ASPARAGUS STIR-FRY ◆ RICE ◆ ◆ ◆

*This is one of the recipes I picked up on my trip to China in 1987. The chef at the Golden Flower Hotel in Xi'an, the town famous for the thousands of life-size terra cotta warrior figures recently discovered, was trained by a master chef before the Cultural Revolution. In 1987 he was one of the few well-qualified chefs left in China.*

*In China the recipe is made with chicken, but turkey breast works nicely too. And it takes 22 minutes, not 20, to prepare.*

## GOLDEN FLOWER TURKEY WITH BAMBOO SHOOTS AND CHILI

12 ounces white meat turkey
1 egg white
2 teaspoons cornstarch
1 tablespoon Chinese black vinegar or balsamic vinegar
1 tablespoon reduced-sodium soy sauce
1½ teaspoons sugar
White pepper to taste
1 5-ounce can bamboo shoots
2 stalks celery or 4 ounces sliced (ready cut) (about 1 cup)
6 ounces whole red bell pepper or 5 ounces sliced (ready cut) (about 1 cup)
3 scallions
4 tablespoons peanut oil
1½ tablespoons hot chili paste with garlic
6 tablespoons chicken stock

1. Wash and dry turkey and cut into strips about ⅛ inch wide and 2 inches long. Mix with egg white and cornstarch and set aside.

2. Combine vinegar, soy sauce, sugar and white pepper and set aside.

3. Drain liquid from bamboo shoots and set aside.

4. Finely chop celery and red pepper; thinly slice scallions.

5. Heat 2 tablespoons oil in wok or skillet until it shimmers. Stir-fry bamboo shoots, celery, scallions and red pepper about 2 minutes; remove and set aside. Wipe out wok.

6. Heat remaining oil in wok until it shimmers. Stir-fry turkey until it turns white.

7. Add chili paste; stir-fry. Add vinegar mixture and stir-fry. Return vegetables to wok and stir in chicken stock; stir-fry to mix well. Serve over rice.

**Yield:** 2 servings

## ASPARAGUS STIR-FRY

12–14 asparagus

1. Wash asparagus and break off tough stem at point where it bends naturally.

| | |
|---|---|
| 1 teaspoon peanut oil<br>2 teaspoons Oriental sesame oil<br>6 tablespoons chicken stock | **2** Heat oils in skillet and add asparagus. Stir-fry for 2 minutes.<br><br>**3** Add stock; cover and simmer about 4 minutes longer.<br><br>**Yield:** 2 servings |

---

**RICE**

½ cup long-grain rice
1 cup water

Combine rice and water in heavy-bottomed pot and bring to boil. Reduce heat, cover and simmer until water has been absorbed, 17 minutes total cooking time.

**Yield:** 2 servings

---

## ◆ *Game Plan* ◆

*Cook rice.   Cut up turkey and mix with egg white and cornstarch.*
*Combine vinegar, soy sauce, sugar and white pepper.*
*Drain bamboo shoots; finely chop celery and red pepper; slice scallions.*
*Prepare asparagus.*
*Stir-fry bamboo shoots, celery, scallions and red pepper.*
*Stir-fry asparagus.   Stir-fry turkey.*
*Add chicken stock to asparagus; cover and simmer.*
*Add chili paste to turkey and stir-fry. Add vinegar mixture and stir-fry.*
*Return vegetables to turkey with chicken stock and stir-fry.*

---

### PANTRY

| | | |
|---|---|---|
| *Egg* | *Reduced-sodium soy sauce* | *Hot chili paste with garlic* |
| *Cornstarch* | *Sugar* | *Chicken stock* |
| *Chinese black vinegar or*<br>    *balsamic vinegar* | *White Pepper*<br>*Peanut Oil* | *Oriental sesame oil*<br>*Long-grain rice* |

---

### SHOPPING LIST

| | | |
|---|---|---|
| *12 ounces white meat*<br>    *turkey*<br>*5-ounce can bamboo shoots* | *2 stalks or 4 ounces*<br>    *chopped or sliced*<br>    *(ready-cut) celery*<br>*Bunch scallions (3)* | *6 ounces whole red bell*<br>    *pepper or 5 ounces*<br>    *sliced (ready-cut)*<br>*12–14 asparagus* |

# MIDDLE EASTERN TURKEY AND PEPPER SAUTÉ ◆ COUSCOUS WITH MUSHROOMS AND SCALLIONS ◆

*If you want to dress up the meal a bit, serve it with a chutney.*

## MIDDLE EASTERN TURKEY AND PEPPER SAUTÉ

5 scallions
1 jalapeño or serrano chile
8 ounces whole red bell pepper or 7 ounces sliced (ready-cut) (1½ cups)
12 ounces turkey breast, skinless and boneless
2 tablespoons corn, safflower or canola oil
1 teaspoon minced garlic in oil
½ cup chicken broth
¼ cup raisins
½ teaspoon ground ginger
½ teaspoon ground cinnamon
1 teaspoon ground cumin
½ teaspoon ground turmeric
Chutney (optional)

1 Clean and trim scallions and cut in thirds. Seed and trim jalapeño or serrano chile. With food processor running put scallions and ½–1 whole chile through feed tube and process.

2 Change blade to slicer. Seed and trim whole red pepper and slice in food processor; drain.

3 Wash and dry turkey and slice in 1- or 2-inch cubes.

4 Heat oil in skillet large enough to hold all ingredients. Sauté scallions, red pepper, jalapeño, turkey and garlic in skillet, cooking about 8 minutes, until red pepper and jalapeño are softened and turkey has turned white.

5 Add chicken broth, raisins, ginger, cinnamon, cumin and turmeric and stir; cook another 5 minutes or so, until seasonings have melded with other ingredients. Serve with chutney, if desired.

**Yield:** 2 servings

## COUSCOUS WITH MUSHROOMS AND SCALLIONS

2 scallions
1½–2 cups chicken broth

1 Clean scallions; cut in 3 pieces and with food processor running, put through feed tube; process.

| | |
|---|---|
| 4 ounces whole or sliced (ready-cut) mushrooms (1 cup) | **2** Bring chicken broth to boil in covered pot (follow package directions for amount of liquid needed). |
| 1 cup couscous, precooked | **3** Wash and trim mushrooms and slice on slicing blade of food processor. |
| 2 tablespoons pine nuts | **4** When broth boils, stir in scallions, mushrooms, couscous and pine nuts. Remove from heat; cover and allow to sit about 5 minutes, until liquid has been absorbed. |

**2** Bring chicken broth to boil in covered pot (follow package directions for amount of liquid needed).

**3** Wash and trim mushrooms and slice on slicing blade of food processor.

**4** When broth boils, stir in scallions, mushrooms, couscous and pine nuts. Remove from heat; cover and allow to sit about 5 minutes, until liquid has been absorbed.

**Yield:** 2 servings

---

## ◆ *Game Plan* ◆

*Prepare scallions, red pepper, jalapeño and turkey.*
*Sauté in hot oil.*
*Cut up scallions and slice mushrooms for couscous.*
*Add broth, raisins and spices to turkey.*
*Bring chicken broth to boil for couscous.*
*Combine all couscous ingredients with boiling broth.*

---

### PANTRY

*Corn, safflower or canola oil*
*Minced garlic in oil*
*Chicken broth*
*Raisins*
*Ground ginger*

*Ground cinnamon*
*Ground cumin*
*Ground turmeric*
*Chutney, optional*
*Couscous*

---

### SHOPPING LIST

*Bunch scallions (7)*
*1 jalapeño or serrano chile*
*8 ounces whole red bell pepper or*
  *7 ounces sliced (ready-cut)*

*12 ounces turkey breast, skinless*
  *and boneless*
*4 ounces whole or sliced (ready-*
  *cut) mushrooms*
*1 ounce pine nuts (2 tablespoons)*

# ORIENTAL MEAT PATTIES ◆ TANGY RICE AND PEAS ◆ ◆ ◆

*The texture of this is softer than ground beef burgers; otherwise you cannot tell what variety of meat it is because of all the savory seasonings. It also has less fat.*

*Note: You may substitute chopped parsley for the cilantro, but the flavor will not be the same.*

## ORIENTAL MEAT PATTIES

2 teaspoons Oriental
  sesame paste
1 teaspoon Oriental sesame
  oil
2 teaspoons reduced-
  sodium soy sauce
½ of 8-ounce can water
  chestnuts
1-inch piece fresh ginger
12 ounces raw ground
  turkey
2 teaspoons minced garlic
  in oil
  Freshly ground black
  pepper to taste
  Chopped fresh cilantro
  for garnish (see Note)

1. Turn on broiler.

2. In food processor process sesame paste with sesame oil and soy sauce to make smooth paste.

3. With processor running, add water chestnuts and ginger and mince.

4. Combine ground turkey with sesame paste mixture, garlic and black pepper and shape into four patties. Broil 2 inches from source of heat for about 8 minutes.

5. Chop cilantro and garnish patties.

**Yield:** 2 servings

## TANGY RICE AND PEA SALAD

½ cup long-grain rice
1 cup water
  Few pinches turmeric
2 tablespoons coarsely
  chopped fresh cilantro
3½ tablespoons rice vinegar

1. Combine rice, water and turmeric and bring to boil in heavy-bottomed pot. Reduce heat, cover and simmer until water has been absorbed and rice is tender, 17 minutes total.

1½ tablespoons Oriental
sesame oil
3 tablespoons roasted,
unsalted peanuts
8–10 ounces frozen peas

2 Chop cilantro and place in serving bowl with vinegar, oil and peanuts and stir.

3 Approximately 3–4 minutes before rice is cooked,
stir in the peas and cook just until they are tender
and heated through.

4 Stir rice–pea mixture into dressing and serve warm
or at room temperature.

**Yield:** 2 servings

---

### ◆ *Game Plan* ◆

*Cook rice.*
*Heat broiler.*
*Prepare meat patties and broil.*
*Chop cilantro for meat and for salad.*
*Finish salad.*
*Decorate meat patties with cilantro.*

---

#### PANTRY

Oriental sesame paste
Oriental sesame oil
Reduced-sodium soy sauce
Fresh ginger
Minced garlic in oil

Whole black pepper
Long-grain rice
Turmeric
Rice vinegar

---

#### SHOPPING LIST

8-ounce can water chestnuts
12 ounces raw ground turkey
Fresh cilantro (2 tablespoons plus
garnish)

Unsalted, roasted peanuts
(3 tablespoons)
8–10 ounces frozen peas

## CHINESE NOODLES AND TURKEY

16 ounces turkey breast, skinless and boneless
2 teaspoons cornstarch
3 tablespoons reduced-sodium soy sauce
3 tablespoons dry sherry
9 ounces whole red bell pepper or 8 ounces sliced (ready-cut) (1¾ cups)
6 scallions
3 tablespoons grated fresh ginger
1 tablespoon peanut oil
2 teaspoons minced garlic in oil
8 ounces fresh or dried very thin pasta, such as linguine
8 ounces whole or sliced (ready-cut) zucchini (1⅔ cups)
1 cup chicken stock
2 tablespoons sesame oil

1  Boil water for noodles in covered pot.

2  Cut turkey into narrow strips.

3  Make a paste of cornstarch and a little soy sauce. Add remaining soy sauce and sherry and marinate turkey in mixture.

4  Wash and seed whole red pepper. Chop the pepper and scallions. Grate ginger. Stir-fry red pepper, scallions and ginger in peanut oil with garlic for about 30 seconds.

5  Drain marinade from turkey and reserve. Add turkey pieces to vegetables and stir-fry for 2–4 minutes, depending on size of pieces.

6  Cook fresh noodles for about 1 minute; follow package directions for dried noodles.

7  Wash and trim whole zucchini. Chop zucchini and add to turkey mixture. Stir-fry for 1 minute.

8  Drain noodles and rinse with cold water.

9  Add marinade and stock to turkey; cook, stirring 1–2 minutes, until mixture thickens slightly.

10  Stir in noodles and sprinkle with sesame oil.

**Yield:** 3 servings

## ◆ Game Plan ◆

*Follow recipe directions.*
*Serve fresh fruit for dessert.*

### PANTRY

Cornstarch
Reduced-sodium soy sauce
Dry sherry
Fresh ginger
Peanut oil

Minced garlic in oil
Dried thin pasta, such as linguine,
   if fresh not available
Chicken stock
Sesame oil

### SHOPPING LIST

16 ounces turkey breast, skinless
   and boneless
9 ounces whole red bell pepper or 8
   ounces sliced (ready cut)
Bunch scallions (6)

8 ounces whole or sliced (ready-
   cut) zucchini
8 ounces fresh very thin pasta,
   such as linguine
Fresh fruit for dessert

# TURKEY BREAST WITH PAPAYA AND CHILE ◆ BASMATI RICE ◆ ◆

*Basmati rice has a wonderful nutty flavor. It is now available in many super-markets and, of course, can be found in Indian grocery stores, but if you cannot find it, use regular white rice.*

## TURKEY BREAST WITH PAPAYA AND CHILE

20 ounces turkey breast, skinless and boneless
2 tablespoons corn, safflower or canola oil
1 mild green chile
7 ounces whole red onion or 6 ounces sliced (ready-cut) (1¼ cups)
7 ounces whole red bell pepper or 6 ounces sliced (ready-cut) (1¼ cups)
1 teaspoon minced garlic in oil
6 ounces whole mushrooms or 5 ounces sliced (ready-cut)
4 tablespoons white wine vinegar
1 papaya
¾ cup chicken stock
1½ teaspoons Dijon mustard
Fresh cilantro for garnish (optional)

1 Wash, dry and cut turkey breast into 1-inch cubes.

2 Heat oil in skillet and cook turkey over medium heat until it is golden and cooked through.

3 Seed chile and halve; turn on food processor and put chile halves through feed tube. Stop machine and add onion and bell pepper. Process until coarsely cut.

4 Set turkey aside; add onion, bell pepper, chile and garlic and cook about 8 minutes.

5 If mushrooms are whole, wash and slice; add them to pan and cook 2 minutes longer.

6 Stir vinegar into pan, scraping up any brown bits clinging to bottom.

7 Slice papaya and add with stock and mustard to skillet, cooking until papaya is heated through.

8 Chop cilantro. Spoon turkey over rice and sprinkle cilantro over each serving, if desired.

**Yield:** 3 servings

## BASMATI RICE

¾ cup basmati rice
1½ cups water

Combine rice and water; bring to boil. Reduce heat. Cover and cook rice for about 15–17 minutes.

**Yield:** 3 servings

---

◆ *Game Plan* ◆

*Cook rice.*
*Follow directions for turkey recipe.*

---

### PANTRY

Corn, safflower or canola oil
Minced garlic in oil
White wine vinegar

Chicken stock
Dijon mustard
Basmati or regular white rice

---

### SHOPPING LIST

20 ounces turkey breast, skinless
  and boneless
1 mild green chile
7 ounces whole red onion or 6
  ounces sliced (ready-cut)
7 ounces whole red bell pepper or 6
  ounces sliced (ready-cut)

6 ounces whole mushrooms or 5
  ounces sliced (ready-cut)
1 papaya
Fresh cilantro for garnish
  (optional)

# "VEAL" IN CREAMY ORANGE SAUCE ◆ COUSCOUS SALAD ◆ ASPARAGUS ◆ ◆ ◆ ◆ ◆ ◆ ◆ ◆ ◆

*The "veal" is really turkey, but you can't tell the difference in this lovely orange sauce.*

*It will take some pretty fancy footwork to prepare this meal in 20 minutes, but even if it takes you 25, it will be worth the effort.*

*This is the kind of dinner you can be proud to serve to guests.*

---

## "VEAL" IN CREAMY ORANGE SAUCE

12 ounces turkey breast, skinless and boneless
1–2 tablespoons olive oil
½ cup fresh orange juice
1 teaspoon cornstarch
⅓ cup plain low- or non-fat yogurt
¼ cup low- or non-fat cottage cheese
Freshly ground black pepper

1 Wash and dry turkey breast and cut into pieces about 2 by 3 inches.

2 Heat oil in skillet and brown turkey pieces on both sides for about 5 or 6 minutes.

3 Mix a little orange juice with cornstarch to make a paste; then stir the paste into remaining juice.

4 When turkey is brown, reduce heat and add orange juice mixture. Simmer about 2 minutes to thicken and finish cooking turkey.

5 Blend yogurt and cottage cheese in food processor until smooth. Reduce heat. Carefully stir into turkey mixture but do not boil. Season with pepper.

**Yield:** 2 servings

---

## COUSCOUS SALAD

½ cup couscous, precooked
2 tablespoons lemon juice
2 tablespoons olive oil
⅛ teaspoon cinnamon
1 stalk chopped celery (ready-cut) (½ cup)
2 scallions
1 tablespoon chopped fresh parsley
3 tablespoons raisins

1 Following the directions on couscous package, bring water to boil in small covered pan.

2 Stir in couscous; remove from heat and cover. Allow to sit for 3–5 minutes, until water has been absorbed.

3 In serving bowl mix lemon juice and olive oil with cinnamon.

4 Wash celery, scallions and parsley and chop in food processor. Add to bowl with raisins and pine nuts.

| 1 tablespoon pine nuts or 2 tablespoons dry-roasted unsalted peanuts<br>Freshly ground black pepper to taste | 5 Stir in couscous and season with pepper.<br>**Yield:** 2 servings |
| --- | --- |

**ASPARAGUS**

12–14 asparagus

1 Bring water to boil in steamer.

2 Break off tough ends from asparagus and wash.

3 Steam asparagus about 7 minutes, until tender but firm.

**Yield:** 2 servings

## ◆ Game Plan ◆

Bring water for couscous to boil.  Bring water for asparagus to boil.
Prepare asparagus.  Cook couscous.
Combine lemon juice, oil and cinnamon for couscous.
Chop celery, scallions and parsley and add with raisins and pine nuts to dressing for couscous.
Wash and dry turkey and heat oil to sauté. Sauté turkey. Cook asparagus.
Mix orange juice with cornstarch and add to turkey.
Process yogurt and cottage cheese and add to turkey.
Mix couscous with dressing.

### PANTRY

Olive oil
Orange juice
Cornstarch

Plain low- or non-fat
  yogurt
Whole black pepper
Couscous

Lemon
Cinnamon
Raisins

### SHOPPING LIST

12 ounces turkey breast,
  skinless and boneless
Low- or non-fat cottage
  cheese
1 ounce celery (1 stalk)

Bunch scallions (2)
Fresh parsley (1
  tablespoon)

1 ounce pine nuts
  (1 tablespoon) or dry-
  roasted unsalted
  peanuts (2 tablespoons)
12–14 asparagus

# "VEAL" STEW WITH PEPPERS AND MUSHROOMS ◆ RICE ◆ ◆

*This thrifty version of veal stew uses turkey breast—and no one will be the wiser.*

## "VEAL" STEW WITH PEPPERS AND MUSHROOMS

13 ounces whole onion or 12 ounces sliced (ready-cut) (2¾ cups)

14 ounces whole red (or other color) bell pepper or 12 ounces sliced (ready-cut) (3 cups)

1–2 tablespoons olive oil

2 teaspoons sweet Hungarian paprika

¾ teaspoon hot Hungarian paprika or few dashes cayenne pepper

16 ounces turkey breast, skinless and boneless

½ of 28-ounce can plum tomatoes

1 teaspoon minced garlic in oil

2 teaspoons Worcestershire sauce

2 teaspoons lemon juice Freshly ground black pepper to taste

4 ounces whole mushrooms or 3 ounces sliced (ready-cut) (1 cup)

1 tablespoon cornstarch

1 cup plain low- or non-fat yogurt

1. Slice whole onion and red pepper. In hot oil sauté onion, red pepper and paprikas for about 7 minutes over medium heat.

2. Cut turkey into large chunks. Squeeze tomatoes to break up. Add turkey and tomatoes to skillet with garlic, Worcestershire sauce, lemon juice and black pepper. Clean whole mushrooms and slice. Add mushrooms to skillet and stir. Cover skillet and cook over medium heat for 7–10 minutes.

3. Stir cornstarch into yogurt and add to stew. Cook, over low heat, stirring occasionally, until sauce thickens.

4. Serve over rice.

**Yield:** 3 servings

## RICE

1 cup long-grain rice
2 cups water

Combine rice and water in heavy-bottomed pot. Bring to boil. Cover and cook over low heat until rice is cooked, about 17 minutes total.

**Yield:** 3 servings

---

## ◆ Game Plan ◆

Cook rice.

Chop whole onion and red pepper. Cook onion, red pepper and paprikas.
Prepare turkey and tomatoes and add to onion with garlic and seasonings.
Prepare whole mushrooms and add. Cover and cook.
Combine cornstarch and yogurt. Add to stew and finish cooking.

---

### PANTRY

Olive oil
Sweet Hungarian paprika
Hot Hungarian paprika or
  cayenne pepper
Canned plum tomatoes
Minced garlic in oil

Worcestershire sauce
Lemon
Whole black pepper
Cornstarch
Plain low- or non-fat yogurt
Long-grain rice

---

### SHOPPING LIST

13 ounces whole onion or 12
  ounces sliced (ready-cut)
14 ounces whole red (or other
  color) bell pepper or 12 ounces
  sliced (ready-cut)

16 ounces turkey breast, skinless
  and boneless
4 ounces whole mushrooms or 3
  ounces sliced (ready-cut)

# BROILED VEAL CHOPS ◆ SPAGHETTI WITH TOMATO AND GOAT CHEESE ◆ ◆ ◆ ◆ ◆ ◆ ◆

## BROILED VEAL CHOPS

3 half-inch-thick loin veal
  chops
  Freshly ground black
  pepper

1 Heat broiler. Cover broiler rack with double thickness of aluminum foil.

2 Rub chops with pepper and broil 2 inches from source of heat for about 8 minutes. Turn and broil for about 4 minutes longer on other side for medium-rare.

**Yield:** 2 servings

## SPAGHETTI WITH TOMATO AND GOAT CHEESE

3 quarts water
  28-ounce can plum
  tomatoes
1 cup tomato puree
½ teaspoon sugar
6 large fresh basil leaves
1½ teaspoons minced garlic
  in oil
1 tablespoon white
  vinegar
  Freshly ground black
  pepper to taste
1 ounce stemless dried
  mushrooms
½ teaspoon dried thyme
4 ounces spaghetti
1 tablespoon olive oil
3 ounces soft goat cheese

1 Boil water for spaghetti in covered pot.

2 Drain most of liquid from tomatoes and reserve for other use. Crush tomatoes with fingers and combine with puree, sugar, basil, garlic, vinegar, black pepper, dried mushrooms and thyme. Cook over high heat for 15–18 minutes.

3 Cook spaghetti according to package directions; drain and toss with oil. Mix with tomato sauce and sprinkle with crumbled goat cheese.

**Yield:** 2 servings

## ◆ Game Plan ◆

Heat broiler.
Boil water for spaghetti.
Combine sauce ingredients and cook.
Broil chops.
Cook spaghetti.
Turn chops.
Drain spaghetti and toss with sauce; sprinkle with cheese.

### PANTRY

Whole black pepper
Canned plum tomatoes
Canned tomato puree
Sugar
Minced garlic in oil

White vinegar
Dried mushrooms
Dried thyme
Spaghetti
Olive oil

### SHOPPING LIST

3 half-inch-thick loin veal chops
Fresh basil (6 large leaves)

3 ounces soft goat cheese

# VEAL WITH LEMON AND BLACK OLIVES ◆ FRESH TOMATO– ZUCCHINI SAUCE WITH PASTA ◆ ◆

*I confess that I put together this menu because I had some superb veal scallopini in the freezer, the result of having ordered it by mail for my annual Christmas mail-order story for* The New York Times.

*It isn't easy to get this kind of veal in the stores and it isn't cheap, but if you love veal and are in the market for some, I urge you to get in touch with Summerfield Farms (see Mail Order Products on page 236). Their veal is the best I have ever eaten.*

## VEAL WITH LEMON AND BLACK OLIVES

12 ounces veal scallops
¼ cup Greek, Italian or French pitted black olives, packed in oil or brine (about 12 large)
2 tablespoons olive oil
1 lemon
½ cup dry white wine Freshly ground black pepper to taste

1. Wash and dry veal.

2. Pit black olives.

3. Heat oil in skillet large enough to hold veal and quickly sauté, about 30 seconds on each side.

4. Reduce heat and squeeze lemon over veal; add wine and olives. Sprinkle with pepper. Cook for about 1 minute, turning veal once, and serve.

**Yield:** 2 servings

## FRESH TOMATO–ZUCCHINI SAUCE WITH PASTA

3 quarts water
16 ounces ripe tomatoes, regular or plum, depending on season
16 ounces whole zucchini or 15 ounces sliced (ready-cut) (3½ cups)

1. Bring water to boil in covered pot.

2. Wash and trim tomatoes and zucchini.

3. Quarter onion.

4. Heat oil in skillet large enough to hold all the vegetables.

9 ounces whole onion or 8
  ounces sliced (ready-cut)
  (1¾ cups)
1–2 tablespoons olive oil
1 teaspoon minced garlic in
  oil
1 teaspoon dried thyme
1 teaspoon dried oregano
  Freshly ground black
  pepper to taste
4–6 ounces small pasta
  (shells, penne or other
  small pasta)

5 Chop whole or sliced onion in food processor and add with garlic to oil.

6 Using slicing blade of processor, slice tomatoes and zucchini. After onion has cooked about 3 minutes, add tomatoes and zucchini with thyme, oregano and pepper to skillet. Cover, reduce heat to medium and cook, stirring occasionally until vegetables are cooked.

7 When water boils, add pasta and cook according to package directions. Drain and serve with tomato-zucchini sauce.

**Yield:** 2 servings

---

◆ *Game Plan* ◆

*Boil water for pasta.*
*Make sauce for pasta.*
*Cook pasta.*
*Pit olives for veal dish.*
*About 5 minutes before pasta is ready, prepare veal dish.*
*Just before veal is finished, drain pasta.*

---

### PANTRY

Greek, Italian or French black
  olives, packed in oil or brine
Olive oil
Lemon
Dry white wine
Whole black pepper

Minced garlic in oil
Dried thyme
Dried oregano
Small pasta (shells, penne or other
  small pasta)

---

### SHOPPING LIST

12 ounces veal scallops
16 ounces ripe tomatoes, regular or
  plum

16 ounces whole zucchini or 15
  ounces sliced (ready-cut)
9 ounces whole onion or 8 ounces
  sliced (ready-cut)

# $\mathcal{B}$OB JAMIESON'S MEATLOAF HAMBURGERS ◆ MASHED POTATOES ◆ BROILED TOMATOES ◆

*Bob Jamieson may have a recipe for hamburgers, but this isn't it. His fabulous meatloaf cannot be made in 20 minutes, and I hope he will forgive me for taking liberties with his recipe and turning it into one that makes these delicious hamburgers.*

*What would meatloaf be without mashed potatoes? Unfortunately, to make potatoes in 20 minutes you cannot prepare them the most nutritious way: cooking them whole, with their skins on. Here, the potatoes are peeled and cut into small cubes.*

*In season use regular ripe tomatoes and in winter use plum tomatoes.*

---

## BOB JAMIESON'S MEATLOAF HAMBURGERS

5 ounces whole onion or 4 ounces sliced (ready-cut) (1 cup)
12 ounces lean ground beef
2 ounces ground veal
2 ounces lean ground pork
1½ tablespoons Worcestershire sauce
1 tablespoon Dijon mustard
2 tablespoons catsup
1½ tablespoons cracker crumbs
Freshly ground black pepper to taste
1 egg white
1 tablespoon corn, safflower or canola oil (if needed)

1. Finely chop onion in food processor.

2. Combine onion with beef, veal, pork, Worcestershire sauce, mustard, catsup, cracker crumbs and pepper.

3. Beat egg white lightly with fork; mix with other ingredients.

4. Shape meat mixture into 3 patties.

5. If meats are very lean you may need a tablespoon of oil in the bottom of a heavy skillet. Otherwise, just heat skillet and add patties. Cook over medium-high heat until both sides are browned, about 10 minutes total.

**Yield:** 3 servings

---

## MASHED POTATOES

24 ounces boiling potatoes (largest possible for less peeling)

1. Peel potatoes and cut into small cubes. In covered pot, boil in water to cover until tender, about 10–12 minutes.

¾ cup plain low or non-fat yogurt
Freshly ground black pepper to taste and also salt, if desired

2 Drain and stir in yogurt, pepper and salt, if desired, and mash with potato masher or fork. Add more yogurt if needed.

**Yield:** 3 servings

---

## BROILED TOMATOES

12 ounces tomatoes, regular or plum
2–3 tablespoons Dijon mustard
Freshly ground black pepper

1 Preheat toaster oven to 375 degrees or heat oven broiler. Line broiler pan with foil.

2 Wash and trim tomatoes; cut regular tomatoes in half, plum tomatoes lengthwise.

3 Spread with mustard and sprinkle with pepper.

4 Arrange on broiler pan and broil in toaster oven about 7 or 8 minutes, or broil in regular oven about 3 or 4 inches from heat for 3–5 minutes (watch carefully) until tomatoes begin to soften.

**Yield:** 3 servings

---

### ◆ Game Plan ◆

Prepare potatoes and boil.
Preheat toaster oven or oven broiler for tomatoes.
Make hamburger patties.    Pan-fry patties.
Wash, halve and season tomatoes and broil.
When potatoes are ready, drain, stir in yogurt and seasoning and mash.

---

### PANTRY

| | | |
|---|---|---|
| Worcestershire sauce | Cracker crumbs | Corn, safflower or canola oil |
| Dijon mustard | Whole black pepper | (if needed) |
| Catsup | Egg | Plain low- or non-fat yogurt |

---

### SHOPPING LIST

| | | |
|---|---|---|
| 5 ounces whole onion or 4 ounces sliced (ready-cut) | 2 ounces ground veal | 12 ounces tomatoes, regular or plum |
| 12 ounces lean ground beef | 2 ounces ground pork | |
| | 24 ounces boiling potatoes (largest possible) | |

# BEEF AND PEAS WITH SCALLIONS ◆ ANGEL HAIR PASTA ◆ SPINACH WITH SESAME OIL ◆ ◆

## BEEF AND PEAS WITH SCALLIONS

10 ounces frozen peas
18 ounces lean ground beef
3 scallions
¾ cup water
5 tablespoons dry sherry
1 teaspoon sugar
1 tablespoon reduced-sodium soy sauce
1 tablespoon cornstarch

1. Allow peas to sit at room temperature while preparing beef.

2. In large skillet over medium-high heat, cook beef in its own fat until it is brown.

3. Cut scallions into rings.

4. Combine water, sherry, sugar, soy sauce and cornstarch; reduce heat under beef and stir sherry mixture into beef with scallions.

5. Add peas to beef and cook over low heat just until peas are heated through. Serve over pasta.

**Yield:** 3 servings

## ANGEL HAIR PASTA

3 quarts water
6 ounces fresh or dried fine pasta, such as angel hair

1. Bring water to boil in covered pot.

2. Cook fresh pasta 30–60 seconds; follow package directions for dried pasta. Drain thoroughly and serve topped with beef.

**Yield:** 3 servings

## SPINACH WITH SESAME OIL

24 ounces loose fresh spinach or 1½ packages (15 ounces) fresh spinach

1. Wash, trim and drain spinach.

2 teaspoons sugar
2 teaspoons Oriental
  sesame oil

$\overline{2}$ Steam spinach only in the water that clings to its leaves and the sugar just until it wilts, a couple of minutes. Drain thoroughly.

$\overline{3}$ Toss with sesame oil.

**Yield:** 3 servings

---

### ◆ *Game Plan* ◆

*Boil water for pasta.*
*Allow frozen peas to sit at room temperature.*
*Brown beef.*
*Cut scallions.*
*Combine water, sherry, sugar, soy sauce and cornstarch.*
*Cook pasta.*
*Clean and cook spinach with sugar.*
*Add sherry mixture and scallions to beef; add peas.*
*Drain pasta.*
*Drain spinach and mix with sesame oil.*

---

#### PANTRY

*Dry sherry*
*Sugar*
*Reduced-sodium soy sauce*

*Cornstarch*
*Dried thin pasta, if fresh not*
  *available*
*Oriental sesame oil*

---

#### SHOPPING LIST

*10 ounces frozen peas*
*16 ounces lean ground beef*
*Bunch scallions (2)*
*6 ounces fresh fine pasta, such as*
  *angel hair*

*24 ounces loose fresh spinach or*
  *1½ packages (15 ounces) fresh*
  *spinach*

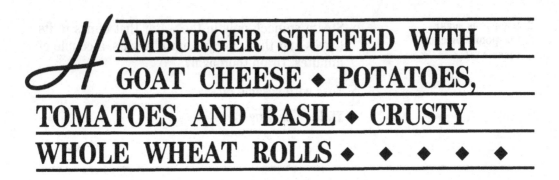

# HAMBURGER STUFFED WITH GOAT CHEESE ◆ POTATOES, TOMATOES AND BASIL ◆ CRUSTY WHOLE WHEAT ROLLS ◆ ◆ ◆ ◆ ◆

*Putting cheese in the middle of a hamburger is nothing new, but using goat cheese is different—and delicious. One night I used goat cheese mixed with sun-dried tomatoes—also superb.*

### HAMBURGER STUFFED WITH GOAT CHEESE

12 ounces lean ground beef
3 tablespoons soft goat cheese

1  Shape beef into 3 patties of equal size.

2  Stuff goat cheese into the center of each patty and mold beef around it.

3  Sauté in heavy skillet over medium-high heat until well browned on both sides and medium-rare in the middle (or as you like it), about 10 minutes total for medium-rare. Serve with 3 crusty whole wheat rolls.

**Yield:** 3 servings

### POTATOES, TOMATOES AND BASIL

12 ounces tiny new potatoes
8 ounces plum tomatoes
3 tablespoons fresh basil

1  Scrub potatoes and cover with water in heavy-bottomed pot. Cover and cook until potatoes are tender, about 18 minutes.

4 teaspoons balsamic
  vinegar
  Freshly ground black
  pepper to taste

2 Wash and trim tomatoes and cut into bite-size chunks. Place in serving bowl and cut in basil. Add vinegar.

3 When potatoes are cooked, cut into halves or quarters and add to bowl. Sprinkle with pepper and serve.

**Yield:** 3 servings

---

## ◆ Game Plan ◆

*Scrub and cook potatoes.*
*Shape ground beef into 3 patties; stuff goat cheese into the center of each.*
*Chop tomatoes and basil into serving bowl; add vinegar.*
*Cook beef patties.*
*Cut potatoes into halves or quarters and add to tomatoes; sprinkle with pepper and serve.*

---

### PANTRY

Balsamic vinegar                    Whole black pepper

---

### SHOPPING LIST

12 ounces lean ground beef          12 ounces tiny new potatoes
Soft goat cheese (3 tablespoons)    8 ounces plum tomatoes
Crusty whole wheat rolls (3)        Fresh basil (3 tablespoons)

# $\mathcal{B}$ARBECUED FLANK STEAK ◆
# WHITE BEAN SALAD ◆ ◆ ◆ ◆

*Preparing this meal is easy and leaves plenty of time for doing most of the cleanup before dinner.*

*The salad calls for canned white beans, but you can use any kind you like, preferably those that are not preserved with EDTA and that do not contain calcium chloride. You can usually find some variety that contains only salt and water. Rinsing off the packing liquid improves the taste considerably.*

## BARBECUED FLANK STEAK

12 ounces flank steak
1½ teaspoons dry sherry
1 tablespoon hoisin sauce
1 tablespoon catsup
1 teaspoon minced garlic in oil

1. Heat broiler. Line broiler pan with double thickness of aluminum foil.

2. Score steak on the diagonal and cut into strips 2 inches wide.

3. Combine remaining ingredients in bowl and add steak, stirring to coat.

4. To serve, remove steak from marinade and place on broiler pan, 2 inches from heat source. Cook 10–12 minutes total, turning once. Brush occasionally with marinade.

**Yield:** 2 servings

## WHITE BEAN SALAD

15- or 16-ounce can Great Northern beans or other small white beans

1. Drain beans in colander and rinse under cold water.

5–6 ounces whole red bell pepper or 4–5 ounces sliced (ready-cut) (1 cup)

1 teaspoon minced garlic in oil

2 tablespoons olive oil

3 tablespoons balsamic vinegar

½ teaspoon ground sage

½ teaspoon freshly ground black pepper to taste

2 Coarsely chop red pepper. Combine with garlic, olive oil, vinegar and sage in a bowl large enough to hold the beans. Add drained beans and mix well. Season with black pepper.

**Yield:** 2 servings

---

### ◆ Game Plan ◆

*Heat broiler.*

*Score meat and cut into strips; prepare marinade and add steak.*

*Rinse beans.*

*Chop red pepper.*

*Broil steak, turning once to brown on both sides, brushing occasionally with marinade.*

*Prepare the rest of bean salad.*

---

#### PANTRY

Dry sherry

Hoisin sauce

Catsup

Minced garlic in oil

Olive oil

Balsamic vinegar

Ground sage

Whole black pepper

---

#### SHOPPING LIST

12 ounces flank steak

15- or 16-ounce can Great Northern beans or other small white beans

5–6 ounces whole red bell pepper or 4–5 ounces sliced (ready-cut)

# BEEF AND BLACK BEANS WITH NOODLES ◆ SAUTÉ-STEAMED SPINACH ◆ ◆ ◆ ◆ ◆ ◆ ◆ ◆ ◆ ◆

*This beef and black bean recipe is an adaptation of one I had at the Golden Flower Hotel, in Xi'an, China.*

*It took me about 21 minutes to do and left more than a dirty spoon or two in its wake. If those who ate it hadn't liked it so much, I might have discarded it. It was such a hit, that you ought to keep it in mind for the night when you are willing to spend a little extra time preparing and washing dishes. Besides, it serves three people.*

*Note: Many supermarkets sell beef that is already sliced into thin strips. You can use it to save time.*

*Salted or fermented black beans are available in Oriental markets and many supermarkets. They keep indefinitely.*

---

## BEEF AND BLACK BEANS WITH NOODLES

4 quarts water

5–6 ounces whole green pepper or 4–5 ounces sliced (ready-cut) (¾–1 cup)

8 ounces boneless sirloin or tenderloin (See Note)

1½ tablespoons salted or fermented black beans

4 scallions

2 teaspoons cornstarch

1 cup chicken stock

1 tablespoon coarsely grated ginger

2 tablespoons peanut oil

1 teaspoon minced garlic in oil

9 ounces very thin fresh Chinese or Italian noodles, such as angel hair

2 tablespoons oyster sauce

1. Boil water for noodles in covered pot.

2. If green pepper is whole, seed and slice into strips about ⅛-inch wide.

3. Wash, dry and slice beef into strips about ⅛-inch thick, ⅛-inch wide and 2 inches long.

4. Rinse salt off beans and set aside.

5. Wash, trim and thinly slice scallions.

6. Combine cornstarch with a few tablespoons of chicken stock; stir into remaining chicken stock.

7. Grate ginger.

8. Heat oil in wok or skillet large enough to hold all ingredients.

9. Stir-fry ginger, black beans and garlic for 30 seconds; add beef and green pepper and stir-fry until beef loses its color.

10. Cook noodles 30 seconds.

11 Stir chicken stock mixture and oyster sauce into beef and stir-fry until mixture thickens slightly.

12 Drain noodles. Run a knife through noodles a few times to cut up. Stir into beef.

**Yield:** 3 servings

---

**SAUTÉ-STEAMED SPINACH**

10 ounces packaged fresh spinach or 15 ounces loose fresh spinach
1 teaspoon Oriental sesame oil
1 teaspoon sugar

1 Wash and trim spinach.

2 Add spinach, oil and sugar to pot. Cover and cook over medium-high heat until spinach wilts, about 1 minute. Drain and serve.

**Yield:** 3 servings

---

## ◆ *Game Plan* ◆

*Boil water for noodles. Prepare green pepper and beef.
Rinse beans; prepare scallions. Mix cornstarch with stock.
Grate ginger. Wash spinach. Stir-fry black beans, garlic and ginger.
Add green pepper and beef; stir-fry. Cook noodles.
Cook spinach with sesame oil and sugar. Finish beef recipe.*

---

### PANTRY

Salted or fermented black beans
Cornstarch
Chicken stock

Fresh ginger
Peanut oil
Minced garlic in oil

Oyster sauce
Oriental sesame oil
Sugar

---

### SHOPPING LIST

9 ounces very thin fresh Chinese or Italian noodles, such as angel hair
5–6 ounces whole green pepper or 4–5 ounces sliced (ready-cut)

8 ounces boneless sirloin or tenderloin or beef that is already sliced into strips

Bunch scallions (4)
10 ounces packaged fresh spinach or 15 ounces loose or fresh spinach.

# ASIL BEEF À LA GERMAINE ◆ EGGPLANT AND BULGUR SALAD

*This beef dish is one of those close ones: you can do it in 20 minutes but it may leave you breathless, so give it 23.*

*Germaine Swanson runs Germaine's, a wonderful Asian restaurant in Washington, D.C. Her recipe is for an hors d'oeuvre in which small beef ovals are wrapped in basil leaves and grilled. This adaptation is a delicious dinner dish.*

*Any leftovers can be eaten for lunch.*

## BASIL BEEF À LA GERMAINE

¼ cup finely minced onion (1 ounce)
1 large scallion
2 heaping tablespoons minced fresh basil
12 ounces lean ground beef
  Freshly ground black pepper
1 tablespoon reduced-sodium soy sauce
  Pinch sugar
2 teaspoons corn, safflower or canola oil

1 Mince onion, scallion and basil in food processor.

2 Combine all the ingredients except for the oil and shape into 4 patties.

3 Heat oil in skillet and sauté patties on both sides until crusty and browned, about 10 minutes for medium-rare.

**Yield:** 2 servings

## EGGPLANT AND BULGUR SALAD

16 ounces eggplant, preferably the small Japanese eggplant
2 tablespoons olive oil
½ cup bulgur
1 cup water
1 teaspoon minced garlic in oil
¼ teaspoon ground cinnamon
¼ teaspoon ground nutmeg
1½ teaspoons ground cumin
½ teaspoon ground turmeric
½ teaspoon ground coriander

1 Heat broiler and cover broiler pan with double thickness of aluminum foil.

2 Wash eggplant and slice ¼ inch or less thick, but *do not peel.* Brush lightly with oil on each side and broil about 2 inches from heat source until slices begin to brown and soften, 3–4 minutes on each side.

3 Cook bulgur in water until it is tender, about 15 minutes. Drain any water that has not been absorbed and set bulgur aside.

⅛ teaspoon cayenne
   pepper
1 teaspoon red wine
   vinegar
1 cup plain low- or non-fat
   yogurt
½ cup raisins
¼ cup chopped fresh
   cilantro or parsley

4 In serving bowl combine garlic, spices, vinegar, yogurt and raisins.

5 Stir cooked bulgur into yogurt mixture.

6 Coarsely chop cooked eggplant, leaving the skin on, and add to yogurt mixture.

7 Coarsely chop cilantro or parsley; sprinkle on salad and serve.

**Yield:** 2 large servings

---

♦ *Game Plan* ♦

*Heat broiler.*
*Slice eggplant and brush with oil; broil.   Cook bulgur.*
*Prepare ingredients for beef and shape into patties.*
*Combine garlic, spices for salad in serving bowl.*
*Turn eggplant.   Cook beef patties.   Add vinegar, yogurt and raisins to*
*spices.*
*Stir bulgur into salad.   Cut eggplant into chunks and add to salad.*
*Turn beef patties.   Chop cilantro and sprinkle on salad.*

---

## PANTRY

| | | |
|---|---|---|
| Whole black pepper | Bulgur | Ground coriander |
| Reduced-sodium soy sauce | Minced garlic in oil | Cayenne pepper |
| Sugar | Ground cinnamon | Red wine vinegar |
| Corn, safflower or | Ground nutmeg | Plain low- or non-fat |
|    canola oil | Ground cumin |    yogurt |
| Olive oil | Ground turmeric | Raisins |

---

## SHOPPING LIST

| | | |
|---|---|---|
| 1 ounce onion (¼ cup) | 12 ounces lean ground beef | Fresh cilantro or parsley |
| Bunch scallions (1) | 16 ounces Japanese or |    (¼ cup) |
| Fresh basil (2 heaping |    regular eggplant | |
|    tablespoons) | | |

# HERBED LAMB CHOPS ◆ SPINACH LINGUINE WITH ANCHOVIED SPINACH ◆ ◆ ◆ ◆ ◆ ◆

*This menu has had several incarnations, but none of them seemed right until I tasted Leslee Reis' anchovied spinach, which she served with lamb for the annual James Beard dinner to raise money for New York City's Meals-on-Wheels program.*

*Leslee was one of the finalists in 1987 chosen to cook for the dinner. She has three restaurants in Evanston, Illinois, and she describes the food there as "assertive."*

*Spinach with anchovies and garlic certainly fills the bill, but I've combined it with spinach linguine to round out the meal.*

*Note: Hot chile oil with garlic is available at Oriental markets and in some supermarkets. Big eaters will want 3 ounces of linguine; others will be happy with two. The proportions of the rest of the recipe remain the same whether 4 or 6 ounces are used.*

## HERBED LAMB CHOPS

16 ounces loin or rib lamb
   chops (3 or 4 chops,
   depending on thickness)
1 teaspoon dried marjoram
   Freshly ground black
   pepper

1 Heat broiler and line broiler pan with double thickness of aluminum foil.

2 Wash, dry and trim excess fat from chops.

3 Rub marjoram and pepper into both sides of chops. Place chops on pan and broil 2 inches from source of heat, about 4–5 minutes per side for ¾-inch-thick chops and 6 minutes per side for 1½-inch-thick chops.

**Yield:** 2 servings

## SPINACH LINGUINE WITH ANCHOVIED SPINACH

3 quarts water
10-ounce package fresh
   spinach or 15 ounces fresh
   loose spinach
5 anchovy fillets

1 Boil water in covered pot.

2 Wash and trim tough stems off spinach. Dry in paper towels.

1–2 tablespoons olive oil
2 teaspoons hot chile oil
  with garlic (see Note)
2 teaspoons minced garlic in
  oil
4–6 ounces fresh spinach
  linguine

3̲ Rinse, dry and finely mince anchovy fillets.

4̲ Heat olive and chile oils in large, heavy pot.

5̲ Add anchovies and garlic and cook over high heat,
   stirring, until garlic begins to brown.

6̲ Add spinach and stir. Cover and cook until wilted,
   2–3 minutes.

7̲ Cook linguine for about 2 minutes.

8̲ Drain linguine and add to spinach; toss well.

**Yield:** 2 servings

---

## ◆ *Game Plan* ◆

*Heat broiler.    Boil water for linguine.*
*Line broiler pan with double thickness of aluminum foil.*
*Wash and trim spinach and dry.*
*Wash, dry and trim fat from chops; rub with marjoram and pepper.*
*Broil chops.*
*Mince anchovies and add with garlic to hot oils and sauté.*
*Turn chops.    Add spinach to anchovies and garlic.*
*Cook linguine; drain and combine with spinach.*

---

### PANTRY

*Dried marjoram*            *Olive oil*
*Whole black pepper*        *Hot chile oil with garlic*
*Anchovy fillets*           *Minced garlic in oil*

---

### SHOPPING LIST

*16 ounces rib or loin lamb chops*          *4–6 ounces fresh spinach linguine*
*10-ounce package fresh spinach or*
*  15 ounces fresh loose spinach*

# LAMB CHOP SATAY ♦ ASPARAGUS ♦ COUSCOUS ♦ ♦ ♦ ♦ ♦ ♦ ♦

*Not a true satay or saté which is bite-size pieces of meat, but flavors are similar.*

## LAMB CHOP SATAY

4 loin lamb chops
1-inch slice fresh ginger
¼ teaspoon minced garlic in oil
2 tablespoons chopped onion
2 tablespoons creamy natural peanut butter
1 teaspoon lemon juice
1 teaspoon reduced-sodium soy sauce
⅛ teaspoon crushed hot red pepper
2 tablespoons plain low- or non-fat yogurt

1. Heat broiler. Line broiler pan with aluminum foil.

2. Wash, dry and trim fat from lamb chops; arrange on broiler pan.

3. With motor of food processor running, put cut-up ginger through feed tube and process.

4. Add garlic, onion, peanut butter, lemon juice, soy sauce, red pepper and yogurt to food processor and continue processing.

5. Broil chops about 2 inches from heat. After about 5 minutes, turn chops and cook about 4–5 minutes longer, to medium-rare.

6. Serve chops topped with some of the sauce, reserving remaining sauce for couscous.

**Yield:** 2 servings

## ASPARAGUS

12–14 asparagus

1. Wash and trim tough ends from asparagus by bending stalks at point at which they break.

2. Heat water in steamer and steam asparagus about 7 minutes, until tender but still firm.

**Yield:** 2 servings

## COUSCOUS

¾ cup couscous

$\overline{1}$ Following package directions, bring water to boil in small covered pot.

$\overline{2}$ Add couscous; turn off heat and allow couscous to absorb water for 3–5 minutes.

$\overline{3}$ Serve topped with satay sauce.

**Yield:** 2 servings

## ◆ *Game Plan* ◆

*Heat broiler.*
*Trim chops and prepare sauce.*
*Broil chops.*
*Wash and trim asparagus.*
*Heat water in steamer for asparagus.*
*Turn chops.*
*Boil water for couscous.*
*Steam asparagus.*
*Cook couscous.*

### PANTRY

Fresh ginger
Minced garlic in oil
Creamy natural peanut butter
Lemon

Reduced-sodium soy sauce
Crushed hot red pepper
Plain low- or non-fat yogurt
Couscous

### SHOPPING LIST

4 loin lamb chops
Onion (2 tablespoons)

12–14 asparagus

# Couscous with Lamb ◆ Multicolored Pepper

## SALAD ◆ ◆ ◆ ◆ ◆ ◆ ◆ ◆ ◆ ◆ ◆ ◆

### COUSCOUS WITH LAMB

14 ounces whole onion or 12 ounces sliced (ready-cut) (2½ cups)
1 tablespoon corn, safflower or canola oil
12 ounces tofu
2 tablespoons coarsely grated fresh ginger
12 ounces lean ground lamb
1 teaspoon cumin
2 teaspoons turmeric
1 teaspoon minced garlic in oil
⅛–¼ teaspoon cayenne pepper
½ cup dried apricots (approximately 15)
1 tablespoon lemon juice
1 tablespoon unsalted butter
¾ cup couscous
Freshly ground black pepper

1 Coarsely chop onion.

2 Heat oil and sauté onion for about 3 minutes.

3 Dice tofu and grate ginger; add to onion with lamb, cumin, turmeric, garlic and cayenne pepper. Cook and stir occasionally until lamb is browned.

4 Cut up apricots.

5 Following couscous package directions, measure water into pot and add apricots, lemon juice and butter; stir, cover and bring to boil. When water boils, stir in couscous. Remove from heat; cover and allow to sit 3–5 minutes until water has been completely absorbed.

6 Spoon couscous onto plates and top with lamb mixture.

**Yield:** 3 servings

### MULTICOLORED PEPPER SALAD

14 ounces whole red, yellow and green bell peppers or 12 ounces sliced (ready-cut) (3 cups)

1 If peppers are not cut up, wash, seed and cut into quarters and put through food processor with thin slicing blade.

1–2 tablespoons olive oil
2 tablespoons balsamic
vinegar
¼ teaspoon dried rosemary
Freshly ground black
pepper to taste

2  In serving bowl beat oil with vinegar; stir in crumbled rosemary and sprinkle with pepper.

3  Stir pepper strips into dressing.

**Yield:** 3 servings

---

## ◆ *Game Plan* ◆

*Chop onion and sauté in oil.*
*Dice tofu; grate ginger.*
*Add lamb, spices, tofu and ginger to onion.*
*Cut up whole peppers for salad.*
*Cut up apricots and add to water with lemon juice and butter; boil.*
*Make salad dressing and add pepper strips.*
*When water boils, stir in couscous.*
*Top couscous with lamb mixture.*

---

### PANTRY

Corn, safflower or
    canola oil
Fresh ginger
Cumin
Turmeric
Minced garlic in oil
Cayenne pepper

Lemon
Unsalted butter
Couscous
Whole black pepper
Olive oil
Balsamic vinegar
Dried rosemary

---

### SHOPPING LIST

14 ounces whole onion or
    12 ounces sliced (ready-cut)
12 ounces tofu
12 ounces lean ground lamb

Approximately 15 dried apricots
    (½ cup)
14 ounces whole red, yellow and
    green peppers or 12 ounces sliced
    (ready-cut)

# LENTIL AND LAMB SALAD ◆ CORN ON THE COB ◆ ◆ ◆ ◆ ◆

*Lentils, like beans, are ornery creatures; sometimes they cook quickly and sometimes they don't. Some cook in less than 20 minutes; others take as long as 25.*

*There is a simple solution: use red lentils, which are much smaller and cook more quickly, usually in 10 minutes. They are generally available in natural food stores and Indian markets. If you like lentil dishes, it's worth buying a hearty supply of them.*

## LENTIL AND LAMB SALAD

½ cup red lentils
12 ounces lean lamb chops
2 tablespoons olive oil
3 tablespoons red wine vinegar
2 teaspoons Dijon mustard
1 tablespoon fresh marjoram or thyme or 1 teaspoon dried
8 ounces whole red bell pepper or 7 ounces sliced (1½ cups)
8 ounces ripe tomatoes, regular or plum
1½ teaspoons capers
Freshly ground black pepper to taste

1 Place lentils in pot and cover with water. Cover pot and bring to boil. Reduce heat and cook at high simmer until lentils are done, about 10 minutes; they should be tender but still firm. Drain if necessary.

2 Wash and dry chops. In a heavy skillet, pan-fry chops in their own fat until they are crusty brown on both sides and are pink inside, 10–15 minutes depending on thickness.

3 In serving bowl whisk together oil, vinegar, mustard and marjoram or thyme.

4 Wash, seed and cut pepper into small pieces.

5 Wash and halve tomatoes and squeeze out seeds. Dice and add to dressing with red pepper.

6 Rinse capers and mix in.

7 When lamb is cooked, trim away fat and cut meat into strips; add to the salad.

8 Drain and rinse lentils and add to salad. Mix well and season with black pepper.

**Yield:** 2 servings

## CORN ON THE COB

4 ears of fresh corn

$\overline{1}$ Bring water to boil in steamer.

$\overline{2}$ Shuck corn and add to steamer basket. Cook 3–5 minutes and drain.

**Yield:** 2 servings

◆ *Game Plan* ◆

*Cook lentils.*

*Pan-fry lamb.*

*Bring water to boil in steamer.*

*Shuck corn.*

*Make salad dressing.*

*Cut red pepper and tomatoes and add to salad dressing; add capers.*

*Cook corn.*

*Cut lamb and add to salad.*

*Drain and rinse lentils and add to salad; season.*

*Drain corn and serve.*

### PANTRY

Red lentils
Olive oil
Red wine vinegar
Dijon mustard

Dried marjoram or thyme,
  if fresh not available
Capers
Whole black pepper

### SHOPPING LIST

12 ounces lean lamb chops
Fresh marjoram or thyme
8 ounces whole red bell pepper or
  7 ounces sliced (ready-cut)

8 ounces ripe tomatoes, regular or
  plum
4 ears fresh corn

# WARM LAMB AND POTATO SALAD ◆ WHOLE-GRAIN BREAD

*For those evenings when you want something simple and up to date, this meal will do beautifully, and it can be made with leftover beef, too. Fresh or dried oregano or thyme may be substituted for the marjoram. If small potatoes are not available, use large new potatoes. Leave the skins on and cut into slices to cook.*

## WARM LAMB AND POTATO SALAD

12 ounces tiny new potatoes
16 ounces thin-cut lean lamb chops
3 ounces whole mushrooms or 3 ounces sliced (ready-cut) (1 cup)
4 ounces whole red onion or 3 ounces sliced (ready-cut) (1 cup)
Soft lettuce (about ½ head Boston or 1 head of Bibb)
1 dozen cherry tomatoes
3 tablespoons olive oil
2 tablespoons balsamic vinegar
1 teaspoon minced fresh marjoram or ¼ teaspoon dried
2 tablespoons minced fresh parsley
2 teaspoons capers
1 teaspoon Dijon mustard Freshly ground black pepper to taste

1. Scrub new potatoes and cook in water to cover in heavy-bottomed pot, covered, about 18 minutes.

2. In heavy skillet, brown lamb chops well on both sides; lower heat and cook until medium-rare. Remove from pan; remove fat and cut meat into thin strips.

3. Wash whole mushrooms, trim stems and dry caps. Slice on thin slicing blade in food processor.

4. Thinly slice whole red onion, in food processor.

5. Wash and dry lettuce and cherry tomatoes.

6. Combine oil and vinegar in bowl large enough to hold salad ingredients.

7. Mince fresh marjoram and parsley and add to dressing along with capers and mustard.

8. When potatoes are drained, cut in half and add to dressing with lamb slices, onion and mushrooms. Season with black pepper.

9. Tuck lettuce around edges of salad. Decorate with cherry tomatoes. Serve with whole-grain bread.

**Yield:** 2 servings

# ◆ *Game Plan* ◆

*Follow recipe directions.*

## PANTRY

Olive oil
Balsamic vinegar
Dried marjoram, if fresh not
   available

Capers
Dijon mustard
Whole black pepper

## SHOPPING LIST

12 ounces tiny new potatoes
16 ounces thin-cut lean lamb chops
3 ounces whole mushrooms or
   sliced (ready-cut)
4 ounces whole red onion or
   3 ounces sliced (ready-cut)

Boston lettuce (½ head) or 1 head
   Bibb lettuce
1 dozen cherry tomatoes
Fresh marjoram (1 teaspoon)
Fresh parsley (2 tablespoons)
Whole-grain bread

# LAMB CHOPS WITH GRAINY MUSTARD ◆ BULGUR PILAF ◆ BROCCOLI WITH LEMON AND OIL ◆

## LAMB CHOPS WITH GRAINY MUSTARD

3–4 double-rib lamb chops
2 tablespoons grainy
    mustard

$\overline{1}$ Heat broiler.

$\overline{2}$ Spread mustard on both sides of chops.

$\overline{3}$ Line broiler pan with double thickness of aluminum foil. Broil chops about 2 inches from heat source, about 5–6 minutes on each side, turning once.

**Yield:** 2 servings

## BULGUR PILAF

2 scallions
1 tablespoon corn,
    safflower or canola oil
½ cup bulgur
1 cup chicken or beef
    bouillon or stock
2–3 tablespoons raisins
⅛ teaspoon allspice

$\overline{1}$ Slice scallions and sauté in hot oil with bulgur for about 1 minute.

$\overline{2}$ Stir in bouillon, raisins and allspice. Cover and reduce heat. Cook over medium heat about 10 minutes, until liquid has been absorbed and bulgur is cooked.

**Yield:** 2 servings

## BROCCOLI WITH LEMON AND OIL

16 ounces whole broccoli or
    8 ounces broccoli
    flowerettes (ready-cut)
    (3½–4 cups)

$\overline{1}$ Remove flowerettes from stems of whole broccoli. Cook flowerettes in steamer for 5–7 minutes, until firm but tender. If broccoli flowerettes have been

2 tablespoons olive oil
2 teaspoons lemon juice
Freshly ground black
pepper to taste

purchased parboiled, sauté in the oil for 4–5 minutes, stirring occasionally.

2 Drain and sprinkle steamed flowerettes with oil, lemon juice and pepper. Sprinkle parboiled flowerettes with lemon juice and pepper.

**Yield:** 2 servings

---

### ◆ Game Plan ◆

Heat broiler.
Slice scallions and sauté in hot oil with bulgur.
Heat water for whole broccoli.
Spread mustard on chops and broil.
Add remaining ingredients to scallions and bulgur; cook.
Steam raw broccoli or sauté parboiled broccoli.
Turn chops.
Finish broccoli.

---

#### PANTRY

Grainy mustard
Corn, safflower or canola oil
Bulgur
Chicken or beef bouillon or stock
Raisins

Allspice
Olive oil
Lemon
Whole black pepper

---

#### SHOPPING LIST

3–4 double-rib lamb chops
Bunch scallions (2)

16 ounces whole broccoli or 8
  ounces broccoli flowerettes
  (ready-cut)

# LAMB CHOPS AND GOAT CHEESE
## ◆ PANZANELLA ◆ ◆ ◆ ◆ ◆ ◆

*Panzanella is a fabulous Italian peasant dish that calls for stale bread. Bakeries often sell stale bread, but if you cannot find it buy a fresh loaf, slice it and let it sit on the counter for a day.*

---

### LAMB CHOPS AND GOAT CHEESE

3–6 double-rib lamb chops
Freshly ground black pepper
1½–2 teaspoons fresh thyme or ½–1 teaspoon dried thyme
3–6 ounces sharp goat cheese

1. Heat broiler.

2. Trim fat from chops. Wash and dry chops. Sprinkle pepper over chops and broil 2 inches from heat source for 7–8 minutes on one side.

3. Remove stems from fresh thyme leaves and mix with cheese, or mix dried thyme with cheese.

4. Turn chops; top with cheese and thyme and continue broiling until chops have reached desired degree of doneness, about 3–4 minutes longer.

**Yield:** 3 servings

---

### PANZANELLA

8 ounces day-old crusty whole wheat Italian or French bread
24 ounces ripe tomatoes
4–5 ounces whole red onion or 3–4 ounces sliced (ready-cut) (about 1 cup)

1. Place bread in a bowl with cold water only long enough to wet thoroughly; squeeze out excess moisture.

2. Chop tomatoes into small chunks; slice onion into small thin strips; remove basil leaves from stems and chop coarsely.

15 fresh basil leaves
   Freshly ground black
   pepper to taste
¼ cup red wine vinegar
 3 tablespoons extra-virgin
   olive oil

$\overline{3}$ Tear bread into walnut-size pieces; combine with tomatoes, onion, basil and pepper in serving bowl.

$\overline{4}$ Beat vinegar and oil and toss with salad; serve.

**Yield:** 3 servings

---

## ◆ Game Plan ◆

*Heat broiler.*
*Wet bread and squeeze dry.*
*Sprinkle chops with pepper and broil.*
*Chop tomatoes into chunks; slice onion; remove leaves from*
*basil and chop.*
*Remove thyme leaves from stems and mix with cheese.*
*Tear bread into small chunks and combine with tomatoes,*
*onion, basil and pepper.*
*Turn chops and top with cheese and thyme.*
*Beat vinegar and oil and toss with salad.*

---

### PANTRY

*Whole black pepper*
*Dried thyme, if fresh not available*

*Red wine vinegar*
*Extra-virgin olive oil*

---

### SHOPPING LIST

*3–6 double-rib lamb chops*
*Fresh thyme (1½–2 teaspoons)*
*3–6 ounces sharp goat cheese*
*8 ounces day-old crusty whole*
   *wheat Italian or French bread*

*24 ounces ripe tomatoes*
*4–5 ounces whole red onion or*
   *3–4 ounces sliced (ready-cut)*
*Fresh basil (15 leaves)*

# MUSTARD PORK CHOPS ◆
# COUSCOUS WITH PEAS ◆
# GREENS WITH SESAME DRESSING

## MUSTARD PORK CHOPS

1 tablespoon Dijon
  mustard
2 teaspoons lime juice
½–1 teaspoon ground cumin
12–16 ounces thin pork
  chops

1. Heat broiler. Line broiler pan with double thickness of aluminum foil.

2. Whisk mustard, lime juice and cumin.

3. Wash and dry chops and trim away excess fat. Arrange on broiler pan and spread tops of chops with half of mustard mixture.

4. Broil chops 2 inches from source of heat for about 5–6 minutes; turn and brush with remaining mustard mixture and broil for about 5 minutes more.

**Yield:** 2 servings

## COUSCOUS WITH PEAS

½–¾ cup chicken stock
1 teaspoon unsalted butter
1 teaspoon dried thyme
10 ounces frozen peas
½ cup couscous

1. Following directions on couscous package, bring chicken stock, butter and thyme to boil in covered pot.

2. Put peas in a strainer and run under hot water to thaw, about 1 minute.

3. Add peas and couscous to stock and remove from heat. Cover and allow to stand for 3–5 minutes, until water has been absorbed.

**Yield:** 2 servings

## GREENS WITH SESAME DRESSING

4 ounces mixed soft salad
  greens
½ teaspoon sesame seeds
1 tablespoon corn,
  safflower or canola oil
1 tablespoon rice vinegar
1 teaspoon honey
  Freshly ground black
  pepper to taste

1. Wash and dry greens on paper towels.

2. Toast sesame seeds.

3. Mix together oil, vinegar and honey in salad bowl.

4. Stir in greens and mix to coat well.

5. Sprinkle with toasted sesame seeds and pepper.

**Yield:** 2 servings

## ◆ Game Plan ◆

Heat broiler.
Mix topping for chops.
Top chops with mustard mixture and broil.
Wash greens.
Toast sesame seeds.
Boil stock with butter and thyme.
Run peas under hot water.
Turn chops; spread on mustard mixture and broil.
Cook couscous and peas.
Make salad dressing and mix with greens; top with sesame seeds.

### PANTRY

Dijon mustard
Ground cumin
Chicken stock
Unsalted butter
Dried thyme
Couscous

Sesame seeds
Corn, safflower or canola oil
Rice vinegar
Honey
Whole black pepper

### SHOPPING LIST

1 lime
12–16 ounces thin pork chops

10 ounces frozen peas
4 ounces mixed soft salad greens

# $L$ENTIL SALAD WITH GOAT CHEESE AND SLICED TOMATOES • BRATWURST • • • •

*Greens, a wonderful natural food restaurant overlooking San Francisco Bay, serves a version of this salad.*

*Use red lentils; they cook in 10 minutes. They are available at natural food stores and Indian markets.*

## LENTIL SALAD WITH GOAT CHEESE AND SLICED TOMATOES

2½ cups water
1 cup red lentils
1 bay leaf
¼ teaspoon dried thyme
1 teaspoon minced garlic in oil
2 dashes ground cloves
4 ounces whole or sliced (ready-cut) carrots (⅔ cup)
9 ounces whole red onion or 8 ounces sliced (ready-cut) (1¾ cups)
2 ripe medium tomatoes
3 tablespoons olive oil
2 tablespoons plus 2 teaspoons red wine vinegar
Freshly ground black pepper to taste
3 ounces soft goat cheese

1. Bring water, lentils, bay leaf, thyme, garlic and cloves to boil in covered pot.

2. Coarsely chop carrots. Coarsely chop onion. Reserve about ¼ cup onion. Add carrots and remaining onion to lentils.

3. Reduce heat and simmer, covered. Total cooking time should be about 10 minutes; the lentils should be firm but tender. Drain lentils and discard bay leaf.

4. Slice tomatoes.

5. Whisk oil, vinegar and pepper; stir in lentils.

6. Top with reserved onion and sprinkle with crumbled goat cheese. Serve with tomatoes on the side.

**Yield:** 2 servings

## BRATWURST

2–4 bratwurst
Grainy mustard

1. Bring enough water to cover bratwurst to boil in covered pot.

$\underline{2}$ Cook bratwurst in boiling water for 10 minutes. Drain and serve with grainy mustard.

**Yield:** 2 servings

---

### ◆ *Game Plan* ◆

*Cook lentils with spices and garlic.*
*Chop carrots and onion and add to lentils.*
*Boil water for bratwurst.*
*Slice tomatoes.*
*Make dressing for lentils.*
*Cook bratwurst.*
*Drain lentils.*
*Mix into dressing. Top with onion and cheese.*
*Drain bratwurst.*

---

### *PANTRY*

*Red lentils*
*Bay leaf*
*Dried thyme*
*Minced garlic in oil*
*Ground cloves*

*Olive oil*
*Red wine vinegar*
*Whole black pepper*
*Grainy mustard*

---

### *SHOPPING LIST*

*4 ounces whole or sliced (ready-cut) carrots*
*9 ounces whole red onion or 8 ounces sliced (ready-cut)*

*2 ripe medium tomatoes*
*3 ounces soft goat cheese*
*2–4 bratwurst*

# POLENTA WITH SAUSAGES AND MUSHROOMS ◆ MESCLÚN OR MIXED GREENS AND HERBS ◆ ◆ ◆

*Polenta recipes usually specify 40 minutes' cooking time for the polenta. The cornmeal in this recipe cooks in just a few minutes, so that it is a simple matter to make a quick version of the traditional Italian dish.*

*On a trip to New England in the summer of 1987, I was introduced to johnnycake meal from Gray's Gristmill in Adamsville, Rhode Island. Johnnycakes are a specialty of Rhode Island. Gray's, a 200-year-old gristmill, produces johnnycake meal that makes spectacular polenta.*

*It's worth sending away for. You can write Gray's Gristmill (see Mail Order Products on page 239).*

*This recipe has much less sausage than a traditional polenta—enough to give all the flavor without all the fat. I chose bratwurst because it is made with veal as well as pork. Another type of veal sausage or, for that matter, any sausage you like may be used.*

*If you have access to fresh wild mushrooms, they add even more flavor to the sauce, but ordinary mushrooms are very good, too.*

*The same summer that I was introduced to Gray's Gristmill, mesclún appeared on the horizon. Known in France and Italy for years, mesclún is a mixture of wild plants, herbs, lettuces and flowers. Mesclún means mixed salad but to call it that does not do it justice.*

*If you can find mesclún, treat yourself to some. You will be surprised at how delicious a salad can be. I recommend mesclún for this meal; otherwise mix different lettuces together with various fresh herbs.*

## POLENTA WITH SAUSAGES AND MUSHROOMS

2 bratwurst or other sausages
8 ounces whole mushrooms, regular, wild or a combination, or 6 ounces sliced (ready-cut) (3 cups)
1 teaspoon minced garlic in oil
1 tablespoon fresh sage or 1 teaspoon dried
28-ounce can Italian plum tomatoes

1. Remove sausages from casing and cook in large heavy-bottomed skillet over medium-high heat, stirring to brown.

2. Wash, trim and slice whole mushrooms.

3. When sausages are browned, drain off any excess oil and add garlic. Cut fresh sage into pan or add dried sage. Stir and cook 30 seconds.

4. Drain liquid from tomatoes and crush tomatoes with your fingers before adding to sausage along with mushrooms. Cook over medium heat, stirring

2 cups chicken or beef stock
1 cup stone-ground cornmeal, finely ground (johnnycake meal) or instant polenta
1 ounce Parmigiano Reggiano

occasionally until the rest of the meal is ready, about 10 minutes longer.

5 Bring stock to boil in covered pot. Slowly stir in cornmeal with wire whisk so that it does not lump. Reduce heat, cover and cook until liquid has been absorbed. Keep warm.

6 Coarsely grate cheese. You can either add it to the polenta or sprinkle it on top of the sauce.

7 Spoon polenta onto 2 dinner plates. Top with tomato–sausage mixture.

**Yield:** 2 servings

## MESCLÚN OR MIXED GREENS AND HERBS

2–3 cups mesclún or mixed salad greens
1 tablespoon walnut oil
1 tablespoon balsamic vinegar

1 Prepare greens.

2 Beat oil with vinegar and mix thoroughly with salad greens.

**Yield:** 2 servings

♦ *Game Plan* ♦

*Cook sausages.   Prepare mushrooms.   Drain fat from sausage;
add garlic and sage.   Add tomatoes and mushrooms to sausage.
Boil stock and add cornmeal; cook.   Prepare mesclún or mixed greens.
Make salad dressing and mix with greens.   Grate cheese.*

### PANTRY

*Minced garlic in oil
Dried sage, if fresh not available
Canned red Italian plum tomatoes*

*Chicken or beef stock
Stone-ground cornmeal, finely ground (johnnycake meal) or instant polenta*

*Parmigiano Reggiano
Walnut oil
Balsamic vinegar*

### SHOPPING LIST

*2 bratwurst or other sausages*

*8 ounces whole or sliced mushrooms, regular, wild or a combination, or 6 ounces sliced (ready-cut)*

*Fresh sage (1 tablespoon)
2–3 cups mesclún or mixed salad greens*

# MA PO'S BEAN CURD ◆ RICE AND BRUSSELS SPROUTS ◆ ◆

*I don't know who Ma Po was, but recipes under that name reappear every few years, each one different from the previous ones but always having bean curd. This is my version.*

*My editor said she didn't think Brussels sprouts were so great with bean curd. To keep her happy I tried asparagus. Take your choice.*

## MA PO'S BEAN CURD

16 ounces firm tofu
1½ tablespoons coarsely grated ginger
2 teaspoons corn, safflower or canola oil
1 teaspoon minced garlic in oil
4 ounces lean ground pork
2 minced scallions
2–3 teaspoons hot chili paste with garlic (amount depending on degree of hotness desired)
1 tablespoon reduced-sodium soy sauce
1 teaspoon Oriental sesame oil
⅔ cup chicken stock

1. Drain tofu and dry in paper towel.

2. Mince ginger in food processor.

3. Heat oil and quickly sauté garlic and ginger; stir in pork and cook about 1 minute.

4. Mince scallions in processor and add to skillet with chili paste, soy sauce, sesame oil and chicken stock. Cook, uncovered, over low heat.

5. Meanwhile, cut tofu into ½-inch pieces and gently stir into skillet. Cook for about 8–10 minutes, uncovered. If necessary, add a bit more stock. Serve over rice.

**Yield:** 2 servings

## RICE AND BRUSSELS SPROUTS

½ cup long-grain rice
1 cup water
10 Brussels sprouts or 12 to 14 asparagus (see Note below)

1. Combine rice and water in heavy-bottomed pot and bring to boil. Reduce heat, cover and cook for 17 minutes total.

<u>2</u> Meanwhile, wash and trim Brussels sprouts. Cut each in half and place on top of rice for the last 10 minutes of cooking time.

<u>3</u> Spoon rice and Brussels sprouts onto serving plates and top with the tofu.

**Yield:** 2 servings

**Note:** If using asparagus break off tough stem. Cut remainder into one-inch pieces and add to rice for last 7 or 8 minutes of cooking.

---

## ◆ Game Plan ◆

*Cook rice.*
*Drain tofu.*
*Trim Brussels sprouts.*
*Make bean curd dish.*
*Add Brussels sprouts or asparagus to rice.*

---

### PANTRY

*Ginger*
*Corn, safflower or canola oil*
*Minced garlic in oil*
*Hot chili paste with garlic*

*Reduced-sodium soy sauce*
*Oriental sesame oil*
*Chicken stock*
*Long-grain rice*

---

### SHOPPING LIST

*16 ounces firm tofu*
*4 ounces lean ground pork*
*Bunch scallions (2)*

*10 Brussels sprouts or 12 to 14 asparagus*

# PORK TENDERLOIN WITH MAPLE GLAZE ◆ POTATOES, BRUSSELS SPROUTS AND ONIONS ◆ ◆ ◆ ◆ ◆

## PORK TENDERLOIN WITH MAPLE GLAZE

8 ounces pork tenderloin (see Note below)
½ teaspoon dried chervil
½ teaspoon dried thyme
2 tablespoons maple syrup
1 tablespoon grainy mustard

1 Heat broiler. Line broiler pan with double thickness of aluminum foil.

2 Wash and dry tenderloin and cut thick end into ¾-inch-thick slices. Leave the thin end in 1 piece.

3 Mix together chervil, thyme, maple syrup and mustard.

4 Dip each piece of pork into maple syrup mixture.

5 Arrange pork pieces in broiler pan and broil 2 inches from heat source for about 10 minutes; turn and broil 5 minutes longer, until meat is no longer pink.

**Yield:** 2 servings

**Note:** Pork tenderloins are often sold two to the package. Use about one for two people and freeze the remainder.

## POTATOES, BRUSSELS SPROUTS AND ONIONS

9 ounces tiny new potatoes
18 ounces whole onion or 16 ounces sliced (ready-cut) (4 cups)
1 tablespoon olive oil
10 ounces Brussels sprouts
1 teaspoon sugar
2 teaspoons reduced-sodium soy sauce

1 Scrub potatoes and cook in water to cover in covered pot over high heat until tender, less than 20 minutes.

2 Slice whole onion.

3 Heat oil and sauté onion until soft. Spoon into serving dish.

**Freshly ground black pepper to taste**

4 Wash and trim Brussels sprouts. Add to potatoes and cook 7–10 minutes, depending on size. Remove sprouts with slotted spoon when they are cooked, drain and add to serving dish. Continue cooking potatoes.

5 Add sugar, soy sauce and pepper to serving dish.

6 When potatoes are cooked, drain and add to serving dish, cutting into halves or quarters. Mix well.

**Yield:** 2 servings

---

## ◆ Game Plan ◆

Heat broiler.    Cook potatoes.

Cover broiler pan with foil.    Prepare pork.

Prepare maple syrup coating for pork.

Coat pork with maple syrup mixture and broil.

Slice onion and sauté.

Trim Brussels sprouts and add to potatoes and cook.

Turn pork.    When onion is done spoon into serving dish.

Add soy sauce, sugar and pepper to onion in serving dish.

Add Brussels sprouts to serving dish.

Add potatoes to serving dish.

---

### PANTRY

Dried chervil
Dried thyme
Maple syrup

Grainy mustard
Olive oil
Sugar

Reduced-sodium soy sauce
Whole black pepper

---

### SHOPPING LIST

8 ounces pork tenderloin
9 ounces tiny new potatoes
18 ounces whole onion or 16
  ounces sliced (ready-cut)

10 ounces Brussels sprouts

# PORK WITH RED PEPPERS AND ONIONS ◆ NOODLES ◆ TOMATOES WITH MUSTARD DRESSING ◆ ◆ ◆ ◆

*This is a close one—it may take a little longer than 20 minutes.*

## PORK WITH RED PEPPERS AND ONIONS

12 ounces boneless lean pork
 8–10 ounces whole red onion or 7–9 ounces sliced (ready-cut) (1½ cups)
16 ounces whole red bell pepper or 14 ounces sliced (ready-cut) (4 cups)
 1–2 tablespoons corn, safflower or canola oil
 2 teaspoons ground cumin
 3 large scallions
 3 heaping tablespoons coarsely chopped fresh cilantro
 2 tablespoons red wine vinegar
 Freshly ground black pepper to taste

1. Wash and dry pork; trim off fat and cut into strips or cubes. Rub skillet with a little of the trimmed-off fat. Sauté pork quickly in hot skillet until brown on both sides. Do not overcook or meat will become tough. Remove pork and set aside.

2. Cut whole onion and red pepper into fourths and slice with thin slicing blade in food processor.

3. Add oil to skillet in which pork was cooked. When oil is hot, quickly sauté onion and red pepper with cumin until they are soft, about 10 minutes.

4. Wash and slice scallions.

5. Wash, dry and coarsely chop cilantro.

6. Turn off burner. Add vinegar and black pepper to skillet; stir well and heat through. Return pork to pan and stir to mix well.

7. Serve pork and vegetables over noodles and sprinkle with scallions and cilantro.

**Yield:** 2 servings

## NOODLES

3 quarts water
4 ounces medium egg noodles

1. Bring water to boil in covered pot.

2. Add noodles and cook according to package directions.

3. When noodles are cooked, drain and serve under pork.

**Yield:** 2 servings

## TOMATOES WITH MUSTARD DRESSING

12 ounces ripe tomatoes
1½ teaspoons corn, safflower or canola oil
1 tablespoon rice vinegar
1 teaspoon grainy mustard
1 teaspoon dark brown sugar

1  Wash, dry and slice tomatoes thickly onto 2 salad plates.

2  In small bowl beat remaining ingredients and pour over tomatoes.

**Yield:** 2 servings

---

### ◆ *Game Plan* ◆

*Boil water for noodles.   Wash, dry and cut up pork; cook.*
*Cut up onion and red pepper.*
*Set aside pork; heat oil in pan and sauté onion and red pepper with cumin.*
*Slice tomatoes.   Cook noodles.   Cut up scallions and cilantro.*
*Add vinegar and black pepper to onion and red pepper.*
*Make salad dressing and pour over tomatoes.*
*Add pork to onion and red pepper.*
*Drain noodles and top with pork; sprinkle with scallions and cilantro.*

---

### PANTRY

Corn, safflower or canola oil
Ground cumin

Red wine vinegar
Whole black pepper
Medium egg noodles

Rice vinegar
Grainy mustard
Dark brown sugar

---

### SHOPPING LIST

12 ounces lean boneless pork
8–10 ounces whole red onion or 7–9 ounces sliced (ready-cut)

16 ounces whole red bell pepper or 14 ounces sliced (ready-cut)
Bunch scallions (3 large)

Fresh cilantro (3 heaping tablespoons)
12 ounces ripe tomatoes

# TERIYAKI PORK ◆ RICE ◆ CUCUMBERS WITH TOMATO–YOGURT DRESSING ◆ ◆ ◆ ◆ ◆ ◆

## TERIYAKI PORK

12 ounces pork tenderloin slices or boneless pork chops
½ cup chicken stock
2 teaspoons reduced-sodium soy sauce
1 tablespoon honey
4 teaspoons dry sherry
1 teaspoon lemon juice
½ teaspoon minced garlic in oil
½ teaspoon cinnamon
1 tablespoon coarsely grated fresh ginger
1 tablespoon corn, safflower or canola oil

1. Wash, dry and trim fat from pork slices or chops.

2. Combine stock, soy sauce, honey, sherry, lemon juice, garlic and cinnamon in bowl large enough to hold pork.

3. Grate in ginger and add pork, turning to coat.

4. Heat oil in skillet large enough to hold pork. Remove pork from marinade. Brown quickly over high heat on both sides.

5. Add marinade and reduce heat so that marinade simmers; cover and cook until pork is tender, about 10 minutes total cooking time.

6. Arrange rice on 2 dinner plates; top with pork and spoon over sauce.

**Yield:** 2 servings

## RICE

½ cup long-grain rice
1 cup water

1. Combine rice and water in heavy-bottomed saucepan. Bring to boil.

2. Reduce heat; cover pot and simmer until rice is tender, about 17 minutes total.

**Yield:** 2 servings

## CUCUMBERS WITH TOMATO-YOGURT DRESSING

1 ripe medium tomato
4 scallions
2 tablespoons coarsely
   chopped fresh cilantro
½ cup plain low- or non-fat
   yogurt
2 small Kirby cucumbers

1 In food processor puree tomato, scallions and cilantro. Stop machine and add yogurt; process briefly just to blend.

2 Wash, dry and trim cucumbers.

3 Put slicing blade in processor and slice cucumbers directly into tomato mixture. Spoon into serving dish.

**Yield:** 2 servings

---

## ◆ *Game Plan* ◆

*Cook rice. Trim pork. Make marinade and add to pork.*
*Make tomato-yogurt dressing. Cook pork.*
*Slice cucumbers; add to tomato-yogurt mixture.*
*Add marinade to pork and finish cooking.*

---

### PANTRY

Chicken stock
Reduced-sodium soy sauce
Honey
Dry sherry
Lemon juice

Minced garlic in oil
Cinnamon
Fresh ginger
Corn, safflower or canola
   oil

Long-grain rice
Plain low- or non-fat
   yogurt

---

### SHOPPING LIST

12 ounces pork tenderloin
   or boneless pork chops

1 ripe medium tomato
Bunch scallions (4)

Fresh cilantro (2
   tablespoons)
2 small Kirby cucumbers

*For busy people, fewer visits to the grocery store mean more time for things they care about. This list makes it possible to buy many staples used in the recipes without spending endless hours in fruitless searches for the less-than-everyday ingredients—arborio rice, kalamata olives, hoisin sauce, etc.*

*The list also includes many ingredients for special-occasion meals when you want someone else to do the work for you.*

*If you have never shopped by mail or if you have had an unpleasant experience with mail order in the past, this is a good list to begin with because the suppliers are reliable. All of these suppliers have been featured in stories I have written for* The New York Times.

*The original plan was to include prices, but they change so rapidly that by the time the book is in the stores, many will have been outdated. In the end it will actually save time to call or write for latest price lists, additional items, methods of payment and shipment.*

## ◆ *Meats, Poultry and Fish* ◆

**Barbecue from Connecticut.** Don't sneer, this is as good as barbecue directly from Texas, but is made instead by an Englishman in Stratford, Conn. The brisket is lean, tender, perfectly smoked; the kielbasa juicy and spicy. Barbecue sauce comes mild, medium, mad and mean. Keeps for weeks in freezer.

*Stick-To-Your-Ribs, 1785 Stratford Avenue, Stratford, Conn. 06497; tel. (203)377-1752.*

**(Organic) Chicken.** Very little fat and lots of flavor to these white chickens.
*Deer Valley Farm, R.D. 1, Guilford, N.Y. 13780; tel. (607)764-8556.*

**Game.** The place for farm-raised game is D'Artagnan. Its products are superb, and for a 20-minute meal there is nothing to beat the semi-boneless quail. The company has free-range chickens and all kinds of fresh duck as well as rabbit and excellent venison. D'Artagnan also sells fresh New York State foie gras.

*D'Artagnan Inc., 399-419 St. Paul Avenue, Jersey City, N.J. 07306; tel. (800)DARTAGN (New Jersey residents, (201)792-0748).*

**Lobster.** These fresh, frisky lobsters, unlike some that have stayed in the tank too long, are full of sweet flavor. This reliable company delivers when it promises or calls when it can't. Lobsters are one pound and up; priced according to market.

*Marblehead Lobster Company, Beacon and Orne Streets, Marblehead, Mass. 01945; tel. (617)631-0787.*

**Sausages.** With or without nitrites, these are the best sausages you are likely to find anywhere, in just about every ethnic variety you might desire: knockwurst, weisswurst, jalapeño-flavored, andouille, bangers. The company also sells excellent nitrite-free ham and bacon. Keep several weeks in freezer.

*Smokehouse, Inc., 15 Coventry Street, Roxbury, Mass. 02119; tel. (617)442-6840.*

**Smoked Fish.** Lightly smoked, low-salt, superb quality products: tuna, trout, salmon, scallops, mussels. Keeps several weeks in freezer.

*Ducktrap River Fish Farm, Inc., R.F.D. 2, Box 378, Lincolnville, Me. 04849; tel. (207)763-3960 or 3970.*

**Veal.** Rosy, milk-fed veal puts white veal products to shame. (These animals are raised humanely.) Keeps for several months in freezer. This is the veal that prompted me to dream up 20-minute meals using veal. It is expensive and worth every penny for that special occasion.

*Summerfield Farm, SR 4, Box 195A, Brightwood, Va. 22715; tel. (703)948-3100.*

**(Organic) Veal.** See Organic Chicken, Deer Valley Farm, page 235.

---

## ◆ *Fresh Produce* ◆

**Herbs.** For those who have trouble getting fresh herbs, a high-quality assortment is available by mail: French fine-leaf basil, thyme, sweet basil, Greek oregano, rosemary, French tarragon, French sorrel, watercress, chervil, savory, etc.

*Fox Hill Farm, 443 West Michigan Avenue P.O. Box 9, Parma, Mich. 49269; tel. (517)531-3179.*

**Herbs and Salad Ingredients.** Can't get good-looking fresh herbs in your neighborhood, winter or summer? Get in touch with Herb Gathering. Though it is a seed company, it sells fresh herbs as well as edible herb flowers by mail. Choose from bay, chervil, sorrel, tarragon, rosemary, marjoram, shallots, arugula, chives, dill, herbal flowers, chervil, shallots, sorrel, lemon balm, opal basil, salad burnet, thyme. Some items are seasonal.

*Herb Gathering, Inc., 5742 Kenwood, Kansas City, Mo. 64110; tel. (816)523-2653.*

**(Organic) Bananas.** Not the varieties you'd expect to find in the grocery store, these have names like Manzano, Blue Java, Brazilian, Mysore. Cook with them, eat them out of hand; directions come with the bananas telling you what to do with them.

*Seaside Banana Garden, 6823 Santa Barbara Avenue, La Conchita, Calif. 93001; tel. (805)643-4061.*

**(Organic) Kiwis and Persimmons.** The tart sweet kiwis and the Fuyu persimmons are excellent. The company also has Valencia and navel oranges, plums and Asian pears, depending on the time of year.

*Ecology Sound Farms, 42126 Road 168, Orosi, Calif. 93647; tel. (209)528-3816.*

**(Organic) Navel Oranges, Limes, Lemons, Avocados.** Superb flavor.

*Be Wise Ranch, 9018 Artesian Road, San Diego, Calif. 92127; tel. (619)756-4851.*

**(Organic) Produce.** Perhaps because of the proximity of this company to where I live, its products arrived in the best condition of all mail order organic food I ordered. Everything was excellent. The shop has an organic fruit club which ships a different fruit each month of the year.

*Smile Herb Shop, P.O. Box 989, 4908 Berwyn Road, College Park, Md. 20740; tel. (301)474-4288.*

**(Organic) Produce.** Most of the produce sampled is exceptional, full of flavor and good enough to be served without seasoning—but the lettuces did not travel well. In season, the company has just about any fruit or vegetable you could ask for.

It also sells organic dairy products, beef, veal, lamb, pork and chicken, but I have not tasted them.

*Rising Sun, P.O. Box 627, Milesburg, Pa. 16853; tel. (814)355-9850.*

**(Organic) Prunes and Walnuts.** The biggest and sweetest prunes I've ever tasted; walnuts were free of the bitterness they sometimes have. Try any of the company's dried fruits. It also sells grains.

*Country Life Natural Foods, Oakhaven, Pullman, Mich. 49450; tel. (616)236-5011.*

**Shiitake Mushrooms.** Meaty and woodsy in flavor, mushrooms like these put the plain white ones from the supermarket to shame.

*Delftree Corp. 234 Union Street, North Adams, Mass. 02174; tel. (413)664-4907.*

## ◆ *Cheeses* ◆

**Blue.** A creamy American blue cheese that can hold its head up with many imports. Keeps for several weeks.

*Maytag Dairy Farms, R.R. 1, Box 806, Newton, Iowa 50208; tel. (800)247-2458.*

**Camembert.** A superb, perfectly ripened cheese that is ready to eat when it arrives. It will keep for several weeks, unopened, in the refrigerator. It will even keep for several months in the freezer without apparent ill effects. A wedge of this cheese and a piece of fruit, and you don't need anything else for dessert.

*Craigston Cheese Co., 45 Dodges Row, Wenham, Mass. 01984; tel. (508)468-7497.*

**Cheddar.** None of these cheeses is very sharp, but all are creamy and smooth. They freeze well and come Mild, Sharp and Extra Sharp.

*Shelburne Farm, Shelburne, Vt. 05482; tel. (802)985-8686.*

**Goat's Milk Cheese.** York (tastes like rich Cheddar), Capriano, fresh cheese roll with pepper. An excellent assortment of cheeses that freeze very well and can be ready at a moment's notice (maybe closer to an hour). Capriano is like an aged Romano, and what the company calls York cheese is what tastes like rich Cheddar, but since it is made from goat's milk, not cow's, it can't be called Cheddar.

*York Hill Farm, New Sharon, Me.; tel. (207)778-9741.*

**Monterey Jack.** This hard, dry cheese doesn't seem to be in the same family as the unassertive supermarket versions of Jack cheese. Beneath the brown coating, its robust flavor is in the tradition of Parmesan or Asiago, a cheese that is perfect with crusty bread. Keeps for months in the refrigerator.

*Vella Cheese Company, P.O. Box 191, Sonoma, Calif. 95476; tel. (707)938-3232.*

**Mozzarella.** Fresh or smoked cow's milk and fresh or smoked buffalo milk mozzarella. Superb cheese that bears no resemblance to the mozzarellas available in the supermarket. This is the kind of cheese you want to eat uncooked, in slices. Fresh lasts only a few days; smoked a week or so.

*Todaro Bros. Mail Order, 555 2nd Avenue, New York, N.Y. 10016; tel. (212)679-7766*

**Parmigiano Reggiano.** Todaro Bros. has top-quality Parmesan that keeps for months in the refrigerator. Just grate a little when you need it.

See Mozzarella, Todaro Bros., above.

## ◆ *Grains* ◆

**(Organic) Cornmeal**—Johnnycake Meal. Makes the best shortcake I have ever eaten and is perfect in the two polenta recipes in the book. Keep refrigerated, and it will last for months.

*Gray's Gristmill, P.O. Box 422, Adamsville, R.I. 02801; tel. (508)636-6075*

**English Muffins.** Whether you choose plain or cheese, or any of the other superb fat muffins such as honey raisin or cinnamon raisin, you will never return to any other kind. May be kept frozen for months.

*Joyce's Gourmet English Muffin Co., 4 Lake Street, Arlington, Mass. 02174; tel. (617)641-1900*

**Italian Biscuits.** A handsome gold tin holds two pounds of this bakery's best, which is very good indeed: focaccia, flat breads redolent of olive oil; biscotti al formaggio, cheese-flavored crisp breads; biscotti angelica, buttery toasts for caviar or paté; bastoncini, bread sticks and biscotti di vino, to be eaten with wine or espresso. Keep for months in freezer, weeks in tightly sealed container at room temperature.

*DiCamillo Bakery, 811 Linwood Avenue, Niagara Falls, N.Y. 14305; tel. (716)282-2341.*

**Lentils.** Red lentils cook in 10 minutes or less. Keep for months.

*G. B. Ratto, 821 Washington Street, Oakland, Calif. 94607; tel. (800)228-3515 in Calif. and (800)325-3483 elsewhere.*

**Rice.** Arborio rice is called for in several recipes in the book, but this flavorful rice is best known for its use in risotto. The company also sells the slightly nutty-flavored Indian basmati rice. Keeps for months.

*Gourmet Treasure Hunters, 10044 Adams Avenue, Suite 305, Huntington Beach, Calif. 92646; tel. (714)964-3355.*

**Rice.** Arborio, See Lentils, G. B. Ratto, above.

**Rice.** Arborio. See Mozzarella, Todaro Bros., page 238.

**Rice.** Basmati—delicately flavored Indian rice. See Lentils, G. B. Ratto, above.

**Sourdough Bread.** The same place that sells lovely Cheddar cheeses in Vermont has a baker on the farm and they sell an excellent bread. Store in the freezer.

See Cheddar Cheese, Shelburne Farms, page 238.

## ◆ *Condiments* ◆

**(Organic) Almond Butter.** Full of nutty flavor, a delightful substitute for peanut butter. The company sells several other nut butters, including peanut and dried fruit, but I have only tasted the almond butter. Keeps for months in the refrigerator.

*Living Tree Center, P.O. Box 797, Bolinas, Calif. 94924; tel. (415)868-2224.*

**Capers.** In several sizes.

See Rice, arborio, G. B. Ratto, page 239.

**Chiles, Dried.** Mild and hot chile powder for Mexican dishes.

Long shelf life but spices lose some of their potency.

*Pecos Valley Spice Co., 500 East 77th Street, Suite 2324, New York, N.Y. 10162; tel. (212)628-5374.*

**Chinese Ingredients.** Much of what you need to cook the Chinese-style recipes in this book can be found at one source: sesame oil, chile paste with garlic, hoisin sauce, rice vinegar, dried mushrooms, Sichuan peppercorns, fermented black beans and oyster sauce.

*China Bowl Trading Co., 169 Lackawanna Avenue, Parsippany, N.J. 07054;* tel. (201)335-1000.

Also available from Gourmet Treasure Hunters, see Rice, arborio, page 239.

**Chutney.** Perfectly balanced and deeply aromatic, the chutney is made from French butter pears, one of the most succulent varieties grown, though they are rare in this country. Superb with meats and poultry. Keeps for months in cupboard.

*Pettigrew Fruit Company, P.O. Box 526, Walnut Grove, Calif. 95690; tel. (916)776-1614.*

**Chutney.** One of these salt-free chutneys—cranberry dusted with cinnamon, apple touched with onion, or peach with curry and ginger—should go well with any kind of poultry or roast. Keeps for months in cupboard.

*Stowe Hollow Kitchens, Box 6830, North Hollow Road, Stowe, Vt. 05672; tel. (802)253-8248.*

**Dried Mushrooms.** Morels, chanterelles, cepes, porcini, Chinese black, tree ears, oyster, shiitake—dried mushrooms always add an interesting depth of flavor. Keep indefinitely.

See Rice, arborio, Gourmet Treasure Hunters, page 239.

**Dried Mushrooms.** Porcini, shiitake, morels. See Rice, arborio, G. B. Ratto, page 239.

**Japanese Ingredients.** Items such as *wasabi*, the Japanese horseradish powder, and pickled ginger, both essential for making sushi. Keeps indefinitely.

See Rice, arborio, Gourmet Treasure Hunters, page 239.

*Nam Pla* or *Nuoc Nam*. In Thai and Vietnamese cooking, fish sauce is as ubiquitous as soy sauce is in Chinese cooking. Keeps indefinitely.

See Rice, arborio, Gourmet Treasure Hunters, page 239.

**Olive Oil.** Especially extra-virgin olive oil, which is excellent for salads. Keeps for months, once opened, in the refrigerator.

See Rice, arborio, Gourmet Treasure Hunters, page 239, or See Mozzarella cheese, Todaro Bros., page 238.

**Olives.** Kalamata, the Greek olives that can be used in many dishes in this book calling for imported olives. Keep indefinitely, once opened, in the refrigerator.

See Rice, arborio, Gourmet Treasure Hunters, page 239.

**Olives.** See Lentils, G. B. Ratto, page 239.

**Peanuts.** Unsalted or salted, and water-blanched before roasting, which gives them more crunch and more peanut flavor, these peanuts are even more flavorful when eaten directly from the freezer. Store for months in the freezer, for several weeks at room temperature.

*Virginia Diner, Inc., Box 310, Wakefield, Va. 23888; tel. (804)899-3106.*

**Sun-Dried Tomatoes in Oil.** Well seasoned with garlic and oregano, these tomatoes come not from Italy but from Ohio. Indefinite shelf life.

*Genovesi Food Company, P.O. Box 5668, Dayton, Ohio 45405; tel. (513)277-2173.*

See Mozzarella cheese, Todaro Bros., page 238.

**Vinegar.** Balsamic is a sweet, rich vinegar called for in many recipes in the book. You don't need as much oil with it for salad dressings. Indefinite shelf life.

Gourmet Treasure Hunters, see Rice, arborio, page 239.

Todaro Bros., see Mozzarella, page 238.

---

## ◆ *Preserves, Jellies and Jams* ◆

**Cider Jelly.** The tart, deep, winey apple flavor is wonderful on toast and also as a glaze on poultry. Keeps on the shelf for months.

*Woods Cider Jelly, RFD 2, Box 477, Springfield, Vt. 05156; tel. (802)263-5547.*

**Jams.** Wild Thimbleberry preserves, described as part loganberry, part raspberry, are refreshingly tart, but the tartest of all is sour cherry spoon fruit with the deepest cherry flavor. And only 7 calories per teaspoon. Keep for months on cupboard shelf.

*American Spoon Foods, Inc., 411 East Lake Street, Petosky, Mich. 49770; tel. (616)347-9030.*

**Jellies.** Wild chokecherry is the most delicious of the exotic-flavored jellies this company makes. Deep, winey and tart, it turns ordinary toast into a breakfast special. Buffalo berry is almost as tart and delicious. These keep for months on cupboard shelf.

*Kountry Kitchen, 406 South Strevell, Miles City, Mont. 59301; tel. (406)232-3818.*

**Preserves and Toppings.** All of these fruit preserves or conserves, or whatever you wish to call them, are deeply fruit-flavored and sweetened with concentrated fruit juice. They are of looser consistency than the usual preserve, and they make a good sauce. Flavors include Strawberry Fanciful, Raspberry Fanciful, Blueberry Fanciful, plus Blueberry Syrup and Raspberry Syrup, which are excellent when mixed with seltzer for a drink. Keep for months in the refrigerator.

*Wax Orchards, Route 4, Box 320, Vashon, Wash. 98070; tel. (206)682-8251.*

---

## ◆ Desserts ◆

**Cake.** This chocolate truffle cake is the ultimate fudge cake. It is made with chocolate, eggs, sugar, butter and flour. That is all. Keeps for weeks in freezer.

*Jake's Famous Products, 4910 N. Basin, Portland, Ore. 97217; tel. (503)226-1420.*

**Cake.** This lemon rum cake is a poundcake-like dessert, redolent of rum, moist and sweetly sharp. It deserves its name: Sunshine Cake. In addition to the rum and lemon, it is made with butter, eggs, wine and other natural ingredients one expects to find in a homemade cake. Keeps for months in the freezer.

*Matthews 1812 House, 15 Whitcomb Hill Road, Cornwall Bridge, Conn. 06754; tel. (203)672-6449.*

**Cake.** Raisin brandy cake from a favorite recipe of the Belle of Amherst, poet Emily Dickenson, is called the Emily Dickenson Cake. It is good all year round but is particularly appropriate for those who don't like fruitcake.

*Concord Teacakes Etcetera, P.O. Box 134, Concord, Mass. 01742; tel. (508)369-7644.*

**Cake.** Dried plums, walnuts, buttermilk and spices usually associated with the holiday season produce a moist, appropriately named Sugar Plum Cake that is topped with nuts. Keeps for several months in the freezer.

*The Final Blessing, P.O. Box 5946, Sparks, Nev. 89432; tel. (702)826-8686.*

**Cakes.** Poppyseed and banana pineapple are The Cake Lady's two very best flavors. Each has an appealing homespun quality. They keep for months in the freezer.

*The Cake Lady, P.O. Box 30683, Charleston, S.C. 29417; tel. (803)792-5724.*

**Cheesecake.** The brochure accompanying this cheesecake includes a copy of a menu from the late lamented Reuben's Restaurant in Manhattan and says the cheesecakes are the same as those served there. The one we tried certainly tasted as if it was. Rich, sweet and very creamy, without being too heavy, a sliver is enough for a serving. Keeps for several months in the freezer.

*Arnold Reuben Jr.'s Cheesecakes, 15 Hillpark Avenue, Great Neck, N.Y. 11021-9990; tel. (516)466-3685.*

**Cheesecake.** If your fancy turns to a lighter version, the cheesecakes from Eli's are rich and creamy, too. I have tasted their plain versions and their chocolate caramel pecan. They also come in other flavors.

*Eli's Chicago's Finest Cheesecake, Inc., 6510 West Dakin Street, Chicago, Ill. 60634; tel. (312)736-3417.*

**Cookies.** Unreservedly recommended. Buttery, crisp shortbread and soft, mellow ginger-molasses cookies. Keep for several months in the freezer.

*Cookie of the Month, Box 155, R.R. 1, Avondale, Pa. 19311; tel. (215)268-8030; tel. (800) 322-6248.*

**Mocadamia Nut Torte.** Redolent of macadamia nuts with a nice overlay of expresso coffee flavor, this chocolate torte contains butter, sugar, white chocolate chips, flour, eggs, chocolate, espresso, macadamia nuts and vanilla. Keeps for several months in the freezer.

*Gwetzli Foods, P.O. Box 20298, Oakland, Calif. 94620; tel. (415)655-5621.*

**Shortbread.** Unpretentious white box holds 1½ pounds or more of wonderfully rich handmade shortbread fingers decorated with the traditional fork pricks. Keeps for several months in freezer.

*Elizabeth's Best, P.O. Box 294, Mystic, Conn. 06355; tel. (203)599-3279.*

**Swiss Water Process Decaffeinated Coffee.** A variety of excellent decaf coffees including espresso, as well as coffees with caffeine intact.

*Schapira Coffee Company, 117 West 10th Street, New York, N.Y. 10011; tel. (212)675-3733.*

Marian Burros has been writing about culinary concerns for 25 years. Before joining *The New York Times* as a food columnist, and for a time, restaurant reviewer, she was Food Editor at *The Washington Post* and several other newspapers. She was also an Emmy-award winning consumer affairs reporter. She has written nine successful cookbooks. Ms. Burros lives with her husband in New York City and Washington, D.C.

Printed in the United States
By Bookmasters